LA INDIA MARÍA

I0892504

LA INDIA MARÍA

Mexploitation and the Films of María Elena Velasco

SERAINA ROHRER

UNIVERSITY OF TEXAS PRESS *Austin*

Copyright © 2017 by the University of Texas Press
All rights reserved
Printed in the United States of America
First edition, 2017

Requests for permission to reproduce material from this work should be sent to:
Permissions
University of Texas Press
P.O. Box 7819
Austin, TX 78713-7819
utpress.utexas.edu/rp-form

♾ The paper used in this book meets the minimum requirements of ANSI/NISO Z39.48-1992 (R1997) (Permanence of Paper).

LIBRARY OF CONGRESS CATALOGING-IN-PUBLICATION DATA

Names: Rohrer, Seraina, 1977– author.
Title: La India María : mexploitation and the films of María Elena Velasco / Seraina Rohrer.
Description: First edition. | Austin : University of Texas Press, 2017. | Includes bibliographical references and index.
Identifiers: LCCN 2016058955
ISBN 978-1-4773-1344-2 (cloth : alk. paper)
ISBN 978-1-4773-1345-9 (pbk. : alk. paper)
ISBN 978-1-4773-1346-6 (library e-book)
ISBN 978-1-4773-1347-3 (non-library e-book)
Subjects: LCSH: Exploitation films—Mexico—History and criticism. | Sensationalism in motion pictures. | Low budget films—Mexico—History and criticism. | Velasco, María Elena. | Women motion picture producers and directors—Mexico. | Women in motion pictures. | Motion pictures—Social aspects—Mexico.
Classification: LCC PN1995.9.S284 R64 2017
DDC 791.43/653—dc23
LC record available at https://lccn.loc.gov/2016058955

doi:10.7560/313442

FOR THE MEXICAN PERFORMER, DIRECTOR, AND PRODUCER MARÍA ELENA VELASCO (DECEMBER 17, 1940–MAY 1, 2015)

"Ya ni le diga usted nada señora. Mejor me voy. Aquí todo es distinto. No puede aprender l'inglés y español se me está olvidando, y al rato como dice mi tata, no voy a ser ni de aquí ni de allá."

[Don't say anything, Mrs. I better leave. Here everything is different. I am not learning English and I am losing my Spanish, and, as my grandfather would say, in a short while I will be neither from here nor from there.]

CONTENTS

ACKNOWLEDGMENTS

THIS BOOK ONLY EXISTS thanks to the support provided by many institutions and individuals, most importantly María Elena Velasco herself and her children, Ivette Eugenia Lipkies and Iván Lipkies. Of immense help in the research process were Nydia Herrera, former secretary of Diana Internacional Films, S.A. de C.V., and Xóchitl Fernández and Rogelio Agrasánchez Jr., heads of the Agrasánchez Film Archive. I also owe a great deal to Adán Avalos, who generously provided materials and insight into his own research on Mexploitation cinema. The same holds true for David Wilt, who provided access to his in-depth research on Mexican straight-to-video productions.

Numerous scholars—whether they are aware of it or not—have greatly enriched my research and writing with their remarks, questions, and suggestions. These people include Jens Andermann, María Arbeláez, Catherine L. Benamou, Lisa Cartwright, Maricruz Castro Ricalde, Marvin D'Lugo, Mara Fortes, Rosa Linda Fregoso, Norma Iglesias Prieto, Ingrid Kummels, Jesse Lerner, Jaime J. Nasser, Theres Steffen, Dolores Tierney, and Margrit Tröhler. I am grateful for the feedback and help from Sheri Englund.

The staff of the Cineteca Nacional (National Mexican Film Archive) as well as the Film Archive of the Universidad Nacional de México (Filmoteca UNAM) generously provided access to industry journals as well as all press clippings. In particular, support has been provided by José Manuel García Ortega, Leonardo García Tsao, Francisco Gaytán, and Abel Muñoz Hénonin. From 2009 to 2010 I was welcomed as a visiting scholar at the University of California, Los Angeles (UCLA). Special thanks go to the Chicano Studies Research Center, headed by Chon Noriega, along with all other staff, including Francisco Javier Iribarren, Luz Orozco, David O'Grady, and Lizette Guerra. I appreciate their hospitality and support.

Many friends have helped me along the way. I am particularly grateful to my partner, Joël Fisler, and our son, Josiah Rohrer, for their patience and kind words. My friends Jenny Billeter, Andreas Brändle, Rosa Medina, and Simone Schaub, as well as my mother, Marianne Rohrer-Bürgi, have supported me throughout this adventure. My friends in Mexico, Fabiola Torres-Alzaga, Enrique Macías, and Rossana Barro, were generous hosts during all of my research stays there.

Finally, the people at the University of Texas Press have been great; in particular, I would like to thank Jim Burr, Robert Kimzey, Sarah E. McGavick, and freelance copy editor Kathy Lewis.

LA INDIA MARÍA

INTRODUCTION

I FIRST ENCOUNTERED La India María (Maria the Indian) in Mexico's sprawling and colorful street markets. As a Swiss PhD student and a visiting fellow in Chicano studies at UCLA, I lived in Mexico for several years and traveled across Latin America. One of my favorite diversions was wandering in the markets and browsing through the impressive selection of legal and pirated films at many stands. Time and time again, the garish covers on a series of Mexican films featuring a clownish indigenous woman caught my eye. Most vendors responded enthusiastically to my queries about the India María films and character and encouraged me to watch them. "Es muy chistosa" [she is hilarious], they would tell me, or "es un ídolo de los pobres" [she is an idol of the poor]. But a few sellers advised me to skip the films, despite their popularity, warning me that they were "muy malas" [very bad]. I decided to find out for myself.

In the fall of 2005 I sat down to watch one of the best-known India María films, *Okey, Mister Pancho* (1981), for the first time. The film tells the story of how La India María, played by María Elena Velasco, decides to help a wounded American pilot who has fallen from the sky. She agrees to cross the border to the United States illegally and deliver a package that he claims contains medicine for his mother. On her way, she discovers that she is about to become the victim of a drug-smuggling conspiracy. Instead of giving up, however, she asserts herself against a group of thugs. At the end of the film, she returns to Mexico as a crime-busting heroine. *Okey, Mister Pancho* and the naive yet stubborn María character depicted as an over-the-top ethnic stereotype startled me. Unsure what to make of the slapstick comic character, I was irritated by the stereotyping—but at the same time cracking up with uneasy laughter. I found myself convinced that this was quite an uncommon female hero. My Mexican friends who were watching the film with me had all seen *Okey, Mister Pancho* at least once before. During the screening, they erupted into cheers when La India María successfully fooled the police and other authorities.

Fascinated, I watched the remaining fourteen India María features that were available at that time. As I settled into my movie-watching binge, I noticed that most of these comedies follow a formula: La India María is exploited, but in the end she defeats her adversaries and unmasks their corruption. In all of the films, the character battles against existing power structures through her slapstick performance.

I was surprised to learn that María Elena Velasco not only starred in sixteen feature films, as well as numerous TV shows and theater sketches, but also directed five of her own films in order to exercise more control over the India María character. In the mid-1980s she founded a film production company together with her children, Iván Lipkies and Ivette Eugenia Lipkies.[1] Clearly, the India María films stand out, with a female protagonist, director, and producer. Velasco was one of the few women in Mexico's film industry from the 1970s for several decades, working in front of and behind the camera. With rising curiosity, I set out to meet her in person.

After several months of unsuccessful attempts, I finally managed to get in touch with Velasco's son, Iván Lipkies, in 2008. We met in Mexico City and talked for hours about his own work and his mother's career. Lipkies stressed that María Elena Velasco was extremely reluctant to give interviews because of previous negative experiences with journalists. I suspect that the fact that I was a European researcher who had lived in Mexico was key to Velasco's decision to give me a chance. She seemed honored and surprised at the same time that her work had stirred interest in Europe.

In December 2008 I interviewed María Elena Velasco for the first time. We met in a café in Mexico City, where she showed up with her daughter Ivette, her son Iván, and her grandson. During this first encounter, I was confronted with a highly interesting woman, who intelligently reflected on the complex Mexican film industry as well as on her own work. After this initial long interview, I returned in 2009 to deepen our conversation. This time she invited me to her house for a conversation lasting over two hours. In 2011 I was lucky enough to visit the set of Velasco's current movie, *La hija de Moctezuma* (Moctezuma's daughter) (2014), produced by her daughter Ivette and directed by her son Iván. Although I went to the shooting as an observer, I ended up playing the part of an American ambassador when the actor cast in the role did not show up. My observations and experiences on and off the set all fed my emerging research.

Some of the most revealing information was offered in the least formal settings, during breaks or at casual dinners.

Velasco became an indispensable source for this book, along with Iván Lipkies and Ivette Eugenia Lipkies as well as Nydia Herrera, the former secretary of Diana Internacional Films, S.A. de C.V.,[2] all of whom I interviewed several times between 2008 and 2011. Sadly, *La hija de Moctezuma* proved to be Velasco's last film. María Elena Velasco passed away after a short illness on May 1, 2015, at the age of seventy-four. Her iconic character remains controversial. Some critics view La India María as a racist depiction of a negative stereotype of an indigenous woman, while others see the widely beloved character as a sly, transgressive critique of discrimination and the powerful political elite. Despite her lack of critical acclaim, Velasco became one of Mexico's most prolific female director-producers and created a spirited and unforgettable character that Mexican audiences have loved for half a century.

Long before Velasco's death, I began to wonder why her movies have rarely been studied. To date, no books have focused solely on her contributions to Mexican cinema as a performer, director, or producer. Three researchers' scholarship, however, has touched upon her work. More than twenty years ago, in 1992, Carmen Huaco-Nuzum assessed the representation of La India María in one of Velasco's most popular films, *Ni de aquí, ni de allá* (Neither from here nor from there) (1988). In a 2008 article, Carol D'Lugo analyzed the processes of identity construction by comparing the famous Mexican comedic persona Cantinflas, the wrestler El Santo, and La India María. D'Lugo defends Velasco's portrayal of La India María, affirming that she stayed truthful to a character defined by marginality in class, gender, and ethnicity. Mexican film scholar Maricruz Castro Ricalde has written several short audience-reception pieces, some unpublished, on La India María (Castro Ricalde 2004a, 2007). Following in their tracks, I have published three articles on the India María films, which laid the groundwork for this book (Rohrer 2009b, 2009c, 2011).

The India María films, including Velasco's more recent films such as *Las delicias del poder* (The delights of power) (1999), remain typical of the historic period between the late 1960s and the late 1980s derisively referred to as *la crisis* [the crisis] by film critics. They are exemplary of Mexican low-budget films produced at that time. Unlike films from the so-called Golden Age of Mexican cinema (late 1930s to the late 1940s) or works from the 1990s onward, the India María films and other low-budget films with a similar style have generally not attracted scholarly attention. They have been widely overlooked or, more accurately, "deliberately ignored," as film scholar Sergio de la Mora (2009: 247) suggests.[3] During this period, only a handful of Mexican films premiered in renowned international film festivals, even though the production volume of around seventy films per year remained identical to that of preceding decades. Besides comedies like Velasco's featuring family-style or "white" humor, several other categories of popular films—including action, wrestling, and movies starring famous dancers—shared similar aesthetics and production and distribution practices.

During this so-called crisis, perhaps a thousand films were produced, aimed at a wide public in Mexico, Latin America, and the United States. For the most part, film critics viewed these mass-market films as devoid of artistic value, judged them to be merely commercial, and accused them of recycling stories that had proven to be successful at the box office—and contemporary scholarship has generally agreed (Ayala Blanco 1989, 1994: 415; Barriga Chávez 1988a, 1988b, 1991, 1993; Galindo 1990). Despite critics' rejection, these films have enjoyed great popular success across Latin America. From the 1970s onward, they were the big box-office grossers, attracting large audiences to the movie theaters. At the turn of the millennium, they continued to be among the most popular videos at rental stores in US neighborhoods inhabited by Latino migrants (Arbeláez 2001: 642). Today many Latino families and migrant workers continue to watch these films online, on YouTube and other streaming sites. For the Latino community these films remain a means to reflect on—and laugh at—their own situation as immigrants. During my research stays in Los Angeles in 2009 and 2010, I observed how lines of dialogue have become widely known catch phrases. India María film quotations even circulate as mobile phone ringtones.

When I began my research, I knew that this book would feature all sixteen India María films as well as the character's TV and theater appearances. The book's scope grew to include other films from the same period, similar in style and production context. After watching nearly one hundred popular films, television series, and straight-to-video productions of the period, I chose around forty works to represent the wider assortment. These films include titles that were repeatedly recommended by street vendors, taxi drivers, auto mechanics, undocumented workers, friends, gardeners, cleaning personnel, and other fans in Mexico and the United States, representing long-term success with viewers. Certain other titles were exceptionally successful at the box office and on video or DVD at the time of their release. In addition, I have given some priority to films that have resonated in academia.

In the beginning, the scarcity of publications made my research endeavor seem more appealing, but it soon became clear that the lack of information on the subject posed some difficulties. It was a particular challenge to reconstruct how these low-budget films were produced. Mexican film archives lack detailed information, and the few existing publications allowed only a partial reconstruction of production and exhibition practices. In the end, I gathered this elusive practical information from a variety of sources, including my interviews with María Elena Velasco and her children.

The research for the extended corpus of films of the period turned out to be a drawn-out process, lasting from 2008 to 2012. After I determined which producers, distributors, and exhibitors were still accessible; I set up interviews and collected as much information on the films as I could. Like Velasco, all interviewees were surprised that a Swiss researcher would be interested in these films. Because most of them viewed these works solely as entertainment that was not worth archiving, the records that they had kept were scarce. Rogelio Agrasánchez Jr., the son of a prolific producer, was an exception to the rule. To my delight, Agrasánchez had collected all of his father's production files in a private archive in Harlingen, Texas. This material, as well as Agrasánchez himself and Xóchitl Fernández, turned out to be an invaluable resource, providing me with a deeper understanding of the period.

To reconstruct production and exhibition practices, I also drew from sources within Mexico's film industry, particularly the trade journal *Cámara*. The journal considers itself an objective observer, monitoring the industry (*Cámara* 1987a: 1), but it must be stressed that *Cámara* clearly represents and defends the mainstream industry. Since its founding in 1978, the journal has sometimes published voices outside the industry, including conference speeches and letters addressed to the film industry by opinion leaders. Yet in general the publication has something of a self-congratulatory insider tone. With this bias in mind, the journal has proven very helpful on the wider historical period and general practices of the Mexican film industry, offering valuable insights into common distribution and exhibition practices.

Some of my research is also based on newspaper articles that in some cases provide a rich source of information on production, distribution, and exhibition practices. In both newspapers and trade papers, however, I often found contradictory information. As it turns out, political regimes in power during this period of Mexican cinema determined what information could be published; particular publishers were more or less cooperative, depending on their political stance. Figures regarding production volume and other crucial data varied to such a large extent that these sources must be evaluated critically and put into political perspective.

This book is not limited to production and exhibition practices but also takes into account the interdependence of production, exhibition, and reception, using the language of media reception studies. I speak of "viewers"—or "users" in the context of appropriations on YouTube—when referring to people I interviewed, ranging from taxi drivers to women working in street markets, migrant workers who live in the United States, and fans who express their admiration online. When using the term "audience," I mean a group of people watching a film together, either in the cinema or in front of the small screen, defined by a historic moment and a community. Most importantly, I distinguish between audiences in the United States and in Mexico. The term "spectator" is always understood in relation to a theory regarding aspects of how he/she is fashioned by a film.[4] The term "reception" encompasses all activities of negotiating meaning, whereas "appropriation," a term from cultural studies, refers to the ways in which viewers integrate films into their daily lives and at times create something new as a result of the reception process (Fiske 1995: 56, 57).

The ultimate aim of this book became interpreting responses from viewers of India María films, María Elena Velasco and her children, other Mexploitation producers, and industry sources in order to understand the enduring appeal of the ethnically marked comic character of India María, the films in which she appears, and Mexico's low-budget film industry.

Six chapters make up this book. The first chapter lays out the particularities of my main research subject: María Elena Velasco, the character of La India María, and the body of her work. Chapter 2 situates Velasco's work among low-budget comedies, wrestling films, sexy movies, and border action adventures. These films from the same period share many similarities in their style. I reconstruct the political context in which the India María films and other Mexploitation films were produced, through an analysis of different political regimes' policies and their respective practices, with particular attention to Mexico's economic situation and censorship regulations. The chapter also discusses how India María films and other Mexploitation films were produced, analyzing both production costs and labor practices. Chapter 3 reconstructs distribution and exhibition practices in Mexico and the United States, attending to the differences between viewing films in theaters and on the small screen. Chapter 4 centers on the reception of the India María character. I identify and try to explain corrosive judgments as well as viewers' adoration for the character. Chapter 5 takes on India María in the context of the diaspora. India María films play a crucial role in the construction of Mexican and Mexican American diasporic identities by reflecting and reviving migration experiences. The epilogue briefly outlines what has become of Mexploitation today.

CHAPTER 1

LA INDIA MARÍA: FROM VAUDEVILLE TO THE BIG SCREEN

MARÍA ELENA VELASCO WAS BORN on December 17, 1940, in the capital city of the highland state of Puebla. The family of six was working class. Her father, a mechanic, was employed by the railroad. After she finished secondary school, Velasco launched a career in the theater, starting out as a singer and dancer in musical routines. Soon she moved onto vaudeville stages at Mexico City nightclubs (1001 Nights and Burro) or theaters like the Teatro Tívoli, El Iris, and Blanquita, where she appeared as a supporting actress for male comedians. Among them were the renowned comic actors Eulalio González and Adalberto Martínez Chávez—best known by their stage names Piporro and Resortes, respectively. Resortes later joined Velasco in her India María features (Castro Ricalde 2007: 632; Fernández Escareño 1996: 120).[1]

In the theater, Velasco met Julián de Meriche (born Vladimir Lipkies), a leading dancer, actor, and choreographer, whom she married in 1960.[2] Meriche, who worked in over 230 films, encouraged Velasco to create her own character and appear as a solo act. In the late 1960s Velasco brought an early version of the India María character to the stage. The character wore makeup and bangs at that time, and her clothing did not identify her with any specific ethnic group.

VAUDEVILLE HIT

La India María soon became a favorite on vaudeville stages in Mexico City. Although she subsequently became widely known through her television and film appearances, Velasco enjoyed the contact with live audiences and continued to make stage appearances until a few months before her death in May 2015. Throughout her career, she often performed her comic routines at *ferias* [annual fairs celebrated on the day of a village saint] as part of programs including music and bullfights. On other occasions,

1.1 AND 1.2. María Elena Velasco started out her career as a dancer before she created her own character. (Vlady Pictures and Estudios Plata México)

she visited female prisons, where she performed her sketches and comical dances and sang. Sometimes she also performed at private events, such as the Christmas celebrations of Mexican corporations (Rohrer 2008). In the United States, she brought her act to theater stages, including the Million Dollar Hotel in Los Angeles and amusement parks like Disneyland

1.3 AND 1.4. The original version of La India María wore makeup and played her sketches on the vaudeville stages in Mexico City. (Vlady Pictures)

1.5 AND 1.6. In the beginning La India María supported other comedians on the theater stage, dancing and adding humorous asides. (Vlady Pictures)

1.7. La India María meanders through Mexico's history in the play *México canta y aguanta*, regularly stopping for folkloric songs and dancing with corrupt Mexican bureaucrats. (Vlady Pictures)

and Six Flags Magic Mountain (Anonymous 1975, 1976; Grant 1982). In 1994 Velasco returned to the stage, debuting at the Mexico City theater Blanquita, with the musical *México canta y aguanta* (Mexico sings and lives through hard times), for which she wrote the script and directed the musical routines. In this play, La India María is chased by policemen for no obvious reason, while a teacher tries to convince her to learn to read and write. The blockbuster show was sold out over 200 times in Mexico City and subsequently toured the country for more than a year (Villaseñor 1994).

The India María character emerged from the theater scene and constantly returned to it for new life and reinvention. Throughout Velasco's career, her musical and dance routines attracted large audiences that gave her immediate responses to her acting and to the character. She drew great energy from appreciative fans of all backgrounds and social classes and particularly liked to bring her performances to audiences that otherwise might lack the resources to attend. When I asked her about her best professional memories, Velasco answered without hesitating: "¡Las rutinas en vivo! ¡Sobre todo en la cárcel!" [The live performances! In particular the ones in prison!] (Rohrer 2008).

TELEVISION BREAKTHROUGH

In 1971 La India María took to a broader stage with her first television appearance. Interviewees—taxi drivers, market vendors, and people on the street—repeatedly told me that they initially encountered La India María on television.[3] The variety show *Siempre en domingo* (Always on Sundays) (1961–1995), hosted by Raúl Velasco,[4] gave La India María her first big break on television. *Siempre en domingo* aired on Canal de las Estrellas [Channel of the Stars], Televisa's most-watched station. The show was broadcast for more than thirty years, but its highest-rated episodes were in 1971 at the launch of La India María, with approximately 400 million viewers (Betanzo 1998: 19; Castro Ricalde 2004b: 202). With *Siempre en domingo*, La India María moved beyond her considerable stage popularity to win the hearts of television audiences with her naive admiration for the show's host.[5] The episode's gimmick is that María is selling fruit in front of the television studio when Raúl Velasco—whom she calls *güero*, a Mexican term for a person with a light complexion and blond hair or someone who belongs to the upper class—stops to buy an orange or an apple. La India María falls in love with him at first sight and pursues him. She spares no effort to get past security and onto the set, leading to a series of hilarious pratfalls. Once she is on the stage, nobody can stop her. She makes fun of the invited guests, narrates anecdotes from her life as a street vendor, and mocks officials and institutions, monopolizing most of the episode. In all of her appearances, music plays a pivotal role. Often La India María dances to the songs performed by invited musicians or sings herself. *Siempre en domingo* was extremely popular but frequently panned as "poorly crafted": prerecorded material was reused, and fake musicians often appeared with bad lip-synching. Thus, from her first moments on screen, La India María was classed as low-budget popular entertainment.[6]

Later the same year, India María appeared on another television program, *Revista musical Nescafé* (Nescafé show) (1971), as one of its main features. The program was essentially a half-hour commercial for Nescafé, enriched with musical numbers and comic routines. A male presenter led the show in most episodes, while scantily clad blonde women performed dance routines—which La India María constantly interrupted with comic interludes. After *Revista musical Nescafé*, Velasco moved into feature films and rarely appeared on TV. In 1998 La India María temporarily returned to the small screen in *¡Ay María qué puntería!* (María,

1.8. La India María moved into the limelight through her appearances on television, here as the guest star on the news show *24 horas* (24 hours). (Vlady Pictures)

what an aim!). Velasco played the lead role, wrote the script, and directed. The show, a series of comic routines with numerous political sketches, aired on Televisa's channel 2 during prime time (Mendoza de Lira 1998). After the first season of thirteen episodes, the show was canceled because Velasco did not want to produce a second season. La India María made only sporadic TV guest appearances after that (Cuéllar 2003; Flores 2003; Hernández 2004).[7]

COMMERCIAL MUSIC AND MUSICAL COMMERCIALS

Music plays a key role in all of India María's television shows, live performances, and films. Velasco recorded six albums, for which she composed several songs. All were produced between 1968 and 1984 and released as vinyl 45 and 33 records. Two albums feature other famous performers alongside Velasco, while the rest consist of popular and original ballads performed solo by her. One album is entirely based on the ballad *El compromiso* [The compromise] from the film *Okey, Mister Pancho.* Two records released in the 1970s contain ballads that bear no direct relation to

1.9 AND 1.10. Velasco recorded five albums promoted as part of the India María franchise and an additional solo album under her own name. (Vlady Pictures)

the films, but only one album, *Canciones románticas* [Romantic songs] (1984), features Velasco and not her character (Lipkies 2010).

Although Velasco was a good singer, she never achieved independent success as a musician. Audiences always primarily perceived her as a comic performer who spiced up her India María routines with popular tunes. Other actors of the period, most prominently Vicente Fernández, were mostly known for their music. Fernández had his film breakthrough playing a singing taco vendor (a variation of the *charro*, the widely popular singing cowboy) in *Tacos al carbón* (Grilled tacos) (1972, directed by Alejandro Galindo), but he got his start as a musician singing about the beauties of Mexico. In contrast, Velasco's comic acting fame drove her musical career, even though she originally entered the theater as a singer-dancer.

La India María also danced and sang her way through several commercials. Among other products, the character serenaded bouillon cubes for the Swiss company Maggi and several Nestlé products, including the instant coffee brand Nescafé, which she also touted on the television show *Revista musical Nescafé* in 1971.

SUCCESS ON THE BIG SCREEN

In 1972 Velasco's TV appearances led to India María's first feature movie, *Tonta tonta, pero no tanto* (Stupid stupid, but not that much) (1972)—a blockbuster hit. After that Velasco played the leading role in sixteen India María features between 1972 and 2014 (for the complete listing, see the filmography). She starred as another character only once in her career: in the film *Huapango* (2004) she played a dance instructor.

The India María films share many similarities. First and foremost, they are all comedies with an innocent form of humor suitable for entire families. In Mexico these family-friendly comedies are commonly labeled *comedias blancas* [white comedies]. The films often reference well-known Mexican historical events, cultural locations, and artifacts and rely on cultural stereotypes such as the virgin or the revolutionary. The clash of the rural and urban is at the core of most films.

In addition, the films combine the logic of what Tom Gunning (1986: 64) calls the cinema of attractions with the logic of classical narration.[8] Commonly, the storyline's development is interrupted by a sudden display of spectacles—often slapstick gags or musical performances directly addressing audiences—not only on-screen but also sometimes live—as part of the viewing context.

Many of the India María films do not conform to a classical style but diverge from it toward Gunning's cinema of attraction. Most importantly, gags are shown explicitly and at length. Cameras are mostly at eye level: high-angle or low-angle shots are rare, as are tracking shots. Camera movements are mostly motivated by characters or the staged attraction and seldom framed longer than the duration of the action. The camera only pans and tilts when characters move. Characters are mostly framed in long or medium shots; close-ups are rare and only used to enhance certain body parts. The color composition often contains strong contrasts: lighting levels are not modulated from one shot to the next and the colors are bright. Props and costumes often look amazingly unreal. This might also be perceived as a lack of attention to detail in the production design. In addition, soundtracks are not tempered: voices and background noises overlap. Musical tunes are often not harmonically mixed. At times they sound hollow or are interspersed with clangors. Special effects, when used, are too obvious. *El miedo no anda en burro* (Fear doesn't ride a donkey) (1976), directed by Fernando Cortés, for example, contains elements of and references to the horror genre. The makeup and movements of the monsters look incredibly amateurish and thereby become spectacular. In addition, several films use fast-motion to create a comic spectacular effect. The films that Velasco directed and later produced try to create more authentic special effects. In one scene in *Ni de aquí, ni de allá*, a coffeepot and other machines explode. The scene might not seem particularly special, but it triggered two interviews with Velasco in the Mexican press about the dangers and complications of shooting it (Dávalos 1987;

Pacheco 1987). This underlines how important those attractions were in the India María films.

The titles of the films clearly situate the features in the realm of popular culture. Several come from popular proverbs or songs. *Ni de aquí, ni de allá* [Neither from here nor from there], for example, is a common saying underlining the loss of culture and identity of Mexican immigrants in the United States. At the same time, it is the title of a Mexican ballad widely known in Mexico and in the Mexican community in the United States, which is also the title song of the film *Ni de aquí, ni de allá*. *El miedo no anda en burro* [Fear doesn't ride a donkey] is a proverb, signifying that fear cannot be foreseen. Similarly, *¡El que no corre . . . vuela!* [Who doesn't run, flies] refers to cleverness to achieve a goal or to baffle the competition.

The India María films center on three main themes: (1) an adventurous migration; (2) religion; and (3) society's power structures. These themes often coexist in the films, but certain films foreground a single theme.

AN ADVENTURE LEADING HOME

Six India María films adhere to the story formula of the adventurous journey, which according to Joseph Campbell (2004) is a "mono-myth"—a ritualized form or narration valid for all cultures and historic eras. Unable to find work in the country, and in order to better her life, La India María migrates to the city, where she is forced to live on the margins of society. She defies poverty by maintaining honorable principles and a strong sense of optimism. Each film narrates how La India María leaves the Mexican countryside and moves to a big city or even farther, to the United States. When she migrates away from the rural area, where she clearly feels at home and knows the cultural customs and daily routines, she is confronted with an alien environment and encounters characters who try to get in her way. The city itself and the United States become antagonists rather than mere settings. In the opening scenes, La India María is usually depicted riding calmly on a donkey through her hometown or at the outskirts of the big city. In the final scenes, she either returns home to rural Mexico or, as suggested by either the musical score or a voiceover narrator, will eventually return there. Throughout the story, La India María proves her abilities and triumphs. She refuses to accept hypocrisy, thereby uncovering hidden power structures and their machinations.

The following comedies feature adventurous journeys within Mexico: *Tonta tonta, pero no tanto* (1972), *¡El que no corre . . . vuela!* (1982), *El*

1.11. In *Tonta tonta, pero no tanto* (1972) La India María embarks on an adventurous journey but ultimately returns to her hometown. (Diana Internacional Films, S.A. de C.V.)

coyote emplumado (The feathered coyote) (1983), and *La hija de Moctezuma* (2014). Limited to the nation's borders, all of these films are nonetheless marked by oppositions. The country and capital city come to life in scenes depicting daily urban life, from markets and traffic to prisons, church squares, and wrestling matches, all of which place the character of India María in stark relief. Similar cultural clashes lie at the core of two additional adventurous journeys, *Okey, Mister Pancho* (1981) and *Ni de aquí, ni de allá* (1988), this time expanding the journey to the United States and setting up a contrast between the national and the foreign as a way to create comic moments.

HOLIER THAN THOU

Five India María films tell stories related to religion. Unlike the adventurous journey films, the religious-themed films are not based on an already established story formula but instead form a thematic cluster.

In *La madrecita* (The little nun) (1974) and *Sor Tequila* (Sister Tequila) (1980)—films with almost identical storylines—La India María joins a convent, where she has many adventures. In both films, the character challenges outmoded traditions and rules in the church and in the convent. She exposes several taboos through her unconventional behavior, displayed in a series of spectacles.

Three other films approach the subject of religion by playfully comparing La India María to the Mexican embodiment of the Madonna, La Virgen de Guadalupe.[9] *Pobre pero . . . ¡honrada!* (Poor but honorable) (1973),

1.12. In *La madrecita* (1974) and *Sor Tequila* (1980) La India María joins a convent as an unconventional nun. Here she gets drunk in a bar in *La madrecita*. (Diana Internacional Films, S.A. de C.V.)

1.13 AND 1.14. Many India María films allude to the image of the virgin, as here in *Pobre pero . . . ¡honrada!* (1973) (*left*) and in *La presidenta municipal* (1975) (*right*).

Duro pero seguro (Hard but safe) (1978), and *Se equivocó la cigüeña* (The stork was wrong) (1993) position the character La India María as a holy virgin who is able to cure the ill, perform miracles, and even immaculately conceive a child. The plots are quite similar. In *Pobre pero . . . ¡honrada!* she saves lives with holy water. Rumors of her special gift spread quickly, and soon the first bad guys are knocking on her door to take advantage of her. In all three films, religion functions as a scheme controlled by powerful adversaries, which La India María must ultimately challenge. In other films, such as *La presidenta municipal* (The municipal president) (1975), La India María's postures and her clothing allude to the virgin.

SOCIALLY OPPRESSED

Finally, all India María films tell stories of social oppression and eventual class empowerment. La India María clearly belongs to Mexico's lower

1.15. In *La comadrita* (1979) La India María subverts class expectations of social behavior. When she dresses up as a wealthy lady, her actions lead to a series of incidents. (Diana Internacional Films, S.A. de C.V.)

classes—she is of the *pueblo* [people]. A sort of folk hero who was and remains especially loved by the working class, she is instantly familiar to Mexican people from all backgrounds. La India María lives in humble circumstances and earns a meager living. She frequently works as a maid in an upper-class household, as in *El miedo no anda en burro* (1976), *La comadrita* (The child's godmother) (1979), and *Ni Chana, ni Juana* (Neither Chana nor Juana) (1985), throwing class differences into stark relief. Comic moments are mainly created through her refusal to acknowledge other characters' evil nature and her daily resistance to the condescending attitude of her employers. In the course of these stories, she resists her oppressors and voices her opposition to class and ethnic differences—and in the end she unmasks and outwits them.

India María's character subverts the constraints of class and social standing, invariably causing a clash that ultimately allows her to reveal and transcend artificial social distinctions. In *La comadrita*, for example, La India María is hired by a Spanish couple to work as a caretaker in Mexico City. While the rich couple is out of town, her relatives in the countryside fall victim to an attack. After their house burns down, they have nowhere else to go, so La India María allows them to stay in her employers' villa in the city. When India María and the relatives pretend to belong to Mexico's upper crust, their encounters with the rich lead to a number of humorous incidents.

La India María always stays true to her humble roots. Her characterization as an illiterate rural woman of Mexico's lowest working class remains consistent throughout Velasco's TV appearances and films. Despite her modest background, she manages to break free, make a place for herself, and triumph—although not usually by becoming rich herself. As a representative of Mexico's most economically vulnerable class, María is shown to be an ally of the weak and the poor. However, while the stories usually start by emphasizing her social disadvantages—especially her lack of education and financial resources—the character gradually becomes increasingly self-determined, steering the plot, overcoming challenges, and striving for her goals. Throughout the story she acquires narrative agency, an important factor for audience enjoyment, eliciting fantasies of overcoming existing power structures. But, in the end of the films, she stays truthful to her working-class fellows, even if she has made money and gained status.

In the film *La presidenta municipal*, for instance, La India María is accidentally elected to political office (the ballots say "María" instead of "Mario"). Corrupt politicians immediately try to take advantage of her. Yet, soon enough, La India María can see through the men's games. Instead of letting herself be intimidated, she takes action by working against corruption and eliminating her opponents. She imposes taxes on drinking and gambling and demands that men give half of their monthly salary to their wives. This wins her the adoration of the people and women in particular. Similarly, in *Las delicias del poder* (1999), La India María is able to replace the presidential candidate simply because they look alike. India María's television appearances on *Siempre en domingo* and *Revista musical Nescafé* in 1971 also fit into this general category.

It is worth emphasizing that different themes often combine and overlap within a single film. *Tonta tonta, pero no tanto*, for example, contains social oppression themes within the overarching narrative structure of an adventurous journey. In this film, La India María migrates to the city, where she works as a maid and lives through various adventures before returning home to rural Mexico.

INDIA MARÍA: A STEREOTYPE WITH A POINT

Velasco created the India María character for Mexico's vaudeville theaters, where working, middle-class, and at times upper-class audiences packed houses for lively variety entertainment featuring physical comedy and humor filled with ethnic stereotypes, exaggerated dialogue, and dialect. It was Velasco's main aspiration to make people laugh with innocent jokes and slapstick performance (Anonymous 1997b; De la Cruz Polanco 1998; El Soberbio 1989; H. Hernández 1988; Pacheco 1988; V. H. Sánchez 1989; Valencia 1992). Like Cantinflas, India María emerged from theatrical sketch performances, which according to Mexican film scholar Tomás Pérez Turrent (1990: 24) were strongly influenced by Spanish theater traditions. Over time, two forms of humor prevailed on Mexican stages. Comedies using *humor blanco* [white humor] were suitable for the whole family and were highly successful with wide audiences. Plays with *albures* [a dirty form of humor using puns and sexual and explicitly racist statements] mainly attracted an audience of male adults. Both forms relied heavily on well-defined character types, similar to the Italian theater tradition of commedia dell'arte.

The India María character, an indigenous woman belonging to Mexico's lowest social class—naive, humble, and illiterate—is a perfect example of a type created for the amusement of wide audiences with an innocent form of humor. As a member of an ethnic minority and a woman from Mexico's underclass who charms audiences with slapstick pratfalls, the character is an amalgamation of various simplified codes and traits.[10] Yet contrary to the original vaudeville tradition, which often promoted a kind of "laughing at" humor that enlisted audiences in veiled cruelty, racism, or class-based snobbishness, the India María character invited audiences to "laugh with" her. Audiences loved her for it.

The inside joke—based in vaudeville, but a shade warmer and more kindly—depended on Velasco's portrayal, so strongly exaggerated that La India María was revealed as a deliberate stereotype. She resisted all outside influences on principle, even when her opponents took advantage of her poor education to humiliate her. Yet Velasco gave La India María other ways of fighting back. She responded to discouragement and oppression with humor. Through her physical daring, she regularly produced hilarious gags that upset or literally upended her opponents.

Velasco's India María character was inspired by indigenous Mazahua women from rural Mexico commonly called Las Marías, who began to migrate to Mexico City in the 1960s to sell fruit, candy, and trinkets and beg for alms on the streets of the capital.[11] Commenting on the origin of the character, Velasco said, "Viviendo en el D.F. crucé esas mujeres cada día en las calles . . . hasta que un día decidí de interpretar una de ellas. Así nació el personaje" [Living in Mexico City, I walked by these women in the streets every day. . . . until one day it crossed my mind to impersonate one of them. This is how the character was born] (Rohrer 2008).

Besides the indigenous street vendors, Velasco also suggested that other popular María characters shaped her depiction of La India María (Rohrer 2008). One of the most influential was clearly the long-running Peruvian heroine of the *telenovela* called *Simplemente María* (Simply María) (1969–1970). The Peruvian series tells the story of an uneducated woman who moves to the city. She finds a job as a housekeeper, but her boss exploits her and she becomes pregnant. Despite her difficulties, María refuses to give up. She begins to take classes in handicrafts and after many years triumphs as a successful fashion designer. This portrayal of an honest, industrious, and ambitious working-class woman was a huge success with Latin American audiences. Spanning 448 one-hour episodes, *Simplemente María* was broadcast on Monday to Friday throughout Latin America from early 1969 until the end of 1970.[12]

Several India María films quote the street vendors called Marías and the *telenovela* character explicitly or refer to them implicitly, such as *Tonta tonta, pero no tanto*. The film starts with India María's journey to Mexico City in search of her cousin and work. After struggling through many obstacles, she somehow ends up on a television show. The moderator of the program proudly introduces her to audiences as "una María clásica" [a classic Maria], referring to the indigenous street vendors. A political functionary later belittles her as "simplemente María" [simply María]. The politician's humiliating comment—reducing her to a nobody who does not even deserve a last name—refers to La India María's low social status and also points to her association with the hit *telenovela*. Aside from such explicit references, there are also subtler story and plot signals. Although the character India María alludes to stereotypes of the Marías, Velasco subverts and transgresses them through her performance. Velasco's embodiment of the character in particular rejects the victim status and powerless tears common to many cultural depictions of the María figure in *telenovelas* and other popular genres such as melodramas. Contrary to the *telenovela*, Velasco's India María was a complete stranger to crying fits.

The *telenovela* María and India María are rare examples of indigenous people being represented by the media. From radio to newspapers and television, Mexico's media largely ignore indigenous concerns, unless covering social unrest in specific geographical areas such as Chiapas or political uprisings such as demonstrations where indigenous people try to voice their demands. Representations of indigenous people were almost nonexistent in feature films during the era from the 1970s and the so-called crisis mentioned earlier (Ramírez Berg 1992: 138).[13] When indigenous characters did appear, they mostly had minor roles such as employees of white protagonists.

During the Golden Age of Mexican cinema (late 1930s to the late 1940s), numerous films had featured noble Indians or cowboys who sang about the beauties of Mexico—but the indigenous characters had always been played by "white" actors of European descent. The presence of indigenous characters was aimed primarily at reinforcing Mexicanness—a concept of national identity that was heavily promoted by the Mexican state after the revolution. Depiction of indigenous characters served as a strategy to forge national solidarity and unity among populations divided by race, language, and regional affiliations (Hershfield and Maciel 1999; Hershfield 1999). Film played a key role in promoting Mexicanness, in part because an emerging national identity coincided with the development of a successful film industry during the Golden Age of Mexican cinema (Hershfield 1999: 81). The Mexican government thus heavily relied on cinema to celebrate and strengthen a national spirit for a wide audience.

Velasco herself, as she created and embodied La India María, clearly departed from such a representation. Although Velasco was a mestiza with an indigenous father and a "white" mother, she always stressed her indigenous features when playing La India María. In fact, Velasco's build and small stature were typical of indigenous Mazahua women. In her films, live performances, and public appearances, Velasco wore clothing typical of these rural indigenous women: a long skirt over an underskirt with lace edges, a thick knitted belt, a brightly colored satin blouse, and traditional jewelry. Her long black hair was neatly braided and adorned with bright ribbons, and she often wore traditional *huaraches* [sandals] or went barefoot.

Notably, while her on-screen presence spanned almost fifty years, La India María changed minimally as a character. Her ethnicity, character traits, dress, and language remained consistent and true to the type. La India María stood for a simplified, stable, and clearly structured representation of a woman of rural indigenous heritage. The lack of character development was completely intentional. Velasco regularly referred to viewers who continued to watch La India María and loved her for her unchanging, dependable nature (Fernández Escareño 1996: 124). In an interview dating from 1974, when the character had existed for less than five years, Velasco took a firm position on her characterization of La India María:

> Periodista: "¿Quiere decir que La India María aprende inglés? ¿O que cabe una transformación o evolución en su personaje?" La mujer cordial [Velasco] se exalta: "¡Nunca! Yo soy La India María y no puedo renunciar a mi burro Filemón, ni a ser La India María. Hay que sincerarse en este oficio."
> [Journalist: "Does this mean that La India María will learn English? Or that she will transform and develop?" The friendly lady [Velasco] exclaims: "Never, I am La India María and I could never leave my donkey Filemón or stop being La India María. You simply have to be honest in this business."] (De La Fuente 1974)

Significantly, Velasco answered the question as her character. As her career progressed, Velasco began differentiating herself from her depiction of the character and her various roles as actress, director, and producer of India María films. While at the beginning she may have intentionally blurred the distinctions, Velasco eventually even began emphasizing differences among them, while always maintaining India María as a sympathetic indigenous character type.

CHARMING WITH SLAPSTICK AND SLANG

Velasco's performance style was clearly grounded in classic slapstick comedy, an acting style popular on Mexico's vaudeville stages and later on television and the big screen.[14] In her films, the actress crawls, hops, bounces, jumps, and dances through the story. She and her character do karate (*Okey, Mister Pancho*), wrestle (*¡El que no corre . . . vuela!*), scale trees and walls (*Sor Tequila*), and perform acrobatic feats and win a motorcycle race (*La comadrita*). Velasco embodied her character through postures, gestures, and movements typical of slapstick and characterized by repeated gags and general horseplay. Velasco's characterization of La India María became instantly recognizable through physical repetition and reduction of complexity, but each performance also tested the limits of India María's type, pushing it into the absurd. In many scenes, slapstick acting and exaggerated physicality blur the lines between the character and her bodily presence.

Velasco's India María can be compared to Charlie Chaplin's Tramp—both characters lean toward the burlesque through the physical expression of nervousness and hyperactivity. The characters both represent marginal figures who suffer from social and economic exclusion, yet the physical comedy and low social status combine to make these characters remark-

1.16. The numerous slapstick scenes in *¡El que no corre . . . vuela!* (1982) include a car race and numerous fights in and outside the ring. (Cineteca Nacional)

ably lovable. Like Chaplin, Velasco used acrobatic stunts—pitting herself against the laws of physics—as a way to depict La India María's protest against external oppression. In *¡El que no corre . . . vuela!*, for example, La India María is pushed around, stumbles out of an overcrowded subway, and is nearly hit by a car several times. Her ostentatiously slapstick displays continue in jail. There she sprays a group of women with a high-pressure hose, provokes mass hysteria, and initiates a large-scale pillow fight that sends feathers flying. This scene is followed by a long sequence with fights in a marketplace and a kitchen, featuring crowds who use fruits and pans as missiles. Later India María drives a car recklessly and bowls over everything in her path, including nuns, policemen, and vending stalls. Special effects—including a blind man's eyes that spin in endless circles—exaggerate the fantastic nature of these episodes. A fifteen-minute fight in a wrestling ring concludes the film, creating a spectacle of the body that associates María with Mexico's favorite national sport.

With exuberant physical escapades, La India María is able to criticize the powerful and turn unfavorable events to her advantage. The fantasies of empowerment that the character elicits transgress typical representations of indigenous women and undercut ethnic stereotypes and social hierarchies. Velasco's brand of physical comedy and emphasis on the body—both on and off screen—made this ethnically marked character a working vehicle for commenting on and overcoming cultural and historical categories of disadvantage.

These elements of Velasco's performance, however, have raised criticism of La India María as a negative racial stereotype (Barriga Chávez 1988a). Scholars, film critics, and at times politicians accuse Velasco of presenting an overly simplified depiction of an indigenous woman but at the same time often criticize her for "overacting"—emphasizing her character's clumsiness, for example (Ayala Blanco 1989: 71; Oehmichen Bazán 2005: 201). Like those of Chaplin's bumbling but kind-hearted Tramp, India María's physical pratfalls are an intrinsic part of her social commentary—as well as a clear reflection of her origins in the vaudeville theater tradition.

The character's speech reveals the same contradiction. She speaks in broken Spanish, provoking misunderstandings and using puns that often result in double entendres and add extra layers of meaning. By giving La India María a heavy accent, Velasco constantly stresses the character's marginality. María's outsider position is reinforced by her occasional long diatribes about social injustice, reminiscent of Cantinflas, who became known for his "demo-babble," a comic imitation of political speech aimed at pacifying the masses. Velasco often inserts a few lines in native languages, such as Chichimeca and Nahuatl, without translating them into Spanish. While India María's speech is often grammatically incorrect, nuances emerge with the use of double entendres and hidden meanings evoked by phrases in her native language. These double entendres and partially accessible parentheses in the dialogue mark the character as the Other and at the same time serve as potentially subversive inside jokes for those who understand them. When La India María verbally confronts other character types, such as corrupt bureaucrats, Velasco uses the encounter to criticize ethnic, gender, and class discrimination, the absurdity of the law, and rampant bureaucracy. In such moments, the character draws attention to herself, but the laugh is not at the character's naiveté. Instead, audiences laugh with plucky and brave María as she points out inequalities and stands up for herself—in her own colloquial slang.

CHAPTER 2

MEXPLOITATION

SOON AFTER MY DISCOVERY of the India María films, I started to immerse myself in a variety of low-budget films. I quickly discovered that, while India María may be uniquely funny and charming, María Elena Velasco's films share many characteristics with other films produced between the late 1950s and the late 1980s. Beyond shared plot elements, all of the films were made with low budgets and surprised me with a distinct aesthetic style marked by low production values. In the opening scene of the Vicente Fernández film *Tacos al carbón* (1972), for example, the main character Champi, a poor taco vendor, is introduced with an over-the-top simulation of a thunderstorm, featuring totally fake and cheap-looking lightning. Instead of being neatly crafted, the film is marked by countless technical flaws. These aesthetic markers appear across all categories of low-budget Mexican film. In terms of characterization, Champi is shallow and lacks psychological motivation. The acting comes across as wooden. In comedies like the India María films, slapstick scenes—for instance, a fistfight over territory for vending stalls—provide most of the humorous moments, while witty dialogue is less common.

Spanish speakers commonly use the terms *cine popular* [popular cinema] or *churro* [literally, a deep-fried pastry] to describe the India María films and similar comedies such as *Tacos al carbón* as well as other low-budget Mexican movies, including wrestling films starring famous *luchadores* [wrestlers] such as El Santo, sexy films featuring scantily clad women, and violent border stories of migrants crossing to the United States and drug trafficking. Like the India María films, these movies consistently focus on characters from the lower rungs of society. *Cine popular* refers to films that were—and still are—successful with moviegoers, from Mexico's Golden Age melodramas to the cheap productions of the

1960s and more recent decades. While the term had a positive connotation during the Golden Age, it gradually shifted to a more negative understanding, as it is attached to the films of the so-called crisis in Mexican cinema. In Mexico today, films are commonly divided into "popular" cinema for the masses (low art) and "quality" cinema (high art), a division that was introduced and heavily promoted by newspaper film critics during the 1970s and 1980s (Castro Ricalde 2004b: 195). The English word "popular" carries an additional layer of political meaning, evoking the culture of common people as a sign of cohesion and social transformation (Shohat and Stam 1994: 340). It often conveys pejorative aesthetic judgments. To avoid confusion with the nuances in English, I refrain from labeling the films discussed in this book *cine popular.*

A *churro*—the other term commonly used for these films since the late 1950s—is a deep-fried pastry, a popular sweet snack in Latin America and around the world, sold by fast-food chains such as Taco Bell and Del Taco in the United States. Labeling films as *churros* is a nod to the speed and low cost of the pastry's manufacturing as well as its sweet taste but lack of nutritional value (García Riera 1998: 151). All *churros* are said to look and taste the same—not unlike the films that adhere to a simple story formula. Like the term *cine popular*, *churro* is not exclusively used to describe low-budget Mexican films with low production values, but all uses of this word are derogatory and bear culturally determined and overtly negative connotations, implying that the films have little, if any, cultural value. This is not uncommon; popular texts are often discursively linked to base pleasures such as casual sex and, in this case, junk food. They are also often labeled "sugary" or "cloying" (Fiske 1995: 121, 122). Significantly, Mexican American film scholar Adán Avalos (2009: 187) points out that the term *churro* is predominantly employed by Mexico's elites to degrade or deride films consumed by the lower classes. The terms *cine popular* and *churro* don't take into account questions about how the movies are made or how they are screened. Because the aim of my study is to emphasize all areas of cinematic practice, it makes little sense to use terms that could lead to confusion or misunderstanding.

In the Anglo-American context, low-budget films that share certain aesthetic characteristics are commonly termed B movies or exploitation cinema. B movies emerged during the Great Depression in the 1930s in Hollywood (Taves 1993: 313). As their name indicates, B movies are defined in opposition to A movies, which were produced by the main industry studios (A studios) with extensive means (Taves 1993: 314). The Mexican films analyzed in this book were produced later (between the late 1950s and the late 1980s). And there was also no division between an A and B film industry in Mexico.

Like B movies, exploitation films were produced within the classical Hollywood era from 1919 and 1959. They are also a production category opposed to the mainstream industry, dominated by the studios. Film scholar Eric Schaefer (1999: 4–6), whose book defined the "forbidden thrills" of exploitation cinema, suggests that the classical exploitation film usually conformed to a series of attributes. First, the film's subject matter is taboo: sex, prostitution, or drug abuse. Second, the films are cheaply made by independent firms, with low production values. Third, the films are independently distributed. Fourth, the films are exhibited in small theaters and the screenings are often accompanied by carnival-like or other extrafilmic events. Finally, classical exploitation films are continually in release. Sometimes they are sporadically exhibited during a span of up to twenty years. Although Schaefer examines Hollywood exploitation films, the concept of exploitation clearly works in other national and historical contexts, including Mexico and Latin America in later decades (Ruétalo and Tierney 2009: 3).

Like exploitation cinema, the India María films and other Mexican low-budget productions are marked by low production values. Scripts are often recycled, and production costs are kept to a minimum. As in the United States, low-budget Mexican films are usually shown as double features and advertised as two films for the price of one. In venues screening these comedies, as well as wrestling, border, and sexy films, extrafilmic practices were actively encouraged. Theaters spared no effort to transform the theatergoing experience into a carnival. They commonly organized slide presentations or hired performers to attend screenings—like exhibitors of US exploitation films (Schaefer 1999: 6).

Within the films set pieces and excessive spectacles—in the sense of Gunning's (1986: 64) cinema of attraction—are key, interrupting the focus on the narrative. In the India María films and other low-budget comedies, the slapstick performances are the main attraction. In wrestling films, long fights in the ring interrupt the story. In the sexy films, naked bodies are displayed as a visual spectacle. Border action films use violence as an excessive spectacle, highlighting injured and ruined bodies and playing out graphic action scenes in loving detail.

Exploitation has become a common term in recent years, appended to almost any cinematic theme. Generally, it underscores the filmmakers' calculated intent to make a profit from specific subjects or emotions.

Movies with explicit sexual content, for example, are commonly known as "sexploitation." "Blaxploitation" is a term used since the 1970s to describe a genre of low-budget action films featuring an African American cast and exploiting racial stereotypes.[1] At the same time, scholars and film critics have adapted the term to low-budget films of defined geographical regions or countries. Dolores Tierney and Victoria Ruétalo (2009: 2), for example, speak of "Latsploitation" when referring to low-budget films from across all of Latin America. Several scholars and film critics have repeatedly labeled Mexican films produced from the 1950s to the late 1980s as "Mexploitation." Andrew Syder and Dolores Tierney (2005), for example, explore the transnational circulation of Mexican wrestling films. Film scholar Doyle Greene (2005) published a book dedicated to the analysis of wrestling and vampire films. Other scholars have used the term to describe sexy movies or border adventure films. In their contribution to Ruétalo and Tierney's collection of essays, Catherine Benamou (2009) and Sergio de la Mora (2009) focus on the public image of two Mexican actresses famous for their appearances in sexy movies or border adventures. Scholars Norma Iglesias (1991) and Hugo Benavides (2008) shed light on the much-understudied narco dramas and their cultural impact. A recent book by Rosana Díaz-Zambrana and Patricia Tomé (2012) deals with Latin America's horror film tradition, which is closely linked to Mexploitation. Ryan Rashotte (2015) provides insight into numerous border adventure films and their relation to the drug cartels in Mexico. Thus this book clearly fits into a current academic trend of reevaluating low-budget films within Latin America and elsewhere (Tierney 2014: 130). One of my aims here is to explore the national specificity of Mexploitation cinema and contribute to an understanding of an important historic era.

The term "Mexploitation" sometimes has been used to imply films that degrade Mexican culture (Greene 2005, 2007). Given the sometimes negative past connotations of the term "Mexploitation," I am especially cautious with value-freighted terms, such as "poorly crafted," "lowbrow," or "low-quality," which subtly discredit these films. It would be foolhardy to deny, however, that aspects of the films presented in this book—including their aesthetic qualities, their content, their exhibition at "second-class" movie theaters, and even their mode of production—often receive negative attention from politicians, film critics, and some cinema lovers. Despite its sometimes problematic associations, I argue that the term "Mexploitation" best describes the films analyzed in this book, because they share several key characteristics with classical Hollywood exploitation films. I want to state directly that I never employ the term as a diminishment of Mexico's culture or people. Instead I use it to describe a category of low-budget films with identifiable shared characteristics. My understanding of "Mexploitation" includes the recurring characteristics of the films, their production and exhibition practices, and different formats ranging from film to television series and straight-to-video productions.

Despite the similarities between classical exploitation and Mexploitation, differences exist. Most importantly, unlike "exploitation" cinema in the United States, "Mexploitation" is not a category of film production that existed within the Mexican film industry. Mexploitation productions flourished during a time span of roughly thirty years (from the mid-1950s to late 1980s), with highs and lows in terms of production output. Contrary to the situation in the United States, Mexico had no division into a mainstream and an exploitation industry. The low-budget Mexican films were the main output of the industry from the 1950s to the 1980s. Also, the notion of "low-budget" itself shifts at the border, as the majority of films in Latin America and Mexico were and still are produced cheaply. Filmmaking in Latin America simply operates on a smaller scale than in the United States and Europe. Finally, censorship regulations did not have the same consistent influence on cinema in Mexico as in the United States (Ruétalo and Tierney 2009: 4; Schaefer 1999: 136–164).

I suggest dividing Mexploitation cinema into four thematic categories: (1) comedies with a hero from the margins of Mexican society, (2) wrestling films, (3) sexy films, and (4) border films. As noted, wrestling and border films have previously been labeled as Mexploitation by other scholars, but comedies and sexy movies have seldom been considered within this paradigm.

FUNNY FOLK HEROES

Between the Golden Age and the 1980s hundreds of comedies that used an innocent form of humor—including the India María films—reached the small and big screen. Some of the performers, like Velasco, debuted on vaudeville stages before moving to the big screen. Many comedies tell the story of an adventurous migration, tackle religion and church hypocrisy, or foster fantasies of upward mobility. The comedies' formulaic narratives are frequently interrupted by comic routines.

Like the India María films, the majority of comedies revolve around certain key character types that represent Mexican stereotypes, such as the *pelado* [urban male drifter or "bum"] and the *charro* [cowboy], a category that Vicente Fernández dominated for decades. The characters are usually depicted as antiheroes just trying to make a living. By the end of the films, they usually triumph and become full-fledged if bumbling heroes, even though their traits and actions violate traditional expectations for a hero. As with Velasco and Fernández, comedians and their character types entirely shape these comic films. Once a comedy became a hit, a filmmaker could rely on films similar in theme, with the same characters played by the same actors—and sometimes even identical stories—to be solid moneymakers in subsequent years. Another form of lucrative recycling was to shoot sequels or adapt successful stories for television. Remakes of former box-office hits were also common.

Fortino Mario Alfonso Moreno Reyes, known and loved by his stage name Cantinflas, remains unchallenged as Mexican film's most prominent comic performer. Cantinflas had the leading role in more than fifty comedies, and his films were successful at the box office for half a century. He achieved his greatest success during the Golden Age of Mexican cinema (Pérez Turrent 1990: 25). Reyes, like Velasco, was primarily identified with his longtime character, a loveable *pelado* in baggy pants with a rope for a belt and a distinctive mustache. The Cantinflas comedies mostly have simple, linear stories, liberally interrupted by comic routines. An example is *El analfabeto* (The illiterate) (1961, directed by Miguel M. Delgado). The film tells the story of a poor illiterate man named Inocencio. He is informed by letter that he is the sole beneficiary of a large sum of money but can't read the letter. While he is learning to read, greedy opportunists are after his money. In the end, however, he learns to defend himself and claims his inheritance. When Cantinflas and La India María are on screen, the underdog always wins—a potent fantasy of empowerment that has appealed to popular cinema audiences for generations. Mexico's audiences in particular have a long history of appreciating stage and film caricatures of ordinary working-class men and women, repressed by the elite, who turn their circumstances around by making fun of authorities ranging from police to bureaucrats. While many of Cantinflas's films belong to this category, some also treat aspects of religion. In *El padrecito* (The little monk) (1964, directed by Miguel M. Delgado) Cantinflas stars in the lead role as a priest, similar to La India María in *La madrecita* (The little nun) (1974) or *Sor Tequila* (Sister Tequila) (1980). In fact, the plots of the three films are almost identical.

Roberto Gómez Bolaños, known as Chespirito [Little Shakespeare], was another comedian famous for his family-friendly innocent humor. Bolaños primarily worked in television. Between 1972 and 1979 alone, he appeared in around 250 half-hour television episodes. Two of the characters that he developed were among the most popular characters across Latin America and among Latinos in the United States: El Chavo del Ocho

2.1 AND 2.2. *El Chanfle* (1979) with Chespirito and *El barrendero* (1982) with Cantinflas are both examples of very successful Mexploitation films. Both performers starred in numerous films, in television series, and on theater stages. (Agrasánchez Film Archive)

[The Lad from the Eighth], an orphan who lived in a poor neighborhood in Mexico City, and El Chapulín Colorado [The Colored Grasshopper], a clumsy superhero. El Chavo del Ocho is an infantile boy played by an adult. He lives in a poor neighborhood and often gets in some kind of argument with the local landlord, the only wealthy character. Whenever El Señor Barriga enters the set, El Chavo finds a way to hit him and then makes an excuse that he did not actually mean to do any harm. The episodes often end in slapstick chaos, with all of the characters behaving like children: the final scenes degenerate into clownish fists flailing and talcum or dirt flying in a raucous mess. El Chavo del Ocho offers a fantasy of poverty that allows the downtrodden characters to come out on top—or at least to get in a good punch (Nasser 2008: 143, 158).

Bolaños's superhero character Chapulín never gets anything right, despite his good intentions. In every episode, he sets out to solve people's conflicts, ranging from everyday to extraordinary problems. Armed with a plastic hammer, he confronts his enemies to rescue innocent victims—who constantly insult him or wish that they had called more reliable superheroes such as Superman or Batman. Both characters reveal Mexico's power structures in ways that echo the India María films.

While several male performers—among them Cantinflas and Chespirito—were highly successful, Velasco remains a female exception. Other comic actresses mostly figured in supporting roles never reached the same recognition as male stars. Like Velasco, these actresses often played consistent character types, including the *corcholata* [drunken prostitute] and the *pelangocha* [wisecracking secretary] (Obscura Gutiérrez 1997: 177). Evita Muñoz, called Chachita, played a witch in a number of comedies between 1982 and 1985. As in Velasco's roles, Muñoz conveyed her humor through dialogue and performance; she mispronounced words, played with them, or used sentences with double entendres (Obscura Gutiérrez 1997: 177). Muñoz's jokes often contained crude humor, however, and the films were part of the dirty comedy humor known as *albures*.[2]

Finally, it has to be mentioned that comedy and comic themes frequently spiced up other low-budget genres. Wrestling, sexy, and border films themselves often overlap. It is sometimes quite difficult to determine clearly in what "category" a particular film should be placed. Often the most successful elements of each category such as nudity, dance routines, and wrestling were combined. The results included comedies spiced up with nudity that take place in border locales, with a fighting scene added in the final showdown. In a similar way, the India María films straddle various genres, including elements of wrestling films (*¡El que no corre . . . vuela!*), border movies (*Okey, Mister Pancho*, *Ni de aquí, ni de allá*), and dance routines. Despite the overlapping of genres, each Mexploitation category has unique characteristics and stars.

WRESTLING WITH THE STARS

Since the late 1950s, countless films have been set in the world of professional wrestling and starred famous fighters (*luchadores*), with successful franchises based on real wrestlers, including Blue Demon, Mil Máscaras [Thousand Masks], and El Santo. These wrestlers often appeared in different media—television, comics, and cinema—over years or even decades. As in the Batman or James Bond franchises, the popular hero was the main element in a multifaceted marketing strategy that included film as one element (Peralta 1999: 35). Scholars and critics have characterized wrestling films as a mix of genres, ranging from melodrama to comedy, science fiction, and horror. Heather Levi points out what moviegoers could expect:

> What distinguished the wrestling films from other movies was the insertion of one or more scenes of *lucha libre* [wrestling] into the narrative. The wrestlers would spend most of the screen time battling evil, solving mysteries, or untangling domestic complications, the plot interrupted by gratuitous *lucha libre* matches tucked into the narrative like awkward dance numbers. (Levi 2001: 337)

Most wrestling films do not seamlessly integrate the in-the-ring fights into the ongoing narrative. Wrestling heroes begin by fighting monsters or other opponents outside the ring—this is the main plot, in terms of both screen time and narrative development—then all of a sudden go back to their day job of wrestling in the ring. The footage of wrestling matches frequently is taken from actual fights and integrated into the narrative acts as padding, which Eric Schaefer (1999: 68) has described as a common practice of exploitation production—a cheap way of filling running time. These wrestling sequences, often lasting five to ten minutes, contain scant plot development; the real focus is on the physical spectacle.

What is striking and widely noted about *lucha libre* movies is the extent to which they utilize conventions and the iconography of Hollywood horror movies, science fiction films, and Westerns. They include similar characters, such as mad scientists, vampires, and other B-movie staples, and some explicitly refer to whole scenes or scenarios from established classics (Syder and Tierney 2005: 38). Wrestling films so freely borrow from other films, in fact, that they constitute a "recycling culture" (Greene 2005: 16). Many of these films incorporate indigenous themes, characters, or settings. Homegrown monsters such as the Aztec mummy or La Llorona [The Crying Woman] embody a cultural thread very specific to the Mexican context (Syder and Tierney 2005: 39). The mash-up of genres and characters ranging from wrestlers, to mad scientists, to Aztec mummies was highly popular with Mexican audiences.

Before they made it to the big screen, these professional fighters established reputations and fame in the ring as either *técnico* [fair] or *rudo* [ruthless] wrestlers, representing either good or evil (hero or antagonist). Often they changed their moral stance over the course of their career—sometimes even during the course of a fight. Attending *lucha libre* matches was among the favorite leisure activities of the urban lower classes in the 1940s and 1950s, before the series and films were produced and became widely popular (Bertaccini 2001: 79; Levi 1999: 180). With the introduction of television, the wrestling matches and fictional *lucha libre* serials were aired on the then-new medium, opening additional spaces and prac-

2.3. The wrestler El Santo became famous in the ring and through a comic strip published regularly in various Mexican newspapers before starring in a myriad of films, here in *Misterio en las Bermudas* (1979). (Agrasánchez Film Archive)

tices for the reception of *lucha libre*—notably, middle-class and upper-class audiences (Levi 2001: 337). Despite this success, in 1954 wrestling shows were banned from television for being too violent, particularly for young viewers. Since then fictional wrestling stories onscreen have been highly successful at movie theaters for over three decades. Today wrestling matches and wrestling films continue to draw people to the arena. Wrestling shows are held once a week in many cities. But wrestling films are mostly watched at home on DVD or online.

It is impossible to discuss Mexican wrestling films without mentioning "El Santo, el Enmascarado de Plata" [the Saint with the Silver Mask]—Mexico's most famous wrestler of all time, loved by generations of fans around the world. For almost three decades, he was omnipresent in films, the arena, comic strips, radio, and television as well as in the print press. He acted in over fifty wrestling films and has become a legend in Mexican culture. In the 1960s he starred in at least one film per year, constantly fighting the evil of the world, overcoming existing power structures and threats from outer space. El Santo debuted in the ring, after which a comic strip was dedicated to him and regularly published in the press, before he finally started to appear on screen (Bertaccini 2001: 95).

Just as in the comic strips, in his films El Santo defeats monsters, vampires, and other evil creatures. Some of his films merge the formula of the adventurous migration journey with fantasies of upward mobility. In *Santo en la frontera del terror* (Santo on the border of terror) (1981, directed by Rafael Pérez Grovas) for example, El Santo undertakes a dangerous journey to the US border, where he fights against a mad scientist exploiting undocumented Mexican workers. The films scarcely bother to establish the character El Santo, because he was so well known. In *Santo en la frontera del terror*, a single take of the Rio Grande indicates the setting of the film in the border region. This initial shot is directly followed by a wrestling match scene: El Santo, disguised in his wrestling outfit, consisting of only a silver mask and tight pants, is carried into the ring on the shoulders of his fans, who encourage him with loud cheering. The camera frames him from a low angle so that he looks monumental and imposing. When El Santo enters the ring, he is typified as a *técnico* [good guy] as two wrestlers attack him using cheating, unnecessary roughness, and trickery. Spectators consequently invest El Santo with the moral qualities of a fair wrestler who fights for a good cause—even against unfair odds—and know that he will prevail as the hero of the film.

When El Santo ventures on a dangerous journey to the border later in the same film to defeat the mad scientist to free his exploited compatriots, he leaps fences, fights fervently, and puts his body at risk, much as La India María does, thus stressing not humor but bravery. El Santo is further defined by his performance of religious rituals, such as praying and worshiping Catholic symbols. Although El Santo's ethnicity is to some extent neutralized through the wearing of a mask, he is clearly established as being a member of Mexico's lower class by his profession as a wrestler. Significantly, El Santo's aim is mostly to bring escapist relief for the fellow members of his class. His character type is provided with positive features and therefore addresses the Mexican working-class spectators as "their" hero fighting for a good cause. El Santo not only became a symbol of a working-class hero but also represents the fairly straightforward catharsis of wrestling, in which the spectacle of abjection is redeemed through the triumph of good (Levi 1999: 179).

Santo contra las mujeres vampiro (*Samson versus the Vampire Women*) (1962, US 1963, directed by Alfonso Corona Blake) was one of his most successful films (Bertaccini 2001: 103; Wilt 1998: 139). Here El Santo fights against vicious women who try to seduce him with their supernatural sexual powers. Modernization left its mark on the character over time, and toward the end of his onscreen career El Santo faced new enemies. In *Santo contra el asesino de televisión* (Santo versus the murderer of TV) (1981, directed by Rafael Pérez Grovas), he is equipped with the newest technologies to fight his enemy, who is no longer an attractive woman, a mad scientist, or some wild beast but a miscreant trying to destroy the accomplishments of modern society.

The wrestler El Santo remained a mystery to his fans, for he refused to reveal his true identity and always wore the silver mask, even when speaking to the press about his Catholic faith, the importance of fidelity, and family values (Bertaccini 2001: 105). Only once shortly before his death did he reveal his face on television. He was however buried in his wrestling suit and his mask (Levi 1999: 182). El Santo was a hero on and off screen. His consistency made him a good companion for his audience and their everyday habits of media consumption (Bertaccini 2001: 104; Fernández Reyes 2004: 17f.).

El Santo was clearly Mexico's most popular wrestler, but many other wrestling films with professional real-life fighters such as Blue Demon and Mil Máscaras satisfied the high demand for visual enchantment from the ring and other spheres. Female wrestlers became increasingly popular in the 1960s both on and off screen (Wilt 1998: 140). Films such as *Las luchadoras vs el médico asesino* (*Doctor of Doom*) (1962, US 1963, directed by René Cardona) and *Las luchadoras contra la momia* (*Wrestling Women versus the Aztec Mummy*) (1964, US 1965, directed by René Cardona), both starring Lorena Velázquez, depict female wrestlers fighting the evils of the world. Like their male counterparts, female-wrestling heroines exposed their bodies as they grappled with bad guys in and out of the ring, which creates part of the visual pleasure. The partial nudity, however, reflects physical exertion, strength, and independent achievement—a departure from the next popular category.

SEXY AND WE KNOW IT

Miles of skin, erotic allusions, and prostitution are the striking features of the lucrative Mexican "sexy movies" also known as *cabaretera* [cabaret] and *fichera* [token] films, which rely on cabarets, dance clubs, and brothels as the main settings for stories centering on female dancers. Sexy movies or "sex-Mexploitation" films—as they might be called—proliferated widely during the early 1970s to late 1980s, the same period when most of the films of La India María were first released in theaters. As in the India María movies playing on other screens, humor and religion play a role in these films, but the sexy movies mainly use dirty humor as opposed to the innocent form suitable for the whole family.

Professional *cabaretera* and *fichera* dancers played the leading roles in these films, which ultimately led to two discernible film categories. As in the wrestling films, many real-world professionals transitioned onto the big screen. The *fichera* films—derived from the earlier *cabaretera* films, produced before the 1960s—borrowed many plot elements (De la Mora 2006: 109). The *cabaretera* films often combined a series of dance routines with a simple story: a young innocent girl from the countryside comes to the city and gets into trouble. Due to unfortunate circumstances, she is forced to work at a cabaret as a dancer. Often she ends up as a prostitute or becomes a famous dancer—or both (García Riera 1998: 154). Just as in the wrestling films and the India María films, the main attraction is the body as a spectacle. The dance numbers are performed at full length, continually slowing down the narrative to focus on the performance. The actresses performing the leading parts were commonly exotic dancers, who got their start in vaudeville theaters. Cuban stars were common, lighting up the screen with elaborate Afro-Caribbean/Cuban dance numbers. One of the performers was Yolanda Montes. She appeared as the character Tongolele in numerous films in which she ecstatically shook her hips and other body parts (Stevenson 2001). The titles of the films that she performs in often reveal their entire plot. In *Las fabulosas del reventón II* (The fabulous women of the wild party II) (1983, directed by Fernando Durán Rojas) Tongolele performs a series of dance numbers, while trying to open a dance club in Acapulco.

In the 1960s and 1970s *fichera* films combined explicit nudity and soft-core sex with just about any imaginable plot device. The stories often center on topless dancers whom male customers hire with tokens (*fichas*), frequently as the prelude to a sexual encounter. In these films the focus clearly shifted from the earlier *cabareteras*: naked female bodies are shown in long takes, mostly in tight framing. Not only was the sexual content heightened but the male protagonists of such films allowed the viewers vicariously to experience a male heterosexual adventure.[3] Commonly, a Mexican playboy gets into a series of situations that require him to seduce a number of beautiful women. Films such as *Bellas de noche* (Beauties of the night) (1975) and its sequel *Las ficheras: Bellas de noche II parte* (The B girls: Beauties of the night II) (1977), both directed by Miguel M. Delgado, present a variety of narrative lines, all intersecting

2.4, 2.5, 2.6, AND 2.7. Films such as *Tívoli* (1975), *Noches de cabaret* (1978), *Albures mexicanos* (1975), and *Las del talón* (1978) have sparked a trend of sexy movies generating lucrative revenues. (Agrasánchez Film Archive)

at the club where the *ficheras* work. A series of side comedy routines by known actors is inserted to spice up the plot (Ramírez Berg 1992: 126). Other films such as *Noches de cabaret* (Carnival nights) (1978, directed by Rafael Portillo), *La pulquería* (The pulque tavern) (1981, directed by Víctor Manuel Castro), and *La guerra de los sexos* (The war of the sexes)

(1978, directed by Raúl de Anda Jr.) feature a Mexican macho who fears having lost his manhood or being homosexual and pursues one or more women to regain his potency. This loss-of-potency/regained-potency formula is repeated in endless sexy comedies (Ramírez Berg 1992: 126).

A small number of actresses and actors starred in numerous sexy movies, particularly during the period of the *cabaretera* films, produced during Mexican cinema's Golden Age. Their appearance usually guaranteed box-office success. *Fichera* films have also produced female stars. Most controversial was probably Sasha Montenegro, an actress of Italian descent. She launched her film career in *lucha libre* films, obtaining several minor parts in movies starring El Santo. In the 1970s and the 1980s she became one of the most famous *fichera* performers, starring in films such as *Noches de cabaret* and *Pulquería.* Montenegro plays a transvestite dancer who is in fact a woman in *Noches de cabaret* and appears as a sexy doctor in *Pulquería.* Sasha Montenegro moved into the limelight probably not because of her role as a *fichera*, however, but because she carried on a relationship with the Mexican president José López Portillo (1976–1982), who was still married at the time.

Isela Vega was another actress who gained fame for her sexually explicit on-screen performances as a sexy blonde. Unlike Sasha Montenegro, Isela Vega was associated with a multilayered star text. Her body of work is harder to categorize, for she appeared in over one hundred films ranging from soft-core *ficheras* to television series and independent art projects (De la Mora 2009: 245). Although Vega had two husbands, she created an image of herself that was never tied to any man. She also crossed national boundaries; she appeared in a series of Hollywood films, including *The Deadly Trackers* (US 1973/Mexico 1974, directed by Barry Shear), based on a screenplay by Samuel Fuller. She even wrote a script and directed her own film: *Las amantes del señor de la noche* (Lovers of the lord of the night) (1986, directed by Isela Vega).

The performances of Sasha Montenegro and Isela Vega—like those of María Elena Velasco—challenge traditional notions of femininity, albeit in significantly different ways. At the time of their release, many viewed the films as offensive due to their depictions of onscreen sex and in Vega's case "manly" swearing. The characters played by Montenegro and Vega break with images of female archetypes such as the virgin or the submissive suffering woman all too common in Mexican film (De la Mora 2009: 250). Likewise, both women provoked numerous scandals in the press. Montenegro made headlines through her affair with Portillo, and Isela

Vega shocked the public when she posed for *Playboy* magazine as a Mexican female revolutionary (De la Mora 2009: 250). Vega admits to wanting her scandals to be seen as acts of rebellion that shake people up and get them to think critically (Oscar Díaz cited in De la Mora 2009: 245). Both Vega and Montenegro consciously constructed star images that established them as "bad girls" who do not fit into well-established definitions of gender difference in Mexico.

Although these female stars clearly were key for the success of these films, the films also rely on well-known male star performers—notably Jorge Rivero. Debuting in the wrestling genre in the 1960s, he had his breakthrough as a handsome playboy with a troubled sex life in numerous *fichera* films, among them *Noches de cabaret* and *Pulquería.* His good looks and muscular build assured revenues and also led to his appearances in several Hollywood films and *telenovelas.* A number of less strikingly handsome actors also made careers mostly in Mexican sexy movies, among them Eduardo de la Peña and Carlos Marcos Aguilar. They commonly played machos or womanizers in search of sexual adventure. Despite their relative lack of sex appeal, they rarely have any difficulty seducing good-looking women in the fantasy world of the sexy films. The murky and violent underworld of the border region provides a strikingly different kind of fantasy in another popular Mexploitation category.

RUN FOR THE BORDER

The border region between Mexico and the United States is the setting for migration, corruption, drug trafficking, and crimes—and thousands of Mexploitation films (Rashotte 2015: 2). These border films often depict extreme violence and stereotypical characters such as coyotes (people smugglers), desperate migrants, drug dealers, and prostitutes. Rubén Galindo Jr., director and producer of numerous border films, concisely summarized his formula:

> Primero presentas a tu personaje, después lo echas al río y empiezan los problemas, después se intensifican los problemas, y ya justo cuando se va a caer en la cascada, lo rescatas. Esa es la estructura dramática del cine mundial. Todas estas cosas las pones en situaciones de la frontera y ahí está tu película.
>
> [First, you present your character, then you throw him into the river, and the problems start. Then you intensify them, and just before he falls down

the waterfall you save him. That is the dramatic structure of world cinema. Take all these things and put them on the border, and there is your film.] (Iglesias 1991: 66)

This formula, along with a border star actor for the leading role (either one of the Almada brothers or Rosa Gloria Chagoyán, the female star of the genre) and ideally a couple of *corridos* [Mexican ballads] performed by Los Tigres del Norte, nearly assured a box-office border hit. Although condemned by film critics for their oversimplification, repetition of stories, and reuse of actors, these films have strongly influenced and shaped the discourse on migration (Iglesias 1991: 67).

One of the formative border movies is *La banda del carro rojo* (The red car gang) (1976, directed by Rubén Galindo). The film brought national and international fame to the Almada brothers. Both Mario and Fernando Almada appeared in hundreds of border films, always playing simple Mexicans, borderline criminals struggling to survive, or supporters of migrating Mexicans.[4] *La banda del carro rojo* established a common

2.8. Numerous films, including *Gatilleros del Río Bravo* (1984) and here *El fugitivo de Sonora* (1989), star the two well-known Almada brothers and contain all elements of the border action film. (Agrasánchez Film Archive)

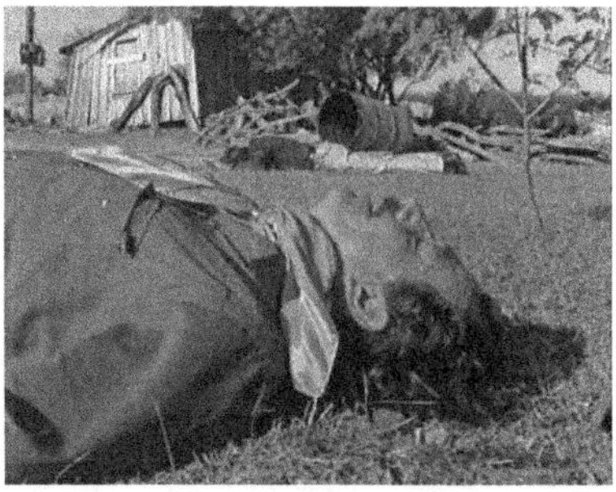

2.9 AND 2.10. The film *La banda del carro rojo* (1976), starring the Almada brothers, is the best-known example of the border action category. Various set pieces halt the development of the story, such as the repeated performance of the title song.

plotline: like several India María films, the film takes fans on an adventurous migration. A group of Mexicans from different social backgrounds migrate to the United States, where they all struggle to survive. When they are offered a fortune to transport drugs across the border, they give in and are willing to participate in an illegal act. Unlike La India María, the characters never fully realize what they have gotten themselves into and ultimately all die.[5]

Like other Mexploitation films, *La banda del carro rojo*'s narrative is repeatedly interrupted and delayed by long chase scenes, gunfights, and a band performing Mexican ballads that reflect on the plot but slow down the narrative. Instead of the expected narrative climax—the drug trafficking across the border—the film's ending is a reprise of the title song lasting over eight minutes, with all four main characters, the border patrol, and the band reappearing. Like the India María films, *La banda del carro rojo* combines the thematic category of adventurous migration with the display of spectacles: here chase scenes or shoot-outs instead of the slapstick performance. In the final battle of the film, all four protagonists are killed in a violent exchange of gunfire. Their bodies are riddled with bullets and splashed with blood. Each death is shown at full length, and the camera is addressed directly.

The film is based on a song of the same title by Los Tigres del Norte, the most famous *corrido* band. The song *La banda del carro rojo* is performed by the band at various times throughout the film, before the final reprise at the film's close. Not only is the same song performed several times, but the mise-en-scène of the two performances is almost identical. The musicians face the firmly positioned camera playing their instru-

2.11 AND 2.12. In *Las braceras* (1981) the border action plot is combined with partial nudity. Rosa Gloria Chagoyán—star of the genre—charms with her actions, here in *La rielera* (1988). (Agrasánchez Film Archive)

ments, and the song is badly lip-synced. Unlike performances in many American musicals, the musical performances in border action films do not figure as moments of emotional excess closely related to the mood of the protagonist but instead foreground the act of performing itself (Altman 2002: 44; Laing 2000: 7). Most Mexploitation films include such pastiches of popular musical hits. Often the popular tunes are separately listed as menu items on DVDs.

Filmmakers frequently combined elements of border movies with plot points from the previously described sexy movies. *Mojado . . . pero caliente* (Wet . . . but hot) (1989, directed by Rafael Portillo) and *Nos reimos de la migra* (Poking fun at the border patrol) (1984, directed by Víctor Manuel Castro) are two examples. *Mojado . . . pero caliente* is a sort of buddy movie about the adventures of two goofy Mexican migrants who encounter plenty of willing women during their adventures. In *Nos reimos de la migra*, a *fichera* showgirl is kidnapped by her uncle who heads a drug cartel in Texas. Three drunks from Mexico City sneak across the border to rescue her. Sexy border films combine border adventures with nudity for a certain joyful excess of body spectacle. Instead of just crossing the border, which is commonly depicted as a miserable physical ordeal, the characters are nearly naked for much of the journey and prance across the border with their minds on romance.

The most renowned female border star is undoubtedly Rosa Gloria Chagoyán. In the course of her career she has performed in over fifty films. She moved into the limelight in the role of a sensuous "warrior, capable of carrying the nation's burden on her shoulders" (Benamou 2009: 172). *Lola la trailera* (*Lola the Truck Driving Woman*) (1983, US 1985, directed by Raúl Fernández)—the film Chagoyán is famous for—tells the story of an innocent and attractive peasant girl who decides to seek revenge for the death of her father, who was killed for refusing to get involved with the drug-trafficking mafia.

The sequels *Lola la trailera 2* (Lola the truck driving woman 2) (1986) and *Lola la trailera 3* (Lola the truck driving woman 3) (1991), both also directed by Raúl Fernandez, were equally successful. A television series with the same title later was produced in which Lola sits behind the steering wheel of a pink truck. The films and the television series follow a similar storyline: the border region becomes an unsafe place due to the evil doings of a series of villains. Timid at first, Lola learns to defend herself against a variety of adversaries: drug dealers, brothel owners, and an evil blonde woman who stands in for "white" evil in general. In the end, Lola restores peace through her own physical feats and modern weapons, finally overcoming unfair power structures. As a grand finale, she mows down her opponents with a machine gun and saves her companion's life. The *Los Angeles Times* sums up: "[The producer's] success was to strip the fiery Rosa Gloria Chagoyán down to her machine gun and little else and to turn her loose à la Rambo against a gang of ruthless dope dealers" (Goldin and Cooper 1986: 12).

To this date, Chagoyán continues to appear across different media in Mexico and the United States. In 2000 she launched a Mexican radio program called *Aventuras de Lola la trailera* (Adventures of Lola the truck driving woman), and she has hosted folk-song contests and appeared at nightclubs (Benamou 2009: 177). Chagoyán's performance in numerous border films brought her admirers from both sides of the border and also led to plenty of imitations, among them *Muerte en Tijuana* (Death in Tijuana) (1991, directed by Hernando Name). Inspired by her character, truck drivers became new heroes. Spinning wheels, big steel trucks, and long roads winding through the deserted border region emerged as filmic motifs.

Film scholar Catherine Benamou has convincingly argued that Rosa Gloria Chagoyán can be seen as a symbol of Mexican identity as the modern version of the iconic figure *la soldadera*—the female Mexican revolutionary soldier. Like La India María, Chagoyán's persona does not neatly fit into gender- and class-bound genre parameters. With interesting parallels to Velasco, Chagoyán has been able to cleverly combine her role as an action heroine and her star image as an everywoman, with an abiding sense of affection for the less fortunate (Benamou 2009: 173). Their characters, too, bear some resemblance: La India María and Lola La Trailera are both clearly portrayed as "of the people" (*del pueblo*). Lola oscillates between seductress and modest yet proud cowgirl. When she brutally kills her opponents, she does so for a good reason. She fights mostly against injustice caused by power hierarchies rigged against the poor. Today Chagoyán regularly appears on radio and TV as a host, giving everyday advice to common folk, further stressing her ordinariness and approachability. In general, she defends women's rights (Benamou 2009: 175, 176). Like the images of most Mexploitation stars, Chagoyán's star image is complemented and brought home to her fans through music and songs performed live at country fairs. Like Velasco's India María, Chagoyán's productions and their reception by a wide audience are informed by both her consistently enacted character and her star image, which together suggest the transgression of traditional gender roles.

MEXPLOITATION STARDOM

Books about Hollywood stars abound, yet few biographies of Mexploitation stars have appeared, perhaps because these actors are still associated with low quality and an audience that doesn't read much. The wrestler El Santo (Rodolfo Guzmán Huerta) is a notable exception and a cottage industry, with at least two biographies currently in print. Although Huerta died in 1984, his fame continues to grow. El Santo has become a folk hero and Mexican icon, with devoted fans around the world (Fernández Reyes 2004; Greene 2005; Syder and Tierney 2005; Wilt 1998). Mexico City's new airport terminal even has a shop exclusively selling El Santo products ranging from DVDs and comics to wrestling robes and backpacks.

Although Mexploitation stars from the 1950s to the late 1980s reliably drew the masses to movie theaters and thereby guaranteed revenues, the industry exerted a relatively low degree of control in the making of their star images. The Mexican film industry never thoroughly regulated the promotion of films. Furthermore, it has not been common practice in Mexico for publicists to control stars' public appearances in the ring, on the stage, or on television. The stars playing certain character types often made films with numerous production companies, contributing to certain inconsistencies in stars' images and the communication of multiple meanings.

Mexploitation stars were paid low salaries compared to Hollywood stars (Goldin and Cooper 1986: 18, 20), but the most important difference between Hollywood and Mexploitation stars was in the trajectory of their star status. Mexploitation narratives fully rely on character-driven plots with a main protagonist. Certain character types such as the wrestler, the mean coyote (human trafficker), and the dancer often reappear in a myriad of films as well as across different media (theater, television, film, comics). The wrestler El Santo, for example, fought in the ring and appeared in a comic strip, on television, and on the big screen. The dancers often performed on theater stages and in films. Unlike most Hollywood stars, Mexploitation stars were directly linked to a certain character type. Usually the character type moved into the limelight first: only subsequently did the person embodying the type become famous. Cantinflas, for example, is primarily associated with his character type, the *pelado*. Only later did audiences become interested in the performer Fortino Mario Alfonso Moreno Reyes. Also, he is called Cantinflas in promotional materials, in gossip, and even when he is referred to as a union member. The same holds true for La India María and El Santo. The blurring or even annulment of the division between the star as a media persona and the character type that he/she impersonates seems especially pronounced in the Mexican context. Because character types typically moved into the limelight before performers, star images fit characters perfectly—indeed they are in effect identical, incorporating all facets of both the character type and as the star's image. Significantly, a high degree of consistency prevails.

MEXPLOITATION, POLITICS, AND CENSORSHIP

The private production companies that produced Mexploitation films, including the companies producing India María films, evolved under very specific political circumstances but did not emerge overnight at a precise historical turning point. Instead, political and industrial circumstances gradually led to this new discernible category, with a majority of the Mexploitation films made between the mid-1960s and the late 1980s. The main goal of this section is to map out the political context in which the Mexploitation films and more precisely the India María films were produced, with particular attention to the interrelation between the Mexican state and the film industry. I argue that certain policies and regulations established prior to the 1960s favored the production and distribution of these films. The section is structured according to presidential terms, because each president had the power to change existing regulations—and did so. Although I focus on Mexploitation films and highlight the factors that contributed to their emergence, I also provide some benchmark data for the Mexican film industry in general. It is worth remembering that these movies were not marginal but made up the majority of films produced in Mexico for three decades. Throughout these years Mexploitation films and the industry that produced them were sometimes supported by the regime in power and at other times actively hindered by it.

From the late 1930s to the late 1940s the Mexican film industry flourished because the country successfully established a mode of film production and distribution with its own studio and star system. Filmmaking in this era became one of the country's largest industries—after the lamination, steel, auto, beer, and cotton wool industries (García Riera 1998: 123). People of all social levels eagerly attended the movies to see the internationally applauded and often romanticized filmic representations of Mexico (Noble 2005: 91; Paranaguá 1998: 33). When *María Candelaria (Xochimilco)* (*Portrait of Maria*) (1944, directed by Emilio Fernández and starring Dolores del Río) won the Grand Prize and the prize for cinematography at the Cannes Film Festival in 1946, Mexican cinema reached its peak of international fame. Mexico basked in praise as a great cinema nation, with its industry no longer hiding in the shadows of its neighbor, the United States. By the following year, however, when *María Candelaria (Xochimilco)* won yet another prize at the International Film Festival in Locarno, Switzerland, Mexico's film industry was already undergoing several changes.

Most evidently, the industry's relation to the United States was being redefined. During World War II, the Mexican film industry enjoyed a favorable position; it received technical and financial support from its northern neighbor, which led to substantial growth and resulted in Mexico becoming the leading cinema nation in Latin America. Argentina—the most productive film nation before World War II—was in disfavor due to its feared Axis sympathies, with sanctions such as the limitation of film stock imposed by the United States. Consequently, Argentina's film production dropped drastically, and Mexico took over the position as the leading exporter of Spanish-language films (Ramírez Berg 1992: 38). World War II was a slack period not only for Argentina but also for Hollywood. Hollywood produced and exported significantly fewer films during this era. Shortly after the war the US industry redefined its strategy and set the recovery of the Latin American market as one of its primary goals. As a result, financial and technological support for Mexico, mainly consisting of raw film stock, was withdrawn (De la Vega Alfaro 1999: 165). This development was a harsh setback for Mexico's industry. The volume of Mexican film production temporarily dropped from seventy-one feature films in 1946 to fifty-seven in 1947 (De la Vega Alfaro 1999: 165). Although the number of films produced increased again, and even surpassed the output of previous years, the Mexican industry became wary of innovation. It had experienced a boom and knew what films worked with audiences. Instead of trying to find new stories or support technological inventions, producers relied on proven box-office hits. They gradually invested less per film produced, which resulted in a large number of films with repetitive stories and low production values (De la Vega Alfaro 1999: 165). By the mid-1950s the majority of commercial producers recycled stories and made films with extremely low budgets. This low-budget production mode prevailed until the late 1980s.[6] Initially the most common film categories were comedies, wrestling films, and films with dancers. Comedies and dance productions remained popular until the end of the period in the late 1980s. Border action films were produced in abundance beginning in the late 1970s.

The Mexican film industry has always been inextricably linked and dependent on state policies and regulations. The political regime in power decided on film policies and everyday practices of the industry. Due to the limitation of a single six-year term for each presidential administration, business practices changed regularly, turning the industry upside down (Maciel 1999: 197). Although laws existed, they were often ignored or bypassed. Mexican film scholar Víctor Manuel Ugalde Romero (1983: 3) expresses the uncertainty prevalent within the industry at the end of each six-year term:

> Preocupación que vino a sumarse, entre otras muchas, a las expectativas que siempre surgen en el último año del mandato presidencial. ¿Sobre quienes serán los nuevos hombres que dirigirán los destinos del cine nacional, y por ello, que nuevos criterios normarán la práctica cinematográfica? [Another concern is added to the expectations that always come up in the last year of a presidential term. The question is: who will be the new men in charge, who will decide about the destiny of the national cinema and introduce new criteria that will regulate cinematic practices?]

Ugalde Romero's observations point to the importance of analyzing laws and policies that affected Mexico's media, alongside the prevailing business practices for each presidential term, for a full understanding of Mexican cinema.

Three key areas of policy—distribution, financing, and censorship—significantly contributed to the rise and wide proliferation of Mexploitation films. The first influential distribution policy was established during the presidential term of Manuel Ávila Camacho (1940–1946) in the era of Mexico's Golden Age of Cinema. The regulations introduced were aimed at maintaining and strengthening the film industry's newly gained position as one of Mexico's strongest industries (García Riera 1998: 123). Most importantly, Mexican theaters were obliged by law to screen all Mexican films. Producers of any kind of film, including cheap fare, were thereby guaranteed that their products would be distributed and exhibited.

The second major development leading to an increase in Mexploitation production can be found in film funding. In 1942 a bank exclusively providing credit for the national film industry was founded. The Banco Cinematográfico remained unique to the Mexican context. To my knowledge, no other national film industry has ever had its own financial institution. Due to the bank's interest in high profits, financing was initially granted to lucrative films. The bank provided credit for promising commercial productions, among them Mexploitation films. By the 1960s the Banco Cinematográfico was fully nationalized and generated financing for the majority of feature films (García Riera 1998: 123). During Luis Echeverría's presidential term (1970–1976), however, credits to private producers aiming at profits were systematically denied. The bank was finally dismantled under José López Portillo (1976–1982) (Mora 2005: 140). Although the bank funded fewer Mexploitation films after Echeverría came into office, it continued to play an important role. The credit granted by the bank in the early years undoubtedly gave an initial boost to the Mexploitation industry.

Censorship regulations were officially established under the film law in 1949 and had an immediate impact on production processes. Representatives of the censorship board were entitled to "supervise" all cinematic production, which meant that they had the right to review the scripts, visit the sets, and preview the final films before their release (Maciel 1999: 198). The state at times even had a say in which theaters a film would be screened at; the censorship board could force producers to premiere in run-down cinemas or outside of the capital (Maciel 1999: 198). Contrary to the US Production Code Administration (1934–1968), which clearly defined what could be shown in Hollywood mainstream cinema, Mexican censorship rules were more freely interpreted. Nevertheless, three particular violations were not tolerated. First, religious symbols, such as the Virgin of Guadalupe, were not to be depicted negatively. Second, the censors consistently prohibited films about the military's dark past. Third, critical statements in films about high-level political officials of the regime in charge were forbidden (Maciel 1999: 203). As a result, the film industry exercised deliberate self-censorship out of fear that the films would not pass the censor board. Producers became reluctant to take up any social or political controversy, and critiques of the state dwindled (Greene 2005: 6f.).

In general, Mexploitation films rarely faced problems with the censorship board, simply because they were considered devoid of social or political commentary.[7] This also holds true for the India María films. Nevertheless, before the start of each shoot, all scripts had to be authorized by a censorship board. The board drafted an official report for every project, consisting of a summary of the plot, comments on cast and crew, and critical considerations. Concerns and objections were listed; depending on their severity, shoots were authorized or vetoed.

Generally, the India María features had little or no difficulty being accepted. For the most part, their content was categorized as harmless or purely intended to entertain. But the censors often foregrounded the profit-making aspect and missed explicit political allusions. The report for *La comadrita* (1979) written on August 4, 1975, merely mentioned that the film contained some illogical dialogue lines such as "somos de izquierda moderada" [we are from the center-left party]. These political lines did not further bother the censorship board representatives, however, because—according to them—the film's goal was to provoke easy laughs with a gullible audience (Borja 1975: 6).

Considerably longer are the critical remarks for the film *Okey, Mister Pancho* (1981). The concerns fall into three categories: "sex and nakedness," "expression with swearwords or of inappropriate nature," and "violence." Despite numerous examples in each category, the censorship board concluded that all of these aspects were of minor relevance. Even a marijuana-smoking hippie and La India María joking around in the Mexican embassy did not keep the board from authorizing the shoot. Other films, including *Sor Tequila* (1980), didn't receive any critical remarks at all (Borja 1976: 4). This is rather surprising, because the film clearly challenges long-established rules in the church and the convent and exploits religious taboos. Although La India María reveals the double standards of religious authorities, the character's aim is nevertheless to set a moral example. For instance, at the end of *Sor Tequila*, La India María convinces several unwed couples to marry officially. This "positive" final message of the film must have convinced the censorship board. The film was released shortly after the election of president José López Portillo—perhaps a stroke of luck. María Elena Velasco had recorded a song to promote Portillo's presidential campaign (Anonymous 1987b). Possibly she faced less severe censorship revisions due to her history of political support.

Different regulations and practices applied to television. After the government passed a law prohibiting content that "went against good customs," all films became subject to inspections (Nasser 2008: 48). Just as with censorship laws for the cinema, the interpretation of television regulations largely depended on the official in charge. Additionally, Mexican private television was closely affiliated with powerful industrial groups and the nation's upper class (Sinclair 1999: 38). To what extent the India María appearances and series were subject to censorship on television remains open to interpretation. Even today Televisa maintains a low profile when it comes to commenting on how censorship practices have shaped the station's programming. While allowing for sparse information, it seems that political remarks might have led to Velasco's exclusion from the show *Siempre en domingo* (1971). When interviewed in 1998 about her collaboration with Televisa, Velasco admitted that she was just barely passing censorship ("estoy al límite" [I'm at the limit]) (Mendoza de Lira 1998). Iván Lipkies claimed that Velasco was banned from Televisa because of a political joke. The Televisa producer in charge of Velasco's project, in contrast, stressed that she had absolute freedom (Mendoza de Lira 1998). I refrain from judging these statements but simply note that Velasco was forced to take into consideration the company's censorship guidelines and the company's beneficiaries, who were closely affiliated with Mexico's conservative Institutional Revolutionary Party (PRI).

In later years La India María faced censorship under the presidency of Vicente Fox (2000–2006), when Velasco's character La India María was epitomized as a negative stereotype of indigenous women (Stevenson 2001). After his election in 2000, Fox had created the new position of director of Indian Affairs whose task was to protect the rights of the indigenous population. The appointed director, Bertha Xóchitl Gálvez Ruiz, who was an Otomi Indian woman, set out to eliminate all stereotypical representations of Mexican Indians on television and in the mass media. María Elena Velasco, her films, and their protagonist, La India María, were an obvious target: for Gálvez, they represented a prime example of a negative depiction of an indigenous woman (Stevenson 2001). According to Gálvez, Velasco's characterization of La India María repeated the stereotype of Indians as simple-minded, fearful, and fascinated but confused by modern contraptions such as washing machines. Consequently, Gálvez tried to ban all India María features and series from exhibition. The outright censorship of such a popular media figure sparked a highly polemical discussion. In the end, the attempt to ban La India María from distribution failed.

ECHEVERRÍA AND THE GRUPO NUEVO CINE

Private companies produced an increasing share of Mexploitation films after the Golden Age. At the same time, a partnership between the state and a cadre of left-leaning Mexican filmmakers began in the late 1960s. A generation of young filmmakers, primarily trained in Europe, aimed at bringing Mexico's realities and social conflicts to the screen. They deliberately distanced themselves from producers who primarily aimed at profits (Ramírez Berg 1992: 6). The first film school was founded at the University of Mexico (Universidad Nacional Autónoma de México) in the 1960s, along with a national film archive (Cineteca) (Mora 2005: 117). El Grupo Nuevo Cine, a group of leftist intellectuals linked to the new film school, including film scholars Emilio García Riera, Carlos Monsiváis, Tomás Pérez Turrent, and Jorge Ayala Blanco,[8] promoted the rise of a new auteur cinema, with an additional focus on preserving older cinema and educating a new generation of filmmakers. The group published a magazine *Nuevo Cine*, launched discussions on film and politics, and called for a more innovative Mexican film culture.[9]

While new auteur films flourished in the early 1970s, particularly under the presidency of Echeverría, commercial production was actively hindered by his regime. Echeverría took up many of the theories and proposed policies of the Grupo Nuevo Cine. After naming his brother, a former actor, as the head of the national film bank, Echeverría began to reshape the industry. He saw the cinema as a means for promoting Mexico to the world and sought to reclaim Mexico's former reputation as a cinema nation (Ramírez Berg 1992: 29). By the end of Echeverría's presidential term, the state controlled, owned, or involved itself in all spheres of cinematic production (Maciel 1999: 199).

Unlike some of his predecessors and successors, Echeverría encouraged a socially engaged and aesthetically innovative cinema (Ramírez Berg

1992: 29). Echeverría personally declared private producers to be the main enemies of innovation. In a speech in 1975 he chastised them and criticized the lack of ideological content in their films: "They seem to me to have intervened in the film industry as in a factory of some product or in banking, without any feeling for general cultural interest" (cited in Pérez Turrent and Turner 1977: 207–209). He bluntly discouraged any private-enterprise productions and made it clear that cinema—under his presidency—was in the hands of the state (F. Sánchez 1989: 99–101). By systematically refusing credit requests from private producers, Echeverría aimed to make it impossible for them to produce films, effectively starving them out of the industry (Ramírez Berg 1992: 44). As a result, some private producers folded, while others migrated to countries in Central or South America. Still others established themselves in the border region between the United States and Mexico (De la Vega Alfaro 1985: 25). During Echeverría's presidency, the production of feature-length films dropped drastically (Mora 2005: 139). By 1974 private participation was almost nonexistent (Ramírez Berg 1992: 45). In 1976 the number of films released fell to sixty-one, of which only a third were privately produced (García Riera 1998: 279). The few private producers who remained in Mexico went to one of the largest production companies, Estudios Américas, "finding a small haven where they could continue to make the same low-cost, low-quality films as before" (Pérez Turrent and Turner 1977: 207).[10]

Velasco's big-screen acting career was launched during Echeverría's presidential term. Echeverría was surprisingly sympathetic toward La India María. Velasco even made a parody of a popular song, using his name. With Cantinflas, she was invited to perform for Echeverría and high-ranking military functionaries. Diana Films, which produced her movies, was one of the few private companies that continued to make films targeting a wide commercial audience during this time. The company's success is rather surprising, as Echeverría excoriated the majority of private productions for their lack of artistic quality or condemned them for their purely commercial interests and their themes. While many private producers left the country or even withdrew from film production, Diana Films managed to produce movies continuously. Nonetheless, Echeverría's reforms left their traces. Due to the lack of government support, Diana Films gradually invested less money per film. Between 1971 and 1976 production costs dropped from around $95,000 (*Tonta tonta, pero no tanto*) to $65,000 (*Duro pero seguro*). Significantly, the company exclusively launched projects that assured revenues. Toward the end of Echeverría's term, Diana Films actively campaigned for the election of a new administration that promised to facilitate private film production. The candidate was José López Portillo, whose lover was the famous *fichera* actress Sasha Montenegro.

PORTILLO: MEXPLOITATION ADVOCATE

When Portillo was elected in 1976, Fernando de Fuentes, the head of Diana Films, initially felt that it was prudent to remain extremely cautious. In a letter to a Spanish producer who had signaled an interest in co-producing *Sor Tequila* and launching other joint projects (Dunlap 1974), he wrote:

> De momento, estimo que convendría dejar este proyecto para más adelante, hasta en tanto se normalice la producción independiente de México o sea hasta ver que explotación comercial y que lineamientos de crédito y de producción tendrán nuestras películas frente al nuevo gobierno, que aunque ha pregonado en varias ocasiones que requiere de la producción cinematográfica privada, no ha dado ningún paso para alentarla en ningún sentido. Creo pues que concretar en este momento una película que no sea las que tienen ya la mitad del camino andado (como es el caso de La India María, Capulina, Piporro) resultaría muy aventurado.
> [For now, I propose to leave this (new) project until circumstances for independent productions are back to normal again or until we can estimate the degree of commercial exploitation and guidelines regarding credit and production that our films will face under the new government, which has signaled its support for private production on various occasions but to date has not taken a single step to actually advance its strategy. Therefore I believe it is too risky to push a project that is not already partly lined up (as is the case of La India María, Capulina, Piporro).] (excerpt from letter by Fernando de Fuentes, March 16, 1977)

Despite the initial skepticism of Fuentes, productions budgets rose again, signaling a more optimistic outlook among private film producers. In 1979 Diana Films began shooting *Okey, Mister Pancho* with a budget of around $240,000.

Portillo's presidential term (1976–1982) proved to be fruitful for private-sector productions. The fears of Fuentes turned out to be unfounded, as this administration actively encouraged Spanish co-productions (Arnaud 1979). Indeed the Portillo administration completely reversed the cinematic policies and practices of his predecessor (Mora 2005: 139). The only similarity that the two presidents shared was a habit of nepotism: both appointed family members to key positions in cinema. When Portillo formed a new mass media department, combining radio, television, and cinema, he appointed his sister, Margarita López Portillo, as the director. A series of drastic revisions followed. The new regime actively encouraged private enterprise productions and withdrew the state's extensive involvement in the industry. Several former executives of the state-run production and distribution institutions were arrested for fraud and corruption. Margarita López Portillo repeatedly spoke out against films that depicted gritty political and social conflicts. She encouraged family films and international co-productions. Ironically, the majority of features being produced during Portillo's administration were border action films and films with sexual allusions (Maciel 1999: 210).

Nevertheless, in 1980 Margarita López Portillo claimed to have successfully saved the Mexican film industry. The numbers seemed to be on her side. A total of 107 Mexican films were produced—88 from the private sector, most with low production values. The volume of state-produced films shrank to almost nothing (García Riera 1998: 304). The films produced in the following years confirmed the trend of numerous Mexploitation films, some premiering at theaters, others going straight to video,[11] and others produced for television.[12]

Intellectuals and defenders of what they called "quality" cinema harshly criticized the Portillo regime and accused Margarita López Portillo of mismanagement (Mora 2005: 143). When the Cineteca Nacional (National Film Archive) was destroyed in a 1982 fire, and thousands of reels, documents, and books were lost, her failure seemed complete in the eyes of her critics. The era was among the most prosperous for commercial producers, however. Audiences across national borders reveled in the low-budget fare, and private producers were highly satisfied, applauding their newly regained freedom to make a profit (Ampudia Girón 1980: 14). According to the industry publication *Cámara*, more than 25,000 workers were employed in the industry in 1979—an increase of 18 percent in two years (Ampudia Girón 1980: 18). Mexican film trade journalist Gabriel Martí (1980: 9) voiced his satisfaction:

> Hasta no hace poco tiempo los trabajadores que participan en el quehacer manual, creativo e intelectual de nuestro cine, habían pasado por una época de crisis laboral principalmente debido a que las puertas de nuestro cine fueron cerradas a los productores fílmicos de la Iniciativa Privada. Sin embargo, ante el llamado cordial que hizo el actual gobierno a través de Doña Margarita López Portillo, Directora General de Radio, Televi-

> sión y Cinematografía (RTC), los cine productores se reincorporaron a la industria fílmica y, desde hace cuatro años a la fecha, dicha producción cinematográfica ha experimentado, para beneplácito de todos y cada uno de los integrantes de nuestro cine, por ende, los del Sindicato de Trabajadores de la Producción Cinematográfica (STPC) y del Sindicato de Trabajadores de la Industria Cinematográfica (STIC). La producción fílmica sostiene en nuestros días una constante escala ascendente.
> [Until recently, the technical and creative workers of our film industry have gone through a labor crisis, primarily because the doors of our cinema were closed to private producers. Nevertheless, the new government, represented by Doña Margarita López Portillo, director of the Radio, TV, and Film Department, introduced favorable new policies and private producers were reincorporated into the industry. In the last four years and to this date the private film industry has experimented and has been able to make progress, to the satisfaction of all members of both the STPC and the STIC unions. Today the film industry is again continuously growing.]

Overall, the Portillos were strong advocates for private producers, whose main output was Mexploitation films. Contrary to previous years, film distribution was no longer limited to the theaters; television and video became increasingly important.

DE LA MADRID: ECONOMIC CRISIS

During the presidency of Miguel de la Madrid (1982–1988), the country's economic conditions worsened drastically. The overall numbers of film produced again dropped, to an average of seventy-one features per year (García Riera 1998: 331). Shortly before De la Madrid came into office, oil prices collapsed, leading to a downturn of the Mexican economy and pushing inflation rates of the peso to over 100 percent relative to the dollar (*Cámara* 1987b: 20). At the same time, prices for technical supplies such as cameras and film stock imported from the United States remained high. With the economical downturn, Mexican producers were forced to pay high taxes (25 percent) to the state (*Cámara* 1987b: 23).[13] As president De la Madrid did not actively encourage the industry to produce Mexploitation films, but neither did he regulate their production.

De la Madrid departed from the Portillo administration by encouraging production of artistically ambitious films. Shortly after he came into office, the Instituto Mexicano de Cinematografía (IMCINE) was founded. The mission of this national film institute was to foster a high-quality national cinema produced by the state. Although initially headed by the retired filmmaker Alberto Isaac, the institute did not produce many films. Its financial resources were mainly spent on administration. After only a year in office, Isaac resigned and was replaced by Soto Izquierdo, a functionary of the ruling party (PRI). Izquierdo supported directors who were his friends or whose work he liked. Servando González, for example, shot an expensive train epic, *El último túnel* (The last tunnel) (1987), the second part to his film *Viento negro* (Black wind) (1965), which Izquierdo is said to have enjoyed. Unfortunately, the film's reception was a total fiasco: it was panned by both film critics and the public (García Riera 1998: 331). Ultimately Izquierdo was accused of violating copyright laws by supplying original film negatives of state-produced cinema to North American Spanish-language video companies for mass distribution (Maciel 1999: 212). The national film institute didn't meet its ambitious goals and proved to be more bad news for films dependent on state funding. Commercial production of Mexploitation films, however, stayed at the forefront of cinematic production throughout the 1980s. Mexico's economic situation worsened at the beginning of the 1990s, and the peso suffered multiple devaluations. Filmmaking became almost impossible, and Mexico's film industry collapsed.

The films featuring La India María were predominantly produced during the presidencies of Luis Echeverría, José López Portillo, and Miguel de la Madrid. Regrettably, I have been able to uncover very little about Velasco's involvement in politics when she began producing her own films. When I interviewed her, she was reluctant to answer any kind of political questions. She never declared any ties to a political party. When Velasco's political satire about a woman running for president, *Las delicias del poder*, premiered in theaters in 1999, however, she used her public platform to call for more female politicians in key positions. According to Velasco, women were underrepresented in politics. The film triggered many articles on gender issues and politics in Mexican newspapers and magazines. While Velasco was notably evasive about politics in general in interviews, I would like to believe that she planned the launch of *Las delicias del poder* in the thick of Vicente Fox's presidential campaign to provide a soapbox on an issue that had touched her work in the film industry for many years.

PRODUCTION IN THE FAST LANE

India María films and Mexploitation films in general are marked by flaws in the filmic text, ranging from technical gaffes to poorly crafted special effects. This recognizable low-budget aesthetic is not coincidental but is the direct result of certain production practices. A set of cheap and efficient production techniques, such as keeping shooting times as short as possible, and the unique circumstances under which India María and other Mexploitation films were made define the Mexploitation style as much as shared plot and character formulas do.

Between the 1950s and the 1980s Mexican cinema productions fell into three major categories: independently produced films, state-supported films, and films by private entrepreneurs. Each production category responded to diverse interests, had different themes, and aimed at a specific audience (Hershfield and Maciel 1999: 194). Independent productions did not receive financial support from the state or generate large revenues.[14] Financing usually came from universities, private investors, or co-production partners in Europe, or the filmmakers worked on commercial projects and invested the profits in their independent films. These films typically relied on alternative distribution and exhibition practices, such as cine clubs, university groups, and trade unions and sometimes film festivals (King 2000: 141). Independent Mexican films often challenged aesthetic traditions, experimented with them, and tested a variety of narrative forms. State-supported production companies and studios produced "artistically ambitious" auteur films to be exhibited on the international film festival circuit. Their aim was to promote politically palatable images of Mexico in the international arena. Finally, private producers made the kind of films that promised commercial success in Mexico and across the border. These audience-pleasing, profit-driven producers are the main makers of the Mexploitation genres: comedies, wrestling films, sexy movies, and border action dramas.

Depending on the political regime in power, some production companies and studios were at times privatized (under Portillo) and in other years nationalized (under Echeverría), so the division into three distinct production categories is sometimes problematic because producers shifted as the political winds changed. Also, mobility across production categories was common in the Mexican industry, which also blurred the lines among the production categories (De la Mora 2009: 247). Books on Mexican film history typically focus on state-supported films, while independent films are occasionally considered. Private-sector productions, however, have been widely overlooked or simply dismissed as poor-quality entertainment for "lumpen working-class audiences" (King 2000: 143). This book is one of the still rare attempts to untangle a jumble of information on Mexico's private film producers and undertake some systematic research on Mexploitation production, like *Aesthetics and Politics in the Mexican Film Industry* (MacLaird 2013), *Narco Cinema* (Rashotte 2015), *Latsploitation, Exploitation Cinemas, and Latin America* (Ruétalo and Tierney 2009), research on Mexican low-budget cinema (Wilt 1996a), and works on border cinema (Iglesias 1991). I hope that other researchers will continue and critically question this new line of inquiry. As I foraged through Mexican film archives and met with Velasco and other private producers, some of my major concerns were the industry's labor force, financing, and censorship practices that are key to discern industry practices.

Velasco's film career can be divided into three production phases. Diana Films initially produced her feature films. After finishing *¡El que no corre . . . vuela!* in 1981, the wish for more artistic freedom caused Velasco to turn her back on Diana Films and collaborate with a different producer for two films in an attempt to gain more control over her work. In the mid-1980s Velasco founded her own production company, Vlady Pictures, which produced four India María films as well as *Huapango* (2004), in which she played a dance instructor. Throughout all these periods—although at times with long gaps between projects—she also worked for and with the television company Televisa as it expanded into film production.

STRONG FAMILIES AND POWERFUL UNIONS

Mexploitation films virtually guaranteed revenues, because they were reliably popular with a large and devoted audience. As a result, producers ranging from well-established private producers (including television producers) to small newcomers all tried their luck. Some of them were only in business for a short time, while others thrived, producing low-budget films for several decades.

Diana Films, which produced the early India María films, and businesses owned by the Calderón, Galindo, and Agrasánchez families were all prolific producers of Mexploitation films. The company Diana Films was already well established in the Golden Age of Mexican cinema. The company had produced a steady stream of box-office hits since the 1940s. The owner of the company, Fernando de Fuentes commonly hired directors and actors that he had previously worked with, including Gilberto Martínez Solares, who directed various films with the renowned comedian Tin Tan (Germán Valdés).[15] Another director, Fernando Cortés, also frequently worked for Diana Films. Both Martínez Solares and Cortés directed several films with La India María. Cortés initially brought the character to the big screen and was in charge of her first seven features; Martínez Solares came into the picture later, when Velasco gradually wished to have more control over her character. Martínez Solares and Velasco co-directed *Okey, Mister Pancho* in 1979 and *¡El que no corre . . . vuela!* in 1981 and also worked together on the scripts for both films (Castro Ricalde 2004b: 202).

The Calderóns and the Galindos also had worked as producers since the Golden Age. Over the years they developed strategies that produced box-office hits within weeks. The Calderóns' formula was to draw the crowds to the theater with naked women, while the Galindos relied on action and violence. The Agrasánchez family entered the film business in 1969, when they bought the Grovas Company. Their output ranged from border dramas to wrestling films. The family founded several other companies over the years, all run by different family members, and these family businesses in turn established additional companies. Administrators, directors, actors, extras, and other crew members in this expanding network were all related and often worked flexibly at several tasks, from directing to making coffee. Directors and actors with track records of bringing in profits were hired. When a successful combination was found, it was repeated for several films (Iglesias 1991: 63). Family homes and properties frequently were used to shoot the films (Iglesias 1999: 234). Production procedures were simple and streamlined. The founder of Agrasánchez commented to the *Los Angeles Times*:

> A film is born with one of my ideas. I write an eight-page treatment, give it to one of my writers, he makes a synopsis, I rewrite it and return it to him. He writes the script. I put down the money. . . . No coterie of production secretaries, script readers, story editors, development executives, directors of creative affairs. No writers waiting to pitch stories. . . . This isn't Hollywood. . . . It's much more direct and businesslike. . . . Don't come to us complaining if the script is bad . . . we don't care. (Goldin and Cooper 1986: 13)

Despite the straightforward process, producers were required to include a minimum number of union workers for each production (often twenty). Private producers disliked the imposed quotas, but they couldn't resist because unions were powerful in Mexico (Iglesias 1991: 69). Producers who decided to film without union workers were harshly criticized, and their films were derided as *piratas* [pirated] (Cabildo 1976).

Diana Films and other private producers primarily employed workers from the union Sindicato de Trabajadores de la Industria Cinematográfica (STIC), mainly composed of below-the-line crew and technicians. Their salaries were considerably lower than those of members of the Sindicato de Trabajadores de la Producción Cinematográfica (STPC), a union that primarily represented well-established directors and cinematographers.

The main reason for the unions' remarkable strength is rooted in the Mexican film industry's boom during World War II, when Mexican workers in many industries organized active unions. Initially STIC was the film industry's only union and represented all film workers, including technicians, writers, and directors. But actors, cinematographers, and other higher paid creative workers were unhappy with the egalitarian treatment of all members. After a bitter internal fight, the creative elite finally split off and formed STPC. Consequently, a national accord regulating the division of labor was released in 1945. It was beneficial for STPC, which from then on was in charge of all feature film productions, while STIC was relegated to less prestigious tasks such as producing, distributing, and exhibiting short films, documentaries, and series (Ramírez Berg 1992: 41). After World War II significantly fewer workers were employed in the film industries, due to the halt in US support to the Mexican industry after the war. Hoping to secure jobs for the people already in the business, the union no longer admitted new members. Young talent was thereby excluded from film productions because everyone working legally on a Mexican film set had to be a registered union member (Mora 2005: 75). At the same time, members of the STIC workers' union were no longer allowed to work for feature film productions. As a result, they systematically began to bypass the regulations defined in the accord. Producers engaged STIC union members in projects that they labeled serials. Later they combined them into one or more feature-length films, avoiding the higher costs that the creative union insisted upon. Patching up serials into feature films was officially forbidden in the accord; nevertheless, it became a common business practice. Eventually the accord was dropped.

In 1973, during the shooting of *El miedo no anda en burro*, Velasco was already considered a star. Numerous fans came to the set to admire their idol or appear as an extra. As Velasco's fame grew, she gradually began to impose demands at Diana Films, intended to give her more influence on the script and the development of her character. She co-directed with Gilberto Martínez Solares for the first time in 1981 on *Okey, Mister Pancho*. In contrast to Hollywood stars, Velasco was never under exclusive contract with Diana Films or any other production company, includ-

2.13. People gather at the filming during the shooting of *El miedo no anda en burro* in 1973. (Diana Internacional Films, S.A. de C.V.)

ing the television producer Televisa. Nevertheless she worked with Diana Films for ten India María productions. When Velasco left Diana Films in 1982, she never openly explained why she chose to leave, but she repeatedly underlined her wish to have more control over her work (Rohrer 2008; Zúñiga Barba 1989).

In 1982 Velasco made the transition from working as an actress to directing solo and later producing her own films by collaborating with family members—none of them previously established in show business. From that point forward, her children, Ivette Eugenia Lipkies and Iván Lipkies, wrote scripts, produced, and at times co-directed her films. When she left Diana Films, she looked for a well-established producer who would grant her more freedom. She chose Producciones Matouk, with whom she produced *El coyote emplumado* (shot in 1982) and *Ni Chana, ni Juana* (shot in 1982). For both features, her son Iván was the executive producer and her daughter Ivette Eugenia worked on the script. Velasco launched her career as a solo director of the two films.

After two productions Velasco left Producciones Matouk and founded her own company, Vlady Pictures, where her son worked as executive producer, while she and her daughter focused on scripts. Their first film was *Ni de aquí, ni de allá* (1988), which became one of Mexico's all-time big-

2.14. In the course of her career, Velasco moved toward writing scripts, directing, and ultimately producing her own films. (Vlady Pictures)

gest box-office hits. The film was distributed by Televisa. Other films were co-financed and distributed by Televicine, Televisa's feature film branch. Vlady Pictures produced five films, but only *Las delicias del poder* was entirely financed by Velasco's company.

For Velasco, working as a family offered several advantages. It was a way to keep costs low and provided increased flexibility in the production process. At the same time, she was able to extend shooting times well beyond the norm: *El coyote emplumado* was shot in five weeks, while *Ni Chana, ni Juana* was shot in an impressive seven weeks (Fernández Escareño 1996: 122; Ramírez 1984). Low-budget film shooting times were commonly held to a minimum, never exceeding four weeks. These longer shoots allowed Velasco to exert the kind of artistic control that she lacked with other producers.

Velasco recruited well-known and experienced workers from the industry for her projects, among them the comedian Resortes. By combining big names with experienced workers and family members, Velasco smartly lined up her productions: she guaranteed professionalism without having to make too many artistic compromises. The level of professionalism on the set, for instance, allowed her to shoot several takes, which was uncommon for Mexploitation productions.

Nevertheless measures were taken to contain costs. When I was on the set of *La hija de Moctezuma* in 2011, I saw that María Elena Velasco's own car and her son's car were used for an action crash scene. For obvious reasons, the scene was filmed in one take—and afterward the two cars were taken directly to a mechanic for repair! Throughout her long career, Velasco retained the energy to perform slapstick routines, but in *La hija de Moctezuma*, her last feature, she relied on stunt performers for physically challenging scenes.

After launching her career as a director and producer, Velasco gradually began speaking out against the shortcomings of the Mexican film industry. She repeatedly deplored the lack of new and innovative comedy scripts that did not rely on dirty jokes (De la Cruz Polanco 2002; Jiménez 2002; Valencia 1992; Zúñiga Barba 1989). She also condemned the practice of recycling scripts and the insertion of material from previous films—a common production practice to fill running time (Rohrer 2009a). But Velasco and her children were notably reluctant to criticize the unions. In my interviews with her she admitted only once that union

2.15. All India María productions included cost-cutting measures. During the shoot of *La hija de Moctezuma*, two family cars were wrecked for an action scene. (Photo by Seraina Rohrer)

2.16. During filming, Velasco and her children sometimes squabbled. Here Velasco and her son are having a discussion on the set of *La hija de Moctezuma* in May 2011. Standing behind Velasco is her double, who was used for stunts in action scenes. (Photo by Seraina Rohrer)

regulations caused her some annoyances (Rohrer 2009a). STIC, the below-the-line union, appears in the credits of *El coyote emplumado*, *Ni Chana, ni Juana*, *Se equivocó la cigüeña*, and *La hija de Moctezuma*. Credits for the other features produced by Vlady Pictures don't list any union. Iván Lipkies stated that the unions refused to work with them at the time. How Vlady Pictures managed to bypass union regulations remains unclear to me.

Over time, Velasco sometimes questioned her assumption that working as a family would facilitate the production process. In 2004 and later in 2011, on the set of *La hija de Moctezuma*, she talked about the challenges of working in a family enterprise. In a published interview, Velasco and her son Iván admitted that they often got on each other's nerves and had arguments on the set. Velasco said that sometimes she had to put her son in his place due to his relative lack of experience (Huerta 2004). I witnessed similar scenes in 2011 when visiting the set during the shooting of *La hija de Moctezuma*: Velasco worked with her son, who directed the film, while her daughter was in charge of production. The advantages of working as a family must have outweighed the irritations, however, because Velasco continued to produce her films with the family members.

Velasco's accomplishments as a director and producer have been widely overlooked or deliberately ignored. In numerous books and articles on Mexican female filmmakers, she is simply not mentioned.[16] This is all the more astonishing because women directors and producers were scarce during the 1970s and 1980s. During this period, only a handful of women worked behind the camera: Marcela Fernández Violante, Busi Cortés, María Novaro, and Isela Vega. With the exception of Vega, these women all attended film school and made auteur films that targeted international festival and art house audiences. Isela Vega, like María Elena Velasco, worked in commercial filmmaking. Vega and Velasco were of the same generation; they learned on the job, as did many other industry professionals working in Mexploitation. While Vega worked behind the scenes for only a few projects (*Los amantes del señor de la noche* [Lovers of the lord of the night] [1986, directed by Isela Vega], *Una gallina muy ponedora* [A hen that lays a lot of eggs] [1982, directed by Rafael Portillo], and *Navajeros* [Criminals with knives] [1980, directed by Eloy de la Iglesia]), however, Velasco proved to be one of Mexico's prolific directors and producers, working not only in cinema but across a variety of formats.

From the Mexican film industry's beginning until today, men have held most key positions. In 1991 Rubén Galindo Jr., the producer of numerous Mexploitation films, went on the record to explain why—according to him—the field of cinema was not suitable for women:

> Es un negocio un poco hostil, es un negocio con un ambiente un poco rudo para una mujer. No es tan atractivo para una mujer estar en un ambiente en que hay desveladas, que hay que estar oyendo gentes decir groserías, estar cargando cables, estar debajo el sol, ¡Vaya!, es difícil porque es un ambiente de hombres.
> [It is a tough business, a rough environment for a woman. In fact, it is not really appealing to a woman to work under these circumstances, with people swearing, having to carry cables, and being in the sun! Well, it is hard, because it is a male environment.] (Iglesias 1991: 68)

Velasco agreed with some of Galindo's characterization of the challenges that women have faced in Mexico's male-dominated film industry. During her first interview with me in December 2008, she reflected on her early work experiences in the industry:

> Yo vengo de la televisión y soy trabajadora. Los directores solamente me dijeron lo que querían que hacía. Después de un tiempo, me cansé. Yo quería tener más control.
> [I came from television and was an ordinary worker. Directors simply told me what to do. After a while, I got tired of it. I wanted to have more control.] (Rohrer 2008)

Velasco's wish to direct her own character led her to an unvarnished awareness of her status within the industry. Throughout her career, she repeatedly underlined how much she valued directing, yet directing forced her to confront numerous challenges by male workers and colleagues who would defy her instructions on the set or in postproduction (H. Hernández 1988; Rohrer 2008).

> Una vez, yo estaba muy infeliz con el montaje de una de mis películas. Entonces, me fui con el encargado y le pregunté de cambiarlo, pero el estaba ofendido, se enojó, sobre todo porque fue criticado por una mujer. Es duro trabajar como directora. Por supuesto no puedo saber todo, pero en mi posición tienes que dar instrucciones.
> [One time, I was extremely unhappy with the edited version of one of my features. I went to the editor and asked him to change it, but he was offended, got angry, more than anything because the criticism came from a woman. It is hard for a woman to work as a director. Of course, I cannot know everything, but in my position one has to give instructions.] (Rohrer 2008)

Even earlier, in 1992, Velasco believed that men controlled the Mexican film industry:

> Actualmente todavía existe algo de machismo y a los señores no les gusta que la mujer invada sus terrenos, pero no me quejo, soy una afortunada. Sobre todo, el público me ha estimulado en toda mi carrerea.
> [Today there is still a bit of machismo around. Men don't like it when women invade their territory, but I can't complain, I am lucky. Above all, the public has motivated me throughout my career.] (Valencia 1992)

Indeed, throughout her career, with the exception of the support that she felt from her fans, Velasco continued to feel that she was knocking on closed doors. Velasco openly and repeatedly discussed the difficulty of her position as a woman in a male-dominated industry, but she did so with a light touch, without belaboring the challenges that she faced. Even so, reflecting on her role in the Mexican film industry prompted her to call for much-needed changes. She often criticized fellow Mexploitation producers, insisting that popular films should not be only about profit but also about quality (Anonymous 1994a; Ramírez 1984, 1985, 1987).

CHEAP FARE

Most Mexploitation producers were eager to cut costs and keep budgets low to minimize financial risk and maximize profits. Working with family members and with STIC union members were two means to bring down spending. Production budgets were very low—but what exactly is meant by a low budget? How did the costs compare to other production categories? Most Mexican films are produced with tight budgets, when compared to Hollywood productions, which ran around $4 million in 1980 and start around $100 million today. From 1946 to 1950 the average cost for a Mexican feature dropped from $111,000 to $67,000, and by 1959 it was as low as $53,000 per film (García Riera 1998: 151). Budgets remained low in the following years, although the actual numbers rose with inflation. In 1970 features cost around $120,000.[17] By the late 1970s average production costs in the private sector had climbed to $190,000. At the same time, state-produced films cost approximately $90,000 more (Ampudia Girón 1980: 19).[18] Finally, throughout the 1980s and into the early 1990s Mexican feature films cost approximately $200,000. This was not only low compared to US productions but also for Latin American films: only Peru and Chile produced films for less (Getino 1998: 53). The gap in production costs between privately produced films and the state-supported ones also increased during the 1980s. In 1987 state-supported films were twice as expensive as privately produced films. In addition, the state ran an expensive administrative machinery, gobbling up almost the same amount of money as the actual film production (Galindo 1987a: 12). Mexploitation films were produced by private entrepreneurs, so it is safe to conclude that their budgets were not padded with extra costs and realistically reflect the actual production costs of these films.

I was fortunate to locate a number of original Mexploitation film budgets in the private collection of Rogelio Agrasánchez Jr., who has carefully kept the company's files. This is a rare exception, because most Mexploitation producers got rid of their materials shortly after production.[19] The average cost of fifty-three Mexploitation films by the Agrasánchez production company, all made in the 1970s and 1980s, was only $80,000—

2.17 AND 2.18. For all Mexploitation films, production was kept simple to cut spending. These pictures were taken on the set of *Superzan y el niño del espacio* (1973). (Photo by Rogelio Agrasánchez Jr., Agrasánchez Film Archive)

markedly lower than the $200,000 average cost of most private productions. In the 1970s Agrasánchez budgets were as low as $40,000. The company's cheapest film was *Superzan y el niño del espacio* (Superzan and the space boy) (1973, directed by Rafael Lanuza), which cost only $32,000. In this case, spending could be kept extremely low because the film was shot in Guatemala. Its main hero, the wrestler Superzan, was a character invented by the producer and played by an unknown actor. By casting an unknown actor instead of a star such as El Santo, the film's budget was significantly lowered. This small pool of financial data provides a fascinating snapshot of Mexploitation film expenditures within the context of privately produced films and the broader Mexican film industry.

Between 1971 and 1982 Diana Films produced ten of the eventual sixteen India María features, starting with the first India María movie, *Tonta, tonta, pero no tanto* (shot in 1971), through Velasco's final film with the company, *¡El que no corre . . . vuela!* (shot in 1981). Budgets for these films were relatively low, ranging from $65,000 for *Duro pero seguro* (shot in 1974), to $241,000 for *Okey, Mister Pancho* (shot in 1979), with average costs around $110,000.[20] Compared to average private production budgets of around $120,000 in the 1970s, the India María films were on average rather cheap, but Diana Films clearly spent more than other low-budget entrepreneurs such as Agrasánchez. The productions *Okey, Mister Pancho* and *Sor Tequila* (shot in 1977) stand out with their budgets of $241,000 and $226,800, respectively—not particularly low-budget at all, by the standards of the day. The high costs reflect the nature of these productions; both films contain scenes requiring expensive props, including a helicopter and an airplane. For previous productions—for instance, *La presidenta municipal* (shot in 1974)—even minor expenses such as karate and bullfighting lessons for Velasco had been justified in the production folder (Rosas 1974). For *Sor Tequila*, money seemed to be less of an issue because the Spanish co-producer, Estudios Balcazar, covered extra expenses. In the case of *Okey, Mister Pancho*, a US distributor recognized the film's potential with Latino audiences in the United States and gave higher distribution guarantees, so the extra costs were easily justified.

Unfortunately, only limited data are available on budgets and other production details for the India María films produced after Velasco left Diana Films. Velasco's second producer, Producciones Matouk, destroyed most files when the business closed after Antonio Matouk's death. Vlady Pictures did not file material systematically, because Velasco never expected that the information would be of historical interest. Based on approximate figures remembered by Velasco and her children, Velasco's budgets were low compared to the industry average (Rohrer 2008). Two articles published in the Mexican press in January and March 1987 noted that production costs for *Ni de aquí, ni de allá* rose to 160 million Mexican pesos (approximately $170,000)—still a rather low figure compared to average production budgets (Anonymous 1987a; Vieyra 1987). Despite the low cost, production processes seem to have been rather complex: Velasco indicated that she worked on *Ni de aquí, ni de allá* for over a year, while the shooting lasted for more than five weeks (Vieyra 1987). An article on the production process commented on Velasco's goals as a producer:

> Otro punto que dice tener a su favor son las posibilidades económicas que le da su productora para filmar, como sucedió en *Ni de aquí, ni de allá* que tiene escenas de un aeropuerto estadunidense, así como de un "freeway" (eje vial, pero bien hecho). "Esas locaciones salen en un ojo de la cara: permisos, sindicatos, seguros, ¡uff! . . . Entiendo que la función del productor es sacar mayor provecho al menor costo, pero le hice ver que aunque obtuviera menos ganancias, una buena producción da prestigio para esta y las películas que vengan."
> [Another point in her favor is the economic framework provided by her production company to make films, as in *Ni de aquí, ni de allá*, which contains scenes at a US airport as well as on the freeway (like large Mexican roads, but well constructed). "These locations cost a lot, they require permits, collaboration with unions, insurance, whew! I understand that producers should keep production costs low, but I am convinced that a solid production helps to gain prestige for the film itself and for future films, even if smaller profits are made."] (Pacheco 1988)

Other Mexploitation producers took more extreme measures to shave costs. For example, they drastically reduced shooting times, which seldom exceeded three to four weeks (Agrasánchez 1971–1984; Pérez Turrent 1995: 141). They often shot several films concurrently, or shootings followed each other seamlessly, so that producers could work with the same crew (Agrasánchez 1971–1984). Some producers looked for locations outside of Mexico, where expenses were even lower. No unions existed in countries such as Guatemala and Costa Rica, so labor was cheap. Producers could work around the clock without having to pay overtime (Rohrer 2010d). Some Mexploitation producers launched co-productions with Puerto Rico, Colombia, Ecuador, Guatemala, and Venezuela. Often Latin American actors were placed under contract, with the aim of recouping money in the Latin American market (Mora 2005: 106f.). Some producers reused previously shot material to extend films—a practice that Velasco deplored. Scripts of old films that had been successful at the box office were sometimes slightly rewritten and then reused. Usually budgets allowed no time for rehearsals, and directors were forced to use the first take. Due to longer shootings with Vlady Pictures, Velasco was able to augment the amount of takes for a scene when she felt it was necessary.

Financing films through distribution guarantees from the Mexican film bank, or later directly from Mexican and US distributors, was a common practice. The audience's familiarity with the cast and the film's themes determined the amount of the credit, and producers covered the remaining costs. In the 1970s US distributors started to play a crucial role in financing. They often guaranteed over two-thirds of the budget, knowing that the films would attract a large Spanish-speaking audience in the United States (Agrasánchez 1971–1984). Latinos in the United States had gradually become the most important consumers of Mexican low-budget fare, assuring between 50 and 70 percent of the Mexican industry's revenues (García Riera 1998: 305; Goldin and Cooper 1986: 11). "Hispanics in the United States are the wealthiest Hispanics in the world," one film industry study enthused (Sinclair 1999: 95). Latinos in the United States paid high admission fees, and the dollar was not subject to inflation. As a result, they became the most important consumer group. Industry profits consistently rose until the late 1980s.

TELEVISA ON THE BIG SCREEN

The television company Televisa broadened its reach in the 1970s when it released its first feature film. As the Golden Age of Mexican cinema came to an end, the Golden Age of Televisa—run and owned by the Azcárraga family—began (Sinclair 1999: 32).

Velasco's La India María character first became widely known through her appearances on the show *Siempre en domingo*, which aired on one of Televisa's channels, the privately owned Canal de las Estrellas. The company's decision to feature her character is not surprising: La India María perfectly fit Televisa's profile of an apparently innocent entertaining character type. La India María's routines always relied on subtle critiques of wealth and power, but with slapstick humor to blunt these serrated edges. The character seemed superficially free of social criticism, a censorship requirement monitored on both state and private channels (Castro Ricalde 2004b: 204).

After Velasco debuted on the big screen and no longer appeared on

Siempre en domingo, Televisa's influence on La India María ceased. The character notably gained agency. It was only in 1987 that Velasco returned to the company—this time to the company's video branch, Videocine, which guaranteed distribution and put down money beforehand for her third feature, *Ni de aquí, ni de allá* (1988). At the time Televisa was becoming an increasingly important financer and producer. Televicine distributed some of Velasco's features across Mexico and the United States on the big and the small screen. Velasco's relationship with her former employer at Diana Films, Fernando de Fuentes, who was at the time heading Televicine, probably facilitated the collaboration between her company Vlady Pictures and Televicine. Teaming up evidently benefited both Velasco and Televicine, which financed the next film produced and directed by Velasco, *Se equivocó la cigüeña* in 1993. Televicine passed on *Las delicias del poder*, which started filming in 1996 (Chiquet 1996; Hernández 1996). In 1998 Velasco returned to the small screen at Televisa for her TV variety show *¡Ay María qué puntería!* and sporadically appeared on other programs. Despite her long-lasting collaboration, she underlined her independence on various occasions, pointing out that she was never an exclusive artist of Televisa and that no other television station had ever offered her a contract (Morales Valentín 2002; Olvera 1996). Nonetheless, even after her death, the actress is often associated with Televisa.

Televisa's entrance into film production in the 1970s is without a doubt one of the most significant developments in the later phase of Mexploitation production. In the 1980s the conglomerate Televisa eventually became one of the main producers of Mexploitation films. Televisa was already one of the main exporters of *telenovelas*, so producing feature films seemed like a logical consequence (Sánchez Ruiz 2000). Televicine, Televisa's film production and distribution branch, expanded in the late 1970s in order to generate additional profits, particularly in the United States. The company's formula was simple: entertainment at modest costs, distributed in both the domestic and the foreign markets, to the big and small screen. Televisa's greatest advantage was its previously established dominance in the Spanish-language market in the United States and across Latin America.[21] *La ilegal* (The illegal) (1979, directed by Arturo Ripstein), one of Televicine's early productions, made net profits of over $1 million shortly after its release in the United States (Ramírez Berg 1992: 213). Similar success greeted the soccer comedy *El Chanfle* (1979, directed by Enrique Segoviano), starring Roberto Gómez Bolaños, called *Chespirito* [Little Shakespeare]. Both comedies and border movies continued to thrive during the 1980s and assured big profits for Televicine. Televicine produced fourteen films in 1979 and twenty the following year (García Riera 1998: 308, 44). At the same time, the company was producing large numbers of *telenovelas* and shows that were highly popular and exported globally (Sánchez Ruiz 1986: 42). A smart marketing strategy was a key factor in the success of Televicine films. The company hired famous television actors to appear in its films. Television audiences already knew Chespirito, for example, from his TV appearances. Lucía Méndez, who played the leading role in *La ilegal*, had previously moved into the limelight in *telenovelas* (García Riera 1998: 308).

CROSS-BORDER PRODUCTIONS

Another crucial boost to the ongoing success of low-budget films came from runaway productions. Between 1970 and 1976 President Echeverría froze credits for private producers. As a result, many low-budget producers moved away from the center of cinematic production in Mexico City. Joining the exodus of Mexploitation producers in the late 1970s, the Agrasánchez and Galindo companies bought properties on the US side of the border and began producing in a "cross-border context," as Janet Wasko and Mary Erickson (2008: 1) have called this production mode.

The Agrasánchez family alone produced dozens of low-budget films in the United States, with an average of one feature film every two months (Goldin and Cooper 1986: 13; Ramírez Berg 1992: 213). The new production location brought numerous advantages. Taxes were lower and union regulations did not apply, so producers felt free to offer lower salaries. The cast and crew worked overtime, which meant that producers were able to work with smaller crews. Films were shot on the producers' properties, and no sets had to be built. The cast and crew were housed on the family property. While salaries were paid in pesos, profits were made in the much more stable dollar. For all of these reasons, production costs of cross-border films were considerably lower than for Mexican productions—and distribution throughout the United States was assured in advance (Iglesias 1991: 62). Additionally, higher ticket prices in the United States guaranteed profits. By the mid-1980s, instead of paying 200 pesos (40 cents) as in Mexico, US moviegoers paid $4 per ticket. With an estimated average budget of $60,000, these films quickly paid back their expenses, bringing in $100,000 in as little as a month in Los Angeles alone (Goldin and Cooper 1986). Box office hits such as *Lola la trailera 2* (1986) reaped a total of $3.5 million in profits—$2.5 million in the United States alone (Goldin and Cooper 1986).

2.19. Many producers moved their businesses to the border region in the United States to bypass regulations and work with family members. Here they are working on the premises of the Agrasánchez family. (Photo by Rogelio Agrasánchez Jr., Agrasánchez Film Archive)

2.20. Mexploitation producers preferred to film with a small crew, here on the set of *Soy chicano y mexicano* (1975). (Photo by Rogelio Agrasánchez Jr., Agrasánchez Film Archive)

These expatriate producers discovered that the border region itself offered many dramatic stories: undocumented migrants struggling to cross the desert, drug trafficking, gangs, and other adventures appealing to the migrant community in the United States (Iglesias 1991: 64). The cross-border producers didn't limit themselves to border films; they also made comedies, sexy movies, and wrestling films. Contrary to many other Mexploitation producers, Velasco never relocated her business headquarters to the United States or acted in a film produced in a cross-border context, although many scenes for *Okey, Mister Pancho* and *Ni de aquí, ni de allá* were shot in Houston and Los Angeles.

By the mid-1980s US unions were lobbying for unionized American workers to be employed in Mexican productions shot in the United States. Starting in 1988, after the passing of the Simpson-Rodino law regulating migration, Mexican casts and crews working on US territory were required to get US work permits, a process that could take up to several months (Iglesias 1991: 69, 78, 83). These increasingly strict labor regulations complicated production, and by 1990 cross-border productions had lost their financial advantage. Within the span of a decade, cross-border productions had boomed and fizzled. Most low-budget producers returned to Mexico City.

Mexican production of low-budget films did not come to a complete stop at the end of the 1980s, but a gradual decline in production volume was obvious by the early 1990s. Despite intensive fund-raising and marketing efforts, Mexploitation film producers couldn't keep up the previous pace of production: shaky finances forced all of the major companies to reduce the number of films that they produced each year. Throughout the 1990s film production became more expensive and less profitable, which ultimately led to the end of Mexico's low-budget film boom. Mexican scholars have argued that the films no longer attracted moviegoers because of the repetition of stories or simply because the audiences preferred Hollywood fare (Agrasánchez 2006: 36; García Canclini and Holtz 1994: 187; Valenzuela Arce 1994: 322). While the audience's taste might indeed have started to shift, the primary reason for the decrease in low-budget film production was simple financing. Mexico's economic crisis and the high inflation rate during the 1980s made film production an increasingly costly undertaking, especially because Mexico's film industry was largely dependent on US technologies. Piracy also cut significantly into producers' profits. Despite the faltering financial picture, some companies and stars continued to make films—among them María Elena Velasco, who completed her final feature, *La hija de Montezuma*, in 2012.[22]

CHAPTER 3

BOX-OFFICE MONEYMAKERS AND SMALL-SCREEN HITS

THE INDIA MARÍA FILMS, like other Mexploitation films, circulated across all of Latin America. In 2005 I accidentally ended up at a screening of Velasco's film *Ni Chana, ni Juana* in a small neighborhood cinema in Cusco, Peru. The India María films were sold in street market stalls in Bolivia, at times packaged with films of Bolivian indigenous women wrestling. The two most important markets, however, were Mexico and the United States. The films have had a unique impact in those two countries. In Mexico they were part of the national industry and circulated as such, while in the United States they were aimed at Spanish-speaking migrants. Audiences generally saw the first-run films in theaters and later enjoyed repeated viewings on video and television.

Contrary to the "classical exploitation cinema" analyzed by Eric Schaefer (1999), the system of distribution and exhibition of Mexploitation films was not opposed to the dominant system but integrated into it. Mexploitation films were distributed like all other Mexican films. In Mexico the films were commonly distributed and exhibited by either private or state-owned companies, depending on the period. In fact, for many years a single company (Películas Nacionales) distributed all national films across the entire country. In the United States, however, several companies competed against each other and bid on the lucrative films primarily aimed at Spanish-speaking audiences.

During the Golden Age of Mexican cinema, the American investor and businessman William O. Jenkins, formerly United States vice-consul in Puebla, owned about 80 percent of the country's theaters (Bertaccini 2001: 38; García Riera 1998: 151; Mora 2005: 77). His monopoly was harshly criticized in the 1950s. State officials and industry representatives accused him of excessive distribution of low-quality films, and some even held him responsible for initially boosting their production (García Riera 1998: 152;

Mora 2005: 78).[1] When the Mexican government finally bought the theaters owned by the Jenkins group in 1960, Mexploitation films continued to dominate Mexico's screens. Contrary to prevailing expectations, Mexploitation distribution became nationalized. Theatrical distribution of Mexican films remained centralized over the next two decades, during the heyday of Mexploitation, with Películas Nacionales as the main distributor. The company also distributed most of the features starring La India María to Mexican theaters.

Películas Mexicanas was in charge of negotiating all foreign territories. Usually the company offered packages of several Mexican films to foreign distributors in the United States and Latin America. These packages varied considerably. At times they grouped the films, sometimes by performers, sometimes by production company or directors, and sometimes by genre. At times they even packaged box-office hits with state-produced auteur films. Particularly during the presidency of Echeverría, exhibitors were forced to show the package and could not acquire only the popular film, which guaranteed high revenues.

Películas Mexicanas negotiated distribution contracts in the United States, where companies such as Clasa-Mohme and Azteca Films dominated the Spanish-language film distribution market. Both Azteca Films and Clasa-Mohme had close ties to the Mexican producers. Nevertheless, they often had to bid for films, even though in certain periods they were owned by the state. In 1960 film export was no longer nationalized. Columbia Pictures challenged the position of Azteca Films and Clasa-Mohme by obtaining the right to distribute Mexican films in the United States. The company actively acquired movies appealing to a wide audience, including films with Cantinflas and most of the India María films (Agrasánchez 2006: 43). Columbia began to distribute these popular films widely across the United States, focusing on cities with large Latino populations such as San Antonio and Los Angeles.[2] In the 1980s Columbia's Spanish-language theatrical distribution business—at the time holding about 40 percent of the Spanish-language market—was purchased by the Mexican multimedia conglomerate Televisa, then the sole owner of broadcast TV stations and the Spanish-language cable network in the United States (Beer 2001: 172; Klain 1980b: 41).

At the same time, American General, Million Dollar, and Protele Films Corporation stirred up the theatrical distribution market (Iglesias 1991: 100, 106f). Additionally, some of the exhibitors founded their own distribution companies; the Los Angeles–based theater chain Metropolitan, for example, became one of the key players in California. Some of the films were distributed by small independent companies, which negotiated terms and conditions directly with the different theaters, often offering package deals with talents accompanying the screenings (Rohrer 2010b). Larger distributors, such as Azteca Films, let exhibitors bid on movies. Whichever theater made the highest offer picked up the premieres; the others acquired second and third runs. About 30 to 40 percent of the box-office income went to the distributors. Exhibitors rarely paid a minimum fee per film; they usually rented the films at prices based solely on attendance (Rohrer 2010b, 2010c).

After the Golden Age, and increasingly in the 1970s and 1980s, attendance at Mexico's movie theaters declined due to competition from television and video, a trend experienced earlier in the United States (Monaco 2001: 40f.). Theaters across Latin America lost almost 50 percent of their audience between 1982 and 1992 (Getino 1998: 27). Numbers dropped from approximately 280 million filmgoers in Mexico in 1983 to 230 million in 1990.[3] With a decrease of 20 percent, the film industry took a significant hit, but Mexico lost considerably fewer spectators than other Latin American countries (Elizondo 1991: 7) and remained one of the world's leading nations in cinema attendance. In 1982 Mexicans between the ages of fifteen and sixty-five visited the theater on average 7.2 times per year (in 1955 the average had been 12.44 visits). In comparison, Octavio Getino (1998: 43) estimates that adults across Latin America attended the theater two or three times a year in 1985.[4]

Going to the movies was a cheap leisure activity, affordable even to relatively low-income earners. Movies were cheaper than other major Mexican pastimes, such as bullfights or the circus (*Cámara* 1982: 12). Until the early 1970s theater admission prices were frozen at a maximum of four pesos (about thirty cents US) by law. Once the regulation was annulled, ticket prices constantly increased and largely depended on the facilities and comfort of the theater. A large gap opened between luxurious cinemas and cheap theaters with minimal comfort. Admission prices also varied considerably between regions. Ticket prices were much lower in the provinces than in cities. In Yucatán theater admission cost as little as two pesos (ten cents) (*Cámara* 1978a: 19), while in Mexico City a ticket cost eighteen pesos (eighty cents) in 1978. In general, Mexploitation films were mainly exhibited in theaters with low admission prices.

SECOND-CLASS CINEMA CROWD PLEASERS

Movie theaters underwent major changes during the era of Mexploitation films. A first shift began around the end of the Golden Age. Audiences were effectively segregated into two tiers, along with the films that they enjoyed.[5] At *cines de primera* [first-class theaters], concentrated in more affluent areas, North American and other foreign films premiered. The *cines de segunda* [second-class theaters] screened reruns of Hollywood productions and Mexploitation films (Maciel 1999: 202; Tuñón 1998: 62).

These theaters differed remarkably. The luxurious first-class theaters were decorated with carpets and paintings on the walls and equipped with comfortable seating and modern projection technologies (Noble 2005: 77). In contrast, second-class cinemas, mostly converted vaudeville theaters (so-called *carpas*), were only equipped with the basics—a screen, a projector, and chairs. These venues often combined screenings with short live vaudeville acts. The middle and upper class usually attended the elegantly equipped theaters, while the working class went to the rudimentary houses with live acts (Noble 2005: 77). Between the late 1950s and the late 1980s exhibition practices led to a more complex categorization of theaters. Some exclusively exhibited foreign films, others screened national productions, and others specialized in auteur films or Mexploitation cinema. Some screened only premieres, while others offered only second releases. Mexploitation films were usually programmed as double or even triple features, a common low-budget exhibition practice worldwide. The first film of the program was usually a more recently released feature. The second and third films were either previously released or simply less crowd pleasing.

In Tijuana, for example, Mexploitation films were exhibited at several theaters. Cinelandia, vividly nicknamed *piojito* [small louse],[6] was located in the center of the market. For decades it was an important meeting place. Screening mainly low-budget Mexican movies, it attracted a cross-section of the lower social classes, who came to the theater not only to see movies but also to eat a bite at the theater's snack bar or just hang out. Films were usually shown all day into the 1990s, and a single ticket allowed the holder to stay for several screenings (Valenzuela Arce 1994: 308).[7] Another Mexploitation movie theater was the Roble, which premiered comedies and border films. After a couple of weeks these films moved on to the cinema Variedades, before ending up at Tijuana's oldest and cheapest theater, Zaragoza, which attracted poor and mostly illiterate audiences (Iglesias 1991: 96–98).

The India María films were primarily shown in venues targeting working-class audiences.[8] These *cines de segunda* offered little comfort but served as important community gathering places. Although movie attendance constantly decreased through the 1970s and particularly during the 1980s, films starring India María guaranteed large audiences. Velasco's films invariably reached high rankings in the box-office statistics published in the industry journal *Cámara*.[9] India María films were often screened first, as the main attraction (Rohrer 2010b, 2010c). Some of them retained top billing for several months (*Cámara* 1982).[10] The large number of copies sent out to exhibitors also points to high demand. *Okey, Mister Pancho*, for example, premiered with nineteen copies in Mexico City (Ugalde Romero 1982a: 11).[11] The film premiered in California with nearly thirty copies. Revenues for the first week added up to $19,000 in California alone. Only slightly lower returns were measured in the following seven weeks (Diana Films 1981). This was quite exceptional; revenues usually drop after a couple of weeks. *Okey, Mister Pancho* was screened in fifteen theaters in San Antonio and Houston (Diana Internacional Films 1981). In 1999 a staggering 60 copies of *Las delicias del poder* were distributed across the Mexican territory, including Mexico City and other big cities in 1999 (Ramírez Hernández 1998). According to Ivette Eugenia Lipkies the number was even higher: 120 copies.

THE PROBLEM OF *ENLATAMIENTO*

Film exhibition practices and theater programming varied significantly between cities and rural areas. Theaters in the countryside screened almost exclusively Mexican films (*Cámara* 1978b: 21, 1980: 16). Significantly fewer national productions were shown in Mexico City, and preference was given to foreign films. Because distributors insisted on premiering their films in Mexico City, exhibitors there had the power to withhold new Mexican films from circulation for years, a problem commonly known as *enlatamiento*. Mexican films often were not released shortly after their completion. They were shown to the public when exhibition facilities had a slot available (Mora 2005: 101). In Europe today films are usually in the theater a few months after the filming wraps. According to producer Alejandro Galindo and his collective, in the mid-1980s Mexican films typically premiered at theaters almost a year after the end of the shooting. In 1986 over one hundred films were withheld from the distribution circuit in the capital entirely (Galindo 1987b: 13). To reduce the numbers of films withheld, exhibitors premiered more films, but each remained in theaters for a shorter time. In 1985 the average Mexican film stayed in Mexican theaters for only six weeks; in 1986 this dropped to five weeks. Exceptions were made for more profitable movies, such as the India María films. Concurrently, the average number of circulation copies increased (Reyna Bernal 1987: 38–39). As a result, more films came out, but the revenue for each one fell due to the reduced theater runs. Ultimately the exhibitors' withholding of films from commercial release made it more difficult for producers to calculate revenues and recover investments: it could take up to a few years until a finished film was finally released.

Seven of the sixteen India María films (*El miedo no anda en burro*, *Duro pero seguro*, *La comadrita*, *Sor Tequila*, *Ni de aquí, ni de allá*, *Las delicias del poder*, *La hija de Moctezuma*) were withheld from distribution or obliged to wait for an exhibition slot. Under Diana Films producer Fernando de Fuentes, the films starring Velasco were withheld four times (*El miedo no anda en burro*, *Duro pero seguro*, *La comadrita*, and *Sor Tequila*). *Enlatamiento* continued to be a problem when Velasco left Diana Films. *Ni de aquí, ni de allá* was released in Mexico later than was probably planned. A journalist speculated in *El Nacional* that *Ni de aquí, ni de allá* was being withheld from distribution in Mexico because US films were receiving preference. The delay for *Las delicias del poder* was even longer; it was shot in 1996, but not released until January 1999. In an article in the Mexican newspaper *Novedades*, Velasco voiced her frustration and even criticized the public disinterest in Mexican fare in comparison to Hollywood blockbusters (Anonymous 1997a). Despite the common belief at the time that the public was responsible for the lack of Mexican films in the exhibition circuit, moviegoers in fact had a limited influence. It is more likely that the interests of the Mexican exhibitors and US distributors conflicted and led to the *enlatamiento* of Mexican films, simply because US distributors offered more attractive contracts and their films generated larger revenue. The *enlatamiento* of Mexican films still prevails today for similar reasons (MacLaird 2013: 34). *La hija de Moctezuma* was shot in 2011 and only released in 2014.

Although rural audiences demanded more Mexican material (*Cámara* 1978b: 21, 1980: 16), films were rarely released first in the provinces because producers preferred to premiere them in the capital, the center of the Mexican press. To respond to the higher demand for low-budget Mexican films in rural areas, old films were simply rereleased. The same strategy was used during temporary downturns in production volume. The India María features were favorites for theatrical reruns, probably because they guaranteed revenues at the box office. *Duro pero seguro*—the fourth feature starring Velasco as La India María—was successfully rereleased when *Ni de aquí, ni de allá* was in production (Vieyra 1987). A journalist commented: "Esto significa que sus películas [las de La India María], como las de Cantinflas pueden exhibirse con igual éxito en cualquier época" [This means that her films (India María's)—like those of Cantinflas—can be exhibited with equal success at any time] (Anonymous 1987a). Other India María films were rereleased at various times. Three years after its premiere in 1985, *Ni Chana, ni Juana* returned to Mexican screens in twenty copies, grossing approximately $12,000 (31 million Mexican pesos) on its first night back in theaters (Fernández Escareño 1996: 122).[12]

DRIVE-INS AND OTHER MEETING PLACES

Mexploitation films found a large and eager audience in the United States. By 1982 an estimated 22 million Latinos were living in the United States, which made it one of the most important Spanish-speaking territories (Sinclair 1999: 95). An estimated 6 million to 10 million migrants were undocumented, and numbers were constantly rising. Between 1970 and 1980 even more people migrated to the United States, a majority of them Mexican (*Cámara* 1984a: 4). They resided in four major regions: the Southwest (Texas, New Mexico, Arizona, southern Colorado, and California), the Northeast (New York, New Jersey, Washington DC, and Philadelphia), the Midwest (Chicago), and Florida. The state of California has the highest density of Spanish-speakers, most of them Mexican. In the 1980s approximately 4 million Mexicans lived in Los Angeles—more than in most Mexican cities (*Cámara* 1984a: 5).

Although movie attendance has decreased across the United States since the 1950s, going to the Spanish-language cinemas remained the favorite leisure activity for Latinos living in the United States in the late 1970s and 1980s. Attending movie theaters was even more popular in Los Angeles than visiting parks and restaurants. Moviegoing was a familiar ritual practiced with family or friends that pulled the Spanish-speaking community together and reminded immigrants of home. For many undocumented migrants—often working in the United States without their families—attending the cinema was the only spare-time activity that they could afford (*Cámara* 1984a: 7). Latinos attended the movies frequently: 62 percent of participants in a 1984 study visited the theater to watch Spanish-language films at least once a month and 15 percent went weekly (*Cámara* 1984a: 7).

Two shifts had a major impact on the theater venues where Mexploitation films were screened in the United States. After World War II and through the 1960s downtown areas were gradually abandoned as commercial centers. The American middle class moved to the suburbs, where new multiplex cinemas located in shopping centers became common and profitable exhibition venues (Monaco 2001: 42, 48). The downtown cinemas constructed in the 1920s were abandoned, converted, and used for other purposes. Those that remained often became art cinemas or porn theaters, while others were reopened to cater to black and Latino populations living in the economically depressed downtown neighborhoods. The increasing number of Spanish-speakers had a profound impact on the reuse of the downtown theaters. Exhibitors turned their attention to this expanding audience and generally made good profits by showing exclusively Spanish-language films (Agrasánchez 2006: 33). None of these films were subtitled in English. In 1951 an estimated 680 screens across the United States—including movie theaters, clubs, schools, and churches—screened Spanish-language films (Agrasánchez 2006: 8). In the 1980s around 500 Spanish-language theaters were generating an estimated $45 million a year (Azteca Films 1980; Klain 1980a). During this period Mexploitation was a highly lucrative business. Most of the theaters were located in Texas, California, and Florida. Colorado, Chicago, and New York had significantly fewer Spanish-language theaters, but enough for the distributor Azteca Films to run a separate office in these regions (Azteca Films 1980).

Velasco's films were in high demand in the cinemas targeting Latino audiences, so India María films were expensive on the distribution market. The exhibitor of a theater targeting Latinos in San Diego commented: "Las más caras son las de Mario Moreno y las de La India María" [The most expensive ones are those by Mario Moreno and the ones by La India María] (Iglesias 1991: 106). Many exhibitors in Mexico, Latin America, and the United States were willing to pay the extra price, knowing that the India María films would fill their venues. For *Pobre pero . . . ¡honrada!* the Los Angeles exhibitor transmitted the revenue numbers to the producer Diana Films and commented: "As you know these grosses are very good. Congratulations!" (Dunlap 1974).

US exhibitors often booked appearances by Velasco, who regularly accompanied her films and staged comic sketches before screenings. This type of performance by famous actors and singers, before or during screenings, made the visit to the cinema exciting and filled theater seats (Amador 1983: 33). Screenings of the India María films and other popular Mexploitation films were regularly accompanied by talent shows called *aficionados* [passionate fans]. Before or after the screening, a band would be ready to back up amateur singers as they performed popular songs in front of a packed house. After each *aficionado* show and at the end of the year, prizes were awarded—ranging from $5 to a car or a record deal (Rohrer 2010a, 2010c, 2010d). The competitions got the public involved and made a visit to the theater an occasion worth remembering (Agrasánchez 2006: 12). The owner of the Bay Theater in San Diego underlines the importance of music in the cinema: "Aquí vienen a cantar sus canciones sintiéndose orgullosos de ellos" [They come here to sing their songs and feel proud of themselves] (cited in Iglesias 1991: 112). Exhibitors sometimes performed short sketches themselves to please the audience. The Texan exhibitor Rick Ruenes, for instance, noted that his entire family had to participate in the talent show staged before the film (Rohrer 2010c). These performances made going to the movie theater a community event, often shared with friends and family (Elizondo 1991: 27). Through these activities, exhibitors kept the audience stimulated and eager to participate. During the film itself, the pumped-up audience often loudly urged heroes to watch out as danger approached or sang along with famous musical themes (Agrasánchez 2006: 15).

Outside of US urban areas, Velasco's films were often shown at drive-in theaters. In 1958 the United States had over six thousand drive-in movie theaters. With the emergence of the cinema multiplex, however, the drive-ins began to lose their Anglo audience, who—according to Monaco (2001: 47)—often considered the drive-ins a second-class movie experience. Drive-ins mostly exhibited second runs, and many of them started to form affiliations with US exploitation companies (Syder and Tierney 2005: 45). The exhibition quality was often poor: the projected image was inferior to a movie theater experience, and the audio came out of small speakers or over the car radio. For Mexploitation films, the poor image and sound were of minor importance, as the production values, aesthetics, and sound quality of these films were already quite low. For the India María films, which were traditionally watched by families, the drive-in had another advantage: kids could easily be brought along and put to bed in the back seat as the evening wore on.[13]

The trajectory of a successful India María feature, *Ni de aquí, ni de allá*, gives a sense of the box-office potential that Velasco's films enjoyed in US theaters. The 1988 film treats illegal immigration to the United States—a popular theme: Latinos living in the United States were the most important audience for Mexploitation films by the 1980s. The higher ticket prices and higher revenues meant that *Ni de aquí, ni de allá* opened first in US theaters. It came out in Mexico City four months later (Fernández Escareño 1996: 123). Indeed, many Mexploitation films were first released in the United States, before they premiered in their home market. *Ni de aquí, ni de allá* became an instant hit in the United States and later in Mexico, where it soon was among the country's most successful films of the decade. The film not only outearned Mexican sexy movies, widely watched at the time, but also attracted more moviegoers than the Hollywood blockbuster *Rambo III* (US 1988, directed by Peter MacDonald) (Castro Ricalde 2004b: 197; García Riera 1998: 344; García Tsao 1990). This achievement is rather astonishing: successful Mexican films in the 1980s usually attracted only about half as many moviegoers as US productions (Medina de la Serna 1988: 9).

Ni de aquí, ni de allá remained in Mexican theaters for more than six months—an extremely long run compared to simultaneously released Mexican features, which stayed in theaters for a maximum of eight weeks (Fernández Escareño 1996: 123; Medina de la Serna 1988: 9). The remarkable appeal of the film was the focus of many newspaper articles. The Mexican newspaper *Novedades*, for instance, ran the headline "Millones de cine espectadores se identifican con La India María" [Millions of spectators identify themselves with La India María] (Vélez 1989). This headline grasps the fundamental appeal of the character as well as the film. La India María remained the *reina de la taquilla* [queen of the box office]—as she was often called—from 1988 to 1993 (El Soberbio 1989; Notimex 1997; Segoviano 1994; Tetzpa Zayaz 1987). In each of these years Velasco earned the industry award honoring Mexico's top box-office grossing actress.[14]

FAVORITES ON VIDEO

Beginning in the 1980s, fans often enjoyed India María and other Mexploitation films at home on video or on television.[15] By the end of the decade the number of theaters screening Mexploitation films had gradually declined in both Mexico and the United States.[16] Fewer films were produced, and some of them went directly to video. Previously exhibited films were no longer rereleased in theaters, as they were readily available on video and TV. This shift in consumption was driven by several developments. Many Mexican households acquired television sets and VCR players in the 1980s, and Mexploitation fans learned to record favorite movies from TV. Video rental stores opened across Mexico and in the border region of the United States. Videos could also easily be copied, and pirated copies were cheap and widely available. Finally, immigration laws in the United States tightened, and many migrants feared roundups at theaters (Iglesias 1991: 102).

By 1989 more than half of Mexico City's homes were equipped with video-players, with the highest density among lower-income families (García Canclini et al. 1994: 161). Numbers remained considerably lower in the provinces (Quintal Avilés and Reyes Domínguez 1994: 280; Sánchez Ruiz 1993: 239). Watching movies on video became an established part of people's media consumption habits.[17] Video rental stores offered a variety of films for members at relatively low costs. While independent small businesses carried a large variety of Mexican films, big corporations such as Videovisión and the US companies Multivideo and later Blockbuster all specialized in US box-office hits, mostly Hollywood productions (Sánchez Ruiz 1993: 241). With the increasing proliferation of videos, Videocine, one of Televisa's distribution branches, bought the right to distribute all India María films in the home video market in Mexico and the United States. The rights were later vested to the company Laguna Films—the video distributor of most Mexploitation films today for various territories, including the United States and most Latin American countries.

In a survey on Mexican audiences, television scholar Enrique Sánchez Ruiz interviewed customers of video rental stores in Guadalajara. When asked what films they remembered renting recently, "Las de La India María" [the ones by La India María] was among the most frequent answers (Sánchez Ruiz 1993: 257). These responses clearly attest to the character's popularity among customers of video rental stores. Interestingly, the interviewees didn't name specific titles but summarized the films under India María's name, which over the years had become a virtual franchise. Similarly, the India María films were among the most rented in video stores in Latino communities in the United States (Arbeláez 2001: 642; Barrios 1989). In 1988 the newspaper *Ovaciones* proclaimed the character's success on the video market, entitling one of its articles "La India María también es campeona en el video" [La India María is also a champion on video] (Galeana 1988).

Other Mexploitation films were also favorite rentals at video stores, with slight regional differences within Mexico. According to Sánchez Ruiz (1993: 242), action, drug trafficking, and sexy movies were among the most rented videos in Guadalajara. Renters in Mérida liked these genres, but comedies ranked even higher (Quintal Avilés and Reyes Domínguez 1994: 282). Action, drama, and comedy were the favorites in Tijuana (Valenzuela Arce 1994: 318). The situation was slightly different in Mexico City. To assure the quality of video circulation, the state launched an initiative to promote quality films on video. Around 300 features were selected, all internationally successful with film critics. These films had further reading materials available (García Canclini et al. 1994: 167). This "culturally valuable" package could be purchased or rented cheaply, and many private video rental stores in Mexico City included these films in their selection.[18] Video stores serving the Mexican and Latino communities in the United States carried hundreds of titles, mostly border films and sexy movies. Today these classics of the Mexploitation genre, as well as more recent low-budget productions, are still widely available for sale and rent in Latino neighborhoods.[19]

Due to the increasing profitability of videos, some Mexican producers abandoned shooting on film for theatrical release, instead producing and releasing films exclusively on video (García Riera 1998: 346). Emilio García Riera estimates that a total of 120 films went straight to video between 1983 and 1988. This business model was clearly lucrative.

The straight-to-video products mostly brought border stories to the screen and reflected ongoing political issues. David Wilt (2009: 158) labels the politically themed videos "reality-based" exploitation. Producers commonly used scandalous hooks in the press to develop their stories. The timely topics assured them of an audience, so promotional efforts could be minimal. The comedy *La ley Simpson me viene Wilson* (The Simpson law makes me Wilson) (1988, directed by José Loza), for example, portrays four undocumented Mexican migrants living in the United States—a near-copy of the famous character Cantinflas, a transvestite, a yard worker, and an innocent maid. The film lampoons the circumstances of undocumented immigrants after the Simpson-Rodino bill was passed in 1986. Also called the Immigration Reform and Control Act, the new law represented a concentrated effort by the US government to reduce illegal immigration. Undocumented migrants who could prove continuous residence in the United States after 1982 were legalized. All others were declared illegal and forced to return to Mexico. The law was passed in the midst of a severe economic crisis in Mexico and relative prosperity in the United States. Many Mexicans, even though they were not legal migrants, chose to remain in the United States to assure an income for their extended families. With extremely low production values and worn-out stereotypes, *La ley Simpson me viene Wilson* is typical of the straight-to-video films: a cheap derivation of already cheaply produced Mexploitation films.

Velasco never made features that went straight to video. As a producer, she insisted on her commitment to and love for the movie theater—her favorite exhibition space (Galindo 1990). For Velasco, video was simply a lucrative addition—a distribution channel that followed a theatrical release and full exploitation of a film's box-office potential.

Beyond providing stories for straight-to-video productions, the Immigration Reform and Control Act was an important factor in the grow-

3.1. Most Mexploitation films are for sale as pirated copies, in street markets in Mexico, in the United States, and across Latin America. (Photo by Adán Avalos)

ing popularity of video exhibition among Latinos living in the United States. Fearing persecution and deportation, undocumented migrants steered clear of movie theaters—previously a popular community gathering place—after the law was passed. Theaters catering to Latinos were targeted by US officials in certain states—and gossip at the time ran rampant.[20] The Mexican producer Rafael Pérez Grovas commented on the law's impact, noting that

> mexicanos ya no van en la misma cantidad de asistentes a las salas de cine mexicano porque se les persiguió mucho, sobre todo en los lugares de reunión. . . . En los lugares de reunión de estas personas, de mojados, llegaba de repente la policía y hacía redadas, y pescaban a los mexicanos que no tuvieran su documentación en regla. Eso hizo que mucha gente se ahuyentara de los cines.
> [Mexicans attend theaters screening Mexican films less frequently, because they were often tracked down, especially in places where these migrants, the wetbacks, met. All of a sudden the police would come and make a raid and arrest the Mexicans who did not have their papers in order. That is why they avoided these theaters.] (cited in Iglesias 1991: 102)

For Mexican audiences—and for undocumented migrants and other Latinos in the United States who decided to stay at home with a video—pirated copies were widely available and even cheaper than rentals. Pirated copies went out for sale at metro and bus stations and markets in cities across Mexico. While the inferior quality of the illegal copies might be an issue for films with high production values, quality does not play a crucial role for Mexploitation films. The circulation of cheap illegal copies across borders contributed significantly to the wide proliferation of these films and influenced the content and aesthetics of exploitation movies in other Latin American countries. Film scholar Gabriela Alemán (2009: 268) points to piracy in the form of transnational elements in Ecuadorian exploitation films, which are considerably indebted to the Mexican border and drug films.

MEXPLOITATION TV

As Mexploitation exploded onto video in the 1980s, fans also began to watch significantly more feature films on television (Getino 1998: 27). According to a content analysis by Enrique Sánchez Ruiz, feature films (including Mexploitation films) made up the second largest segment of Mexican television programming after the news.[21] During prime time (7:00 to 11:00 P.M.), Mexican feature films were the dominant programming (Sánchez Ruiz 1993: 235). In the 1980s private television (Televisa) and state-supported channels imported only about 20 percent of their program content from the United States. Sánchez Ruiz (2000) labeled the 1980s as a period of "Mexicanization," in contrast to the 1990s, when dubbed US content significantly increased to more than 50 percent of the programming schedule.

Films with La India María, a character familiar from her early TV appearances, were frequently aired on the small screen. Audiences seemed particularly fond of her (Sánchez Ruiz 1993: 236).[22] The innocent nature of India María, along with the low production values of her films and TV shows, perfectly corresponded to the television aesthetics of the time. Viewers were already fond of the cheaply made *telenovelas* and warmly embraced the India María features and television programs. Even today Velasco's films are regularly broadcast on television, predominantly on channels owned by Televisa. The films are commonly shown on Sunday afternoon, targeting family times in Mexico and in the United States. Rating statistics and the continuous programming of La India María films affirm their ongoing popularity with a large TV audience.

Another factor contributing to the rise of Mexploitation films on TV was President Echeverría's negative stance on these movies, which he gradually tried to ban from theaters. By nationalizing distribution as well as exhibition companies in the 1970s, the state exerted considerable control over theaters. Although Echeverría tried to intervene in television broadcasting, private entrepreneurs formed lobbying blocs to prevent additional regulations and to challenge the increasing competition from state channels. Televisa filled its private network schedule with comedies and action films, audience favorites that the state-owned channels didn't usually air, which contributed to the increasing presence of these films on television—and underwrote Televisa's financial success.

La India María features usually were first released in theaters and subsequently distributed on VHS and DVD and aired on television. In 1993, however, Televisa decided to premiere *Se equivocó la cigüeña*, which the company's film arm had produced, as a special event on its new cable channel Cinestrenar one week before to the film's premiere at theaters (Ayala Blanco 1994: 415). This one-time early TV release was most likely a strategy to promote the new channel and convince television viewers to subscribe to cable TV. Televisa might also have expected lower ticket sales than usual for this India María feature, because movie attendance was already low by the time of the film's release in 1993.

In the US context, there is a difference between Mexploitation films aired on Spanish-language channels and films that were dubbed and at times reedited and aired on independent American channels. Most Mexican films and *telenovelas* that reached a US audience were aired on the network Univisión—formerly the Spanish International Communication Corporation (SICC)—owned in large part by Televisa. In 1986 the network could claim 409 outlets, reaching 83 percent of Spanish-speaking households or 15 million viewers, with no commercial competition from other networks (Sinclair 1999: 101). The company fed its channels with mainly Mexican content aimed at a Latino audience of different nationalities.[23] Televisa later continued to provide a majority of the content for the Spanish-language market through one of its subsidiaries under the Univisa umbrella. Besides distributing in-house produced features and other Mexploitation films, Univisa became active in video manufacturing and created Galavisión, a cable television network, which became one of the main exhibitors of Mexploitation films in the 1980s.[24]

From the mid-1960s onward, low-budget Mexican horror, fantasy, and science-fiction films dubbed into English were frequent fare on independent television in the United States, mostly through the television branch of American International Pictures (AIP-TV). Producers Jerry Warren and

K. Gordon Murray were the primary importers and distributors of Mexploitation films (Syder and Tierney 2005: 33). Both producers dubbed and sometimes drastically changed the cheaply acquired films to fit the expectations of the Anglo audience, consisting of teenager and genre fans. Often characters were renamed: the wrestling hero El Santo, for example, became Samson in the English version. They also changed the musical scores, replacing Mexican music with rock and roll or other music that they thought would appeal to teenagers and sleepless late-night TV audiences. Warren and Murray underlined their involvement by changing the film credits, adding their own title cards—"supervised by" followed by their handwritten signature—to stand out from the other credits (Syder and Tierney 2005: 48).

Warren and Murray's films were packaged with a variety of other low-budget films from around the globe, all of which were adapted for US late-night audiences using similar techniques. David Wilt (1996a: 40) has argued that more Mexploitation films have been exported than any other Latin American film genre. Nonetheless, the market for the dubbed English and edited versions of Mexploitation films was considerably smaller than the market for the original Spanish versions of these productions. The targeted audiences also varied considerably. The original productions aimed at a wide working-class audience of all ages, largely Hispanic, while the English-language versions were mainly geared toward teens and other nonworking audiences of late-night TV, mostly Anglo (Syder and Tierney 2005: 48).

THE UNSTABLE LATIN AMERICAN MARKET

During the Golden Age of Mexican cinema, Latin America and Spain were important distribution territories for the Mexican film industry. Particularly during World War II, Mexico produced more films than any other country in Latin America, so Mexican films dominated screens across a vast Spanish-speaking territory (Tierney 2007: 1). By the heyday of Mexploitation cinema in the late 1970s, however, distributing and exhibiting Mexican films in parts of Latin America had become increasingly difficult.

Across Latin American, the 1970s and 1980s were marked by instability caused by civil wars and revolutions. Political regimes were overthrown and new ones imposed. Several countries were hit by economic crises, leading to the devaluation of national currencies.[25] In Bolivia, for example, the exchange rate for one US dollar went from 40 Bolivian pesos to 2,000 within a couple of years. Peru experienced a similar currency crisis (*Cámara* 1984b: 2). Inflation rates were at such high levels by 1980 that literally no profits could be made, so private film producers in Mexico no longer viewed these unstable regions as viable markets for their films. With no money to be made with theater releases, Mexploitation films were mostly distributed on video. Even more common were pirated copies sold in local markets.

In other Latin American countries, among them Colombia and Venezuela, where exchange rates were stable, Mexico's private producers continued to follow established practices for distributing their films. In Colombia, as in Mexico, cinemas were divided by class—in Spanish they were known as theaters for *los de arriba* [the ones above] and *los de abajo* [the ones below] (Gómez Ocampo 1997: 177). As in Mexico, Mexploitation films were screened in the cheaper theaters, along with low-budget films from other countries. As in the United States and Mexico, double features were shown for a single ticket price, with films running continuously from morning until midnight. Ticket holders usually could walk into the theater at any time (Gómez Ocampo 1997: 179f.).

Despite the poor market in some parts of the region, reports and letters from distributors across Latin America attest that India María films were released successfully across Latin America, particularly in Venezuela. The first feature starring Velasco as La India María, *Tonta tonta, pero no tanto* (1972), had a strong showing across Latin America. On May 7, 1973, the international distributor Películas Mexicanas, represented by Ignacio Pendás, made this statement about the box-office performance of *Tonta tonta, pero no tanto* in Caracas, Venezuela:

> La película ha respondido extraordinariamente bien, aparte de que el sábado sufrimos un verdadero temporal de agua, que perjudico grandemente las entradas.
> [The film has reached an extraordinary box-office response despite heavy rains on Saturday, which greatly hurt attendance.] (Pendás 1973)

Pendás added a possible explanation for the success:

> El éxito alcanzado se debe a la presentación que hicimos en televisión de La India María . . . el público la ha recibido con grandes muestras de cariño y simpatía.
> [The success achieved is mainly the result of the presentation that we made of La India María on television . . . the public has embraced her with affection and sympathy.] (Pendás 1973)

3.2. Opening night of the first India María film, *Tonta tonta, pero no tanto* in front of a cinema in Caracas, Venezuela, in 1973. The exhibitor sent the picture to the producer at Diana Films to prove that the film was a hit. (Diana Internacional Films, S.A. de C.V.)

Distributors and cinema owners across Latin America responded with similar enthusiasm to Velasco's subsequent films.

Censorship at times hindered wide distribution of wrestling, sexy, and border films across Latin America. Regulations were different in each country; sometimes they varied from state to state. In Ecuador, for example, censorship decisions could differ from Quito to Cuenca (*Cámara* 1984b: 2). As in Mexico, changing political regimes interpreted and revised censorship regulations. Whether existing laws were strictly enforced often came down to the inclination of the person in charge. Over the course of a few decades, Latin America became a territory of decreasing importance for the Mexican film industry. The producer Rafael Pérez Grovas estimated that Latin American territories generated only 10 percent of the revenues of a Mexican production by 1988; it had once been 50 percent (cited in Iglesias 1991: 100).

Very few Mexploitation films and none of the India María films were distributed and exhibited in Europe, even though Películas Mexicanas had a branch in Paris. When Mexploitation films did get picked up, local

3.3. Some exported Mexploitation films were amended to create steamy new versions. *Draculas Tochter und Professor Satanas* (1968) is a German version of *La mujer murciélago* (1968). (Agrasánchez Film Archive)

distributors in effect produced their own custom versions. They chose titles that appealed to their national audience and renamed characters: El Santo, for example, became Superman in Germany. Just as in dubbed US versions, certain scenes were cut and replaced with material that would seem more intriguing to the respective national audiences. For some films erotic scenes were spliced in and steamy new versions were edited. For example, for *Las luchadoras contra el robot asesino* (Wrestling women versus the murderous robot) (1969, directed by René Cardona), a sexually suggestive version named *El asesino loco y el sexo* (The mad killer and sex) was released, featuring an evil monster who ripped off women's clothes. The press book for the film promised "¡La violencia sexual de desborda!" [Bursting with sexual violence!] and included this catchy promotional summary:

> Ávido de dominar el mundo, el Dr. Orlak pretende crear hombres de fuerza extraordinaria que solo obedezcan sus mandates. Su máxima crea-

> ción es Karfay, zombi mudo y de monstruoso aspecto que se solaza en escapar y atacar sexualmente a bellas mujeres. . . . A colores con Joaquín Cordero, Regina Torne, Héctor Lechuga, Malu Reyes, Carlos Agosti. . . . Pronto en su cine.
> [Eager to rule the world, Dr. Orlak aims to create a man with extraordinary powers who only follows his orders. His latest and greatest creation is Karfay, a monstrous-looking silent zombie, who finds solace in escaping and sexually attacking beautiful women. . . . In color, with Joaquín Cordero, Regina Torne, Héctor Lechuga, Malu Reyes, Carlos Agosti. . . . Coming soon to theaters near you.] (promotional materials from the Agrasánchez Film Archive)

It is uncertain how many sexploitation versions—made exclusively for export—existed. The Agrasánchez Film Archive owns promotional materials for some of these films. Additionally, Viviana García Besné revealed production stories of the "Calderón" family business in her documentary *Perdida* (Loss) (2009). Her research resulted in the retrieval of some sexually explicit reels that had been forgotten for decades.

MARKETING MEXPLOITATION

Like the Mexploitation films themselves, movie posters and other advertising that pulled in big audiences had a distinctive low-budget aesthetic. US and Mexican distributors relied heavily on graphic advertising to sell these films. Ads in newspapers trumpeted new theatrical releases, while exhibitors in Mexico and the United States displayed flashy posters, window and lobby cards, and other promotional materials for current and upcoming films in front of and inside theaters. Little effort was made to distinguish one film from another. Instead Mexploitation promotion stressed the key attributes of the films: the body spectacle, the character types, and the names of known performers.

Advertising for the India María features primarily centered on the character, which was already familiar from television and earlier movies. When launching a new movie, distributors sometimes merely reminded audiences of how hilarious La India María was. Appearances by well-known Mexican actors, such as Resortes, were also part of the marketing strategy for India María features. To attract even more spectators across Latin America and within the Latino community in the United States, actors from Venezuela, Colombia, Argentina, and Puerto Rico were cast (Vergara 1972). For example the Puerto Rican actor Rolando Borral, already famous through his appearances in *telenovelas*, played a lead role in *La presidenta municipal* and earned a sizable mention in movie posters and ads.

Mexploitation posters and advertisements commonly depicted the main hero in a variety of scenes. Cartoon drawings often were intertwined with film stills to form newspaper advertisements and posters. Promotional items often feature the main conflict in the story. On a lobby card for *Sor Tequila*, for example, La India María is depicted as a cartoon nun pulling a priest from a helicopter. They are about to fall, yet their gestures and expressions are incongruously filled with joy and excitement: the priest throws his arms happily in the air, while María elegantly swings her legs in an acrobatic attitude. The still from the same film, integrated into the poster, shows La India María arm-wrestling with a bare-chested, artfully perspiring muscleman. While he is flexed and evidently struggling, she seems almost relaxed.

Exhibitors typically placed advertisements in the events section of newspapers. For the India María features, cartoon drawings depicted either a single scene or a series of comical moments from the film. The amusing caricature images emphasize India María's physical features,

3.4. The lobby cards used to advertise India María films, here *Sor Tequila*, always contained both a still and a cartoon scene. (Cineteca Nacional)

3.5. Cartoon drawings were used to advertise India María films (here *La comadrita*) in newspapers. (Cineteca Nacional)

such as her mouth, long braids, and solid build. Some advertisements also explicitly address their audience. The phrase "¡NIÑOS traigan a toda la familia!" [KIDS, bring along your entire family!] in bold white letters enhanced the dark ad for *Okey, Mister Pancho*. An ad for *El miedo no anda en burro* gave spectators a tongue-in-cheek warning about the strong sensations that the film might evoke:

> ¡Se le pondrá la carne de gallina! ¡Los pelos de punta! ¡Le bailaran las rodillas! ¡Le rechinaran los dientes! ¡Se le saldrán los ojos! ¡Se comerá las uñas!
> [You will get goose bumps! Your hair will stand on end! Your knees will tremble! Your teeth will gnash! Your eyes will pop out! You will chew your fingernails!] (publicity material from Cineteca Nacional)

Posters for comedies often played up sweet, childlike attributes of the characters, but promotional materials for wrestling films, sexy movies, and border films visually enhanced different physical features. Posters for the wrestling films emphasized the muscular bodies of the fighters, while sexy movies focused on erogenous zones like buttocks or breasts—which often filled the entire poster in tight close-ups. Some ads featured women

3.6 AND 3.7. The physical features of women and men are enhanced on posters such as the ones for *La loba* (1965, US 1966) and *Solo para damas* (1981). (Agrasánchez Film Archive)

in skimpy outfits striking lascivious poses. Posters for the border films shocked viewers with graphic depictions of extreme violence or the faces of male stars superimposed over guns or other weapons.

To complete the marketing effort, exhibitors sent press books provided by distributors to local radio stations. An announcer would read one or several short advertising texts or catchy lines on the air; some exhibitors also sent prerecorded spots to radio stations. Films featuring La India María were promoted on the radio as a way to reach moviegoers who rarely read newspapers or could not read at all. One radio spot for *La presidenta municipal* grabbed listeners' attention by making an unlikely claim: "La presidenta municipal le quita al pobre para dárselo al rico" [The mayor takes from the poor to give to the rich]. This line asserts that La India María takes from the poor, when the movie's plot is in fact the opposite—but it makes for a memorable commercial.

The radio commercial for *La presidenta municipal* was more elaborate:

> ¿La India María como 'PRESIDENTA MUNICIPAL'??? ¡Increíble! . . . ¡Inaudito! . . . ¿Sí? . . . Pués véala en PRESIDENTA MUNICIPAL para que goce viéndola como resuelve el problema de los braceros . . . ¡importando gringos a Mexico![26] . . . ¡Como combate los altos precios de las tor-

> tillas . . . el pan y los frijoles quitándolos como artículos de lujo! La India María, María Elena Velasco en LA PRESIDENTA MUNICIPAL toda a colores una película divertidísima para toda la família con un reparto formidable encabezado por El Resortes, Pancho Cordova, Fernando Soto Mantequilla, Borolas y muchos más. . . . No se la pierda.
> [La India María as 'municipal president'??? Incredible! . . . Unheard of! . . . Yes? . . . Well, come and see her in PRESIDENTA MUNICIPAL and enjoy watching how she solves problems with migrant workers . . . by importing white Americans to Mexico! How she fights the high price of tortillas, . . . bread, and beans by declaring them luxury items! La India María, María Elena Velasco in LA PRESIDENTA MUNICIPAL in color, a funny film for the whole family with a great cast headed by Resortes, Pancho Cordova, Fernando Soto Mantequilla, Borolas, and many more. . . . Don't miss it.] (press book for *La presidenta municipal*)

The advertisement's wording and sentence structure clearly echo informal speech and stress pleasures that the film promises to deliver. The ad is full of verbal surprises, just as the plot will deliver surprising twists, courtesy of India María.

Playing with proverbs was another common strategy for marketing Mexploitation films on the radio. Sometimes these sayings are challenging for a non-native to decode. *La comadrita* ads used the following phrase: "El compadre pone . . . Dios dispone . . . ¡viene la comadrita y los descompone!" Literally translated, this means: "Man proposes, God disposes, and the godmother [term used for any good friend—here for La India María] turns it all upside down!" Although the meaning is roughly the same in English, the Spanish version rhymes and offers a memorable rhythm that gets stuck in listeners' heads.

Individual radio spots vary from film to film, but the Mexploitation advertisements all follow similar patterns. Catchy sentence-length ads point to the extraordinary spectacle in the advertised film, while longer ads give a few hints about the plot and usually name the most famous actors.

Distributors also provided preview trailers for the theatrical release, at times running close to ten minutes (Grant 1982). These trailers were screened at theaters a few weeks before a film's release. Later they were used for the VHS and DVD releases. The trailers remain an important marketing tool today. At the beginning of every VHS or DVD, several trailers (which sometimes cannot be skipped on DVD) stimulate an interest in upcoming or related films.

The same advertising materials often were used for the VHS and DVD

3.8. Today DVD box sets of Mexploitation films, combining similar films, are widely available on the market.

release. By the time the films were released in that form, the titles of the films—often based on popular sayings or ballads—had wide circulation and a ready audience. Only in rare cases were titles changed for the video and DVD release. Although relatively few marketing efforts were made for these releases, repackaging kept the profit flowing. Compilation box sets, combining a series of films of the same genre or with the same performer, have been common since the VHS era. Individual films on television were generally not advertised at all, but the programming slot framed the films within a certain predefined context.

When exhibitors thought that they had a big hit on their hands, they sometimes made a special promotional splash—mounting posters and loudspeakers on a pickup truck, for example, and driving around local neighborhoods to announce highlights of upcoming shows (Rohrer 2010a,

2010c). Shouting out the names of the character types or the stars playing them was another method for attracting moviegoers. Similarly, personal appearances of Mexploitation stars such as the Almada brothers, Jorge Rivero, Isela Vega, or Rosa Gloria Chagoyán drew crowds to the cinema. But as an everyday pleasure that fans enjoyed for decades, the simple fact that a movie featured India María or Cantinflas was reason enough for people to buy their tickets.

CHAPTER 4

HATED BY CRITICS, LOVED BY THE PEOPLE

SOME OF MY CHICANO FRIENDS use names of characters from Mexploitation films as their nicknames in their blogs on websites for the Latino community in the Los Angeles area. Their affectionate but ironic reference to these characters suggests that they have drawn a different meaning from these films than, for instance, a street vendor who declares that he simply enjoys watching India María films and other Mexploitation films. His view, in turn, differs considerably from those of a drag queen who regularly dresses as the character or film critics who accuse Velasco of using clichéd characters (Barriga Chávez 1988a). The Mexican film historian and critic Paco Ignacio Taibo carried this common critical stance a step further in the *Los Angeles Times Magazine*: "Mexican good taste is being poisoned by those producers who impose horrific, crude films on the viewing audience" (cited in Goldin and Cooper 1986).

My own interest in the India María films stems from both the lack of previous scholarship and their contradictory reception. The main goal of this chapter is to inquire into the ways viewers make sense of La India María. To find out more, I interviewed thirty people who watched the India María films in Mexico and the United States, including taxi drivers, hairdressers, teachers, library clerks, market women, farmworkers, cleaners, and gardeners.[1] Based on these interviews and analysis of the films, promotional materials, and exhibition practices, I outline how different reception modes occur. While some viewers criticize the films and the characters, others admire both the character and Velasco. Some viewers participate in more than one mode of reception and switch between the modes according to the setting or social context.

BAD FILMS

A headline featured prominently on the cover of the Mexican magazine *Super Musical* succinctly sums up the critical reception of India María: "¡Los intelectuales no me quieren, pero el pueblo sí!" [Intellectuals don't like me, but the people do!] (Anonymous 1989a). The memorable headline is certainly a generalization, but India María films, like most Mexploitation films, have repeatedly been the subject of harsh criticism. They are denounced for their "bad quality" and for having a negative influence by degrading viewers' taste.

During the heyday of Mexploitation films in the 1970s and 1980s, many Mexican film critics and media studies scholars insisted on the omnipotence of television and cinema and their power over passive viewers. It is worth noting that often film critics and film scholars held double positions. They wrote articles for newspapers and taught at universities, and some made films.[2] As critics they often saw their main role as revealing mechanisms of influence and warning audiences of negative effects from the media (Castro Ricalde 2004b: 198). Early critics mentioned Velasco's association with the company Televisa, implying that India María was a character type exploited by the conglomerate, which fostered low-quality entertainment at minimal costs. This critical stance has partly prevailed. Some of the people interviewed still associated the India María character with Televisa and criticized Velasco for teaming up with a conglomerate that they held responsible for poisoning people's taste.

The reception of many India María films turns on the film style itself. Since the 1980s, critics have repeatedly pointed to perceived flaws, such as the bland repetition of stories, simplistic themes, low-quality aesthetics, unskillful directing, and "wooden" performances—particularly the gags (Ayala Blanco 1989, 1994: 415; Barriga Chávez 1988a, 1988b, 1991, 1993; Galindo 1990). While critics have largely argued that India María films fail to provide Hollywood-level quality, these films have also been considered "bad" by Mexican standards. Film critic Ezequiel Barriga Chávez (1988b), for example, harshly condemned *Ni de aquí, ni de allá* at the time of its release, taking it as a prime example of the "crisis" of Mexican cinema:

> Basta con una cinta como ésta para darnos cuenta del estado de cosas a que ha llegado esta industria que en otros tiempos fue una de las principales de este país, amén de ser una importante generadora de divisas. Hoy el cine se hace a partir de los argumentos más simplones con unas adap-

> taciones pésimas, un supuesto humor completamente envejecido, personajes que rayan en la caricatura y una realización anodina, incapaz de lograr una sola toma rescatable.
> [A film like this one speaks for itself and makes us realize how bad things have gotten in this industry, which before was among the strongest of the country in addition to generating lucrative profits. Today films are made with the most simplistic scripts, based on horrible adaptations, a humor totally out of date, clichéd characters, badly filmed, not getting a single shot right.]

He concluded his overwrought review by complaining that one never knows at which points in the film to laugh or cry—except from despair over the fall of Mexican cinema (Barriga Chávez 1988b).

India María films and other Mexploitation films undeniably differ from classical cinema, marked by what are commonly considered filmic deficiencies. The stories are straightforward with linear plots but frequently interrupted by excessive and obvious slapstick routines and other spectacles. Cinematography and montage are mostly used pragmatically: camera movements pursue the main goal of framing characters. Some films contain continuity errors. Colors are at times bland, and sometimes it seems as if the process of color grading has simply been skipped. Hence, within established norms determined by mainstream Hollywood cinema, India María films bear marks of what is commonly called "low quality." Some of Velasco's films explicitly engage in a sort of B-movie parody, through a combination of her acting style, a cheap production mode, and resulting aesthetic choices. The film *El miedo no anda en burro*, for instance, parodies the horror movie genre. La India María is threatened by silly monsters that make her scream throughout the entire film. Considering how harmless the creatures are, her fear seems so utterly overblown that it becomes part of the film's comedy. The slapstick not only exaggerates the character's terror and clichéd naiveté but also enlists the audience in the gag by parodying the obvious constraints of the director and producer and their inability to create expensive special effects that would make the monsters at all believable.

Velasco's films are known for their wide distribution and success with their working-class audience. Their popular success might have encouraged some film critics in their condemnation of these films. Whatever the cause, at the time of their release, critics and scholars have formed a unified and often unspoken agreement that India María and most Mexploita-

4.1. In *El miedo no anda en burro* (1976) Velasco breaches her character type. The film thereby becomes a parody of the horror genre. (Diana Internacional Films, S.A. de C.V.)

tion films are successful with audiences but possess little artistic value: indeed, archives have rarely collected or preserved these works.[3]

The negative image of Mexploitation films was nurtured by their producers, who declared that their main goal was to make high profits. Critics felt proven right by such statements. Velasco frequently commented on the state of the Mexican film industry (Garay 1994; A. C. Hernández 1988). She commonly insisted that the film industry was a business, aiming only to generate revenue:

> El cine es una industria. Con esto quiero decir que si se filma una cinta, lo menos que se puede esperar es recuperar lo que se invirtió.
> [Film is an industry. This means that when you make a movie, the least you can expect is that it recoups its investments.] (cited in A. C. Hernández 1988)

Velasco was not alone in her frank statement about the industry's commercial motives. Many Mexploitation producers openly declared that they made films for the money. Rogelio Agrasánchez, a prolific producer who specifically made films to exploit the Los Angeles audience, admitted that he was after "sure-fire instant hits"—not art films. In a 1986 interview with the *Los Angeles Times*, Agrasánchez listed what was necessary for his films' success: "*wetbacks*, violencia, mucha violencia" [wetbacks, violence, a lot of violence] (cited in Goldin and Cooper 1986). With his use of the derogatory English term "wetbacks," Agrasánchez openly signaled his lack of empathy for migrants and underlined that his business was exclusively about profits. Similarly, Rolando Fernández, the producer and director of the *Lola la trailera* films, portrayed himself solely as a businessman:

> Nosotros, mi grupo somos gente de negocios, sabemos cuanto cuesta meterse al mercado, popularizar un nombre, conquistar al público.
> [We are businesspeople and know exactly how much it takes to produce films for the market, create stars, and conquer the public.] (Anonymous 1985b: 5)

Producers were outspoken about their endeavor being commercial, which didn't bother them. To the contrary, they had a sort of inside agreement with their audience—ordinary people who took pleasure in these predictable, fun films where the "little guy" is the hero. Such clear commitments to commercial production, and even Agrasánchez's provocative stance, contributed to the harsh critique that these producers received from film critics.

Some producers of Mexploitation films were clearly aware of the pleasures that are gained from precisely the B-movie aesthetic of their films. Some of them even explicitly enhanced certain of these aspects in order to entertain. This phenomenon is not unique to the Mexican context. Hollywood exploitation and B films often foreground overacting and cheap effects as a marker of difference from stuffy, respectable A films. When the B movies are watched with other fans, these differences create a sort of community solidarity, a shared acknowledgment of and pleasure in the "bad" quality. Numerous scholars have described these reception dynamics, observing that spectators do not simply enjoy watching films or television shows categorized as "bad" but propose their own interpretation, by attacking the criteria used to define "high-quality" films (Cartmell et al. 1997; Grant 2008; Gwenllian-Jones and Pearson 2004; Jancovich 2002; Jancovich et al. 2003; Jenkins 2013; Le Guern 2004; Schaefer 1999; Sconce 1995; Sontag 1999). They have suggested reevaluating these apparently "bad" films as cult, trash, or paracinema, a common way to reinterpret films with supposedly negative artistic attributes.[4]

Like critics, politicians such as President Luis Echeverría held producers responsible for what he considered a proliferation of "low-quality" films. A 1975 speech makes Echeverría's stance clear: "[The private producers] seem to me to have intervened in the film industry as in a factory of some product or in banking, without any feeling for general cultural interest" (Pérez Turrent and Turner 1977: 207–209).

Similarly harsh judgments were made by some filmmakers. At an award ceremony for Mexican films, the internationally acclaimed director Gabriel Figueroa, for example, commented on the boom of Mexploitation films, which he characterized as

> cheap cinema, with no artistic or cultural ambitions, a repetition of the oldest and most time-worn formulas, sub-pornography, facile folklore, routine melodramas, films aimed at manipulating the emotions and frustrations of the lower strata of the population and the nostalgia of Mexicans and of those of Mexican descent in the United States. (cited in Pérez Turrent and Turner 1977: 207)

Figueroa's prepared remark on a public platform epitomized an attitude that was widely accepted among critics in Mexico: Mexploitation films are "bad" because of predictable plots, clichéd characters, and aesthetic qualities. More importantly, Figueroa degraded the audience as an easily manipulated passive mass, with no means to create its own meaning out of these films.

While many filmmakers, politicians, and film critics held producers responsible for the low quality of the films, producers themselves hardly bothered disagreeing—on the contrary, one of them even blamed spectators for the lack of quality. The private producer Raúl Ramírez declared:

> El pueblo no merece nada bueno. Quiere basura y eso le damos. Estás películas [Mexploitation] dejan dinero y por eso las hacemos.
> [The masses don't deserve anything good. They want trash and that is what we are giving them. These films (Mexploitation) generate revenues and this is why we produce them.] (cited in Díaz et al. 2008: 12)

This harsh statement was reinforced by the venues that the films were released in: the so-called second-class movie theaters with low hygiene standards, at times even nicknamed *piojitos* [small lice]. Through the division into luxurious first-class cinemas where Hollywood films were screened and second-house movie theaters, which were often associated to former theater stages, exhibitors contributed the common notion that these films were of low value.

It stands out that scholars, politicians, producers, and exhibitors all blamed one another for fostering "bad-quality" films. While many Mexploitation producers didn't seem to mind the negative judgments, other members of the Mexican film industry gradually became worried about the harsh critical attention. In January 1987 an edition of the industry journal *Cámara* (1987c) was dedicated to these disagreements. Director Gilberto Martínez Solares, known for Mexploitation films such as *Los días de los albañiles* [Days of the bricklayers] (1985–1990, directed) and Velasco's *Okey, Mister Pancho* (1981), blamed critics and film scholars for their patronizing stance on Mexploitation films. He underlined their pivotal role in establishing the values of cultural products and focused on how their opinions shift across time.

> Por lo que siento que los críticos son muy solemnes y que están por lo menos 20 años atrás en los gustos del público, ya que consideran a la comedia como un género vulgar y ordinario. Así llegaron a calificar por ejemplo las comedias que hice con Tin Tan, pero después cambiaron de opinión. Hasta que García Riera y creo también Ayala Blanco empezaron a decir que tenía cierto valor y ya ve, ahora las películas con Tin Tan que dirigí son consideradas como clásicas y hasta como joyas del cine mexicano.
> [I feel the critics are holier-than-thou and at least twenty years behind the taste of the audience. They consider comedy to be a vulgar and ordinary genre. That, for example, is how they categorized the comedies that I made with Tin Tan, but later they changed their minds. Until García Riera and I believe also Ayala Blanco began to see some cultural value and there you go: now the films with Tin Tan that I directed are considered classics or even pearls of Mexican cinema.] (cited in Jiménez Patiño 1987: 16)

Like Martínez Solares, Velasco took deliberate jabs at the critics' corrosive judgments. Her quotation in the 1989 headline cited above ("intellectuals don't like me, but the people do!") (Anonymous 1989a) attests to Velasco's strategy: suggesting that it is impossible to please the critics and simultaneously gain a wide audience, while also implying that critics have relatively little influence on a film's success. In another interview, Velasco took her hypothesis a step further by turning the tables and lambasting intellectuals and critics for making art films that no one wants to watch:

> Los intelectuales quieren hacer un cine que ellos consideran que es el CINE con mayúsculas, pero desgraciadamente a la gente no le gusta. [Intellectuals want to make films that they consider CINEMA in capital letters, but unfortunately people don't like them.] (cited in A. C. Hernández 1988)

Velasco's division between the *pueblo* [people] and the intellectual elite was in fact quite common in Mexico (Castro Ricalde 2006: 88). The critical designation of the "low quality of the India María films" suggested that their consumption was not desirable—which, significantly, made watching the films an act of resistance against the dominant notion of bad taste.

The notion of the popular audience as passive victims prevailed into the late 1980s. Film scholars, historians, and critics posited and reinforced the simplistic division between passive viewers and producers aiming to make profits. In a study of border cinema, for instance, Iglesias (1991: 69) observed a change in the attitude of producers between the Golden Age (until approximately the late 1940s) and the period of Mexploitation (late 1950s to late 1980s):

> Al parecer hace unos años el productor y realizador se sentían orgullosos de hacer cine nacional, se sentían parte del público, por lo que podían decir "produzco para mí o para nosotros" . . . ahora encontramos un abismo entre ellos y nosotros.
>
> [It seems that a few years back producers and directors were proud to make national (Mexican) cinema, they felt they were part of the public and therefore they could say, "I produce for myself or for all of us" . . . now there is a gap between them and us.]

Thus Iglesias lamented that numerous Mexploitation producers had lost their link to their audience, accusing them of living a life set apart from their viewers. She returned to her claim some years later in a study of the audiences for border action films and showed a verifiable distance between Mexican film industry insiders and the majority of these viewers—although her data also call into question her own participation in the "us" of this audience. She found that border action audiences were mostly undocumented migrants who had lived in the United States less than a year and a half (32.5 percent) or less than four years (25.5 percent). She further noted that some 13.3 percent of moviegoers in the United States were illiterate or had little schooling (Iglesias 1999: 237).

Elite critical positions on the India María films have become less polarized since the late 1980s. The most remarkable shift in perception came with the release of Velasco's film *Las delicias del poder* (1999). Critics praised the film for its overt critique of Mexico's political system in the midst of a presidential campaign (Arredondo 1999; Aviña 1999; Betacourt 1999; Morales Valentín 1998). Several important film critics and scholars publicly praised the film for its mockery of mechanisms of power and also supported Velasco's statements to the press. In her interviews, she had called for more women in politics. Velasco had previously voiced similar opinions to the press, but film critics only took note of them in the 1990s.

During this period, Velasco's contribution as a filmmaker was gradually reevaluated, as an invitation to appear at the Women's Film Festival and conference in Tijuana confirms (Fregoso and Iglesias 1998; Hernández 2007). More recently, several female scholars have revisited Velasco's work. Carol Clark D'Lugo (2008) reevaluated Velasco's films by comparing them to the films of Cantinflas. She defended Velasco's portrayal of La India María as a consistent and truthful portrayal of a character defined by marginality in class, gender, and ethnicity. Mexican film scholar Maricruz Castro Ricalde (2004a, 2007) applauded the India María films for their empowering message. This book shares the goal of reevaluating Velasco's notable career and work. I admit my deep admiration for Velasco's career and believe that her movies are important contributions to Mexican culture. I have deeply enjoyed watching La India María films with enthusiastic fans, although I do not consider myself a fan of all of her films.

Nevertheless, I was astonished that showing interest in Velasco's work alone was sufficient to attract negative critical attention. At several conferences in Mexico in 2009 and 2010, when I was completing fieldwork for this book, Mexican scholars criticized me for researching the India María films. Even the newspaper *La Jornada* ran a long article. The journalist was startled to note that India María films had become the object of international academic research (Márquez 2009). *La Jornada* and other left-leaning news sources, such as *Unomásuno* and the magazine *Proceso*, had pointedly overlooked Velasco's work and her films until then. Even when Velasco began directing her own films and generated a massive box-office response, the newspapers simply ignored her (Castro Ricalde 2006:

88). After Velasco's death in May 2015, numerous articles appeared in the Mexican press. Most obituaries and news coverage foregrounded her accomplishment of creating the folk character La India María, while ignoring her work as a producer and director.

A broader reevaluation of Mexploitation cinema has recently emerged in Anglo scholarship, along with the attention to the India María films. One of the most significant contributions is the collection of essays *Latsploitation, Exploitation Cinemas, and Latin America*, edited by Victoria Ruétalo and Dolores Tierney (2009). Adán Avalos (2009) has also contributed to shining a new critical light on Mexploitation films. He has analyzed the role of border films in the migrant community in an attempt to rehabilitate the term *naco*—originally a slur against Indians, peasants, or people with a provincial background. *Naco* generally refers to attitudes, values, and tastes of the lower classes, but in recent years the migrant community has reclaimed the term, using it in a positive sense for cultural products that had previously been labeled as "low quality" (Avalos 2009: 187). The essay on Mexican wrestling films by Syder and Tierney (2005), Greene's *Mexploitation Cinema* (2005), and Rashotte's *Narco Cinema* (2015) also offer important reevaluations of Mexploitation cinema. It is worth noting that my research on La India María has been received with interest among Latino scholars in the United States (Hudson 2010; Zimmermann 2009). This reflects the current trend in Anglo film studies toward reevaluating exploitation cinemas.

While the style of Velasco's films has often stirred criticism, the India María films and other Mexploitation films also produce pleasure precisely through their baldly obvious "bad" quality. There is a fine line, it seems, between "Wow, is this bad!" and "This is so bad, it's funny!"

STAGNATION

It is worth recalling that the reception of India María has been shaped by the character's development over more than forty years—a strikingly long trajectory for both the character and Velasco herself as a pop culture star. Critics at times denigrated Velasco's acting as stagnant because of her career-long dedication to a single role. This perspective reflects an elite attitude toward cultural production, in which actors are required to prove their skills by playing different multifaceted roles in order to "grow" and demonstrate their versatility. Each role is perceived as new challenge that, when successfully met, leads to rewards in the form of critical recognition and an increase in the actor's reputation. Velasco chose not to conform to this model and for many years stuck firmly with the character of La India María. As a result, even though Velasco grew into other industry roles, such as working on scripts, directing, and ultimately producing her own films, critics still perceived her dedication to a single character as a trap that kept her from progressing as a mature actress.

Significantly, Velasco agreed that her dedication to La India María had limited her as an actress. Later in her career, however, she repeatedly voiced a wish to play other characters (Anonymous 1987b; Chiquet 1996; Jiménez 2002; Notimex 1997; Ramírez 1987). A 1992 interview with the newspaper *El Sol del Medio Día* exemplifies Velasco's recognition of the mechanisms at play, which she projected onto the audience:

> Me gustaría crear otro [personaje] completamente antagónico, por ejemplo una mujer de la vida galante o una narcotraficante, para demonstrar al público que tengo la capacidad de interpretar todo tipo de géneros.
> [I would like to play another (character), totally opposite, for instance, a prostitute or a drug dealer, to prove to the audience that I am able to interpret any kind of roles.] (Anonymous 1992b)

At the same time, Velasco was fully aware that her career success and ongoing reputation depended on La India María. She remarked:

> Si acaso, continuo, haré algunas innovaciones [al personaje], pero ninguna manera desaparecerlo. Esto es como si dijeran que Mario Moreno dejo der ser cómico como la ha sido toda su vida y se olvidara de Cantinflas. El público, no sólo de México, sino a nivel internacional lo recordará como Cantinflas y a mí, como La India María.
> [If I continue, I might amend some traits, but I would never abandon the character. It would be as if Mario Moreno would stop being a comedian, after playing Cantinflas for all his life. Mexican as well as international audiences will always remember him as Cantinflas and me as La India María.] (Suárez Ojeda 1992)

More than a decade later, when Velasco finally stepped into a different role as a dance instructor in her son's film *Huapango* (2004, directed by Iván Lipkies), an adaptation of William Shakespeare's *Othello*, the critical acclaim for her acting that she had hoped for never materialized. However, Mexican film industry professionals took this opportunity to acknowledge Velasco's contributions by awarding her an Ariel, the Mexican equivalent of Hollywood's Oscars, for best-adapted screenplay for *Huapango*.

Huapango was the only film in which Velasco played a lead role as a character other than India María. In interviews I conducted in 2008 and 2009 Velasco acknowledged that her career had been entirely marked by La India María. Two years later, in 2011, she told me on the set of her final film, *La hija de Moctezuma*: "Quiero explotar el personaje una última vez más" [I want to exploit the character one last time]. Velasco's choice of words clearly emphasized the economic value of the character, reflecting the fact that the character was the main source of income—and indeed a reliable source of both profit and criticism.

SIMPLY ENTERTAINING

Despite some harsh critical reactions, most Mexican viewers enjoyed the India María films. As the popularity of Velasco's and other Mexploitation films at the box office and on TV attests, viewers were eager for this type of light, predictable entertainment. One of the main advantages of the character India María was that people knew exactly what to expect. Through previous viewing experiences, they were certain that a happy ending was guaranteed—even when some serious topics like migration were part of the plot. Familiar with the formula, they could expect the character to overcome problems and ultimately triumph, and along the way they could enjoy Velasco's slapstick performance. When I asked people what exactly they found entertaining about La India María, interviewees pointed to Velasco's style of slapstick performance, the transgression of gender roles, her resistance to male oppressors, and her ways of mocking politicians and taking on the nation's powerful establishment. Some viewers also admired the films for their transgressions and reversals of ethnic stereotypes.

La India María's potential to entertain is clear from public screenings in Mexico, Bolivia, Peru, and the United States, where I watched the films with large audiences of fans—many laughing throughout the films. As part of my research, I have also watched India María films with different small gatherings, including a housekeeper's family in Los Angeles, a group of field workers in Fresno, and a Mexican market woman and her family. During these screenings, viewers often repeat jokes and dialogue and even sing along during songs. Surrounded by fans' enthusiasm, I sometimes found myself cracking up, unable to resist joining in the audience's reaction.

But what exactly is it that makes viewers of these movies laugh? Clearly the slapstick performance draws attention to the physical body. A comic effect occurs when the limits of the body's vitality become visible. La In-

4.2 AND 4.3. Audiences loved Velasco and her character La India María. Fans waited to meet her on the set of her final India María feature, *La hija de Moctezuma*, shot in May 2011 in Mexico City. (Photos by Seraina Rohrer)

dia María is funny precisely because of the exaggeration of her physicality. Her gestures are clumsy: she continuously stumbles and struggles with everyday objects, constantly producing gags. In all of the films she is established as a burlesque antihero from the first scene. As her character maneuvers or is forced into various compromising situations, comic moments arise through a reduction of the image to the materiality of the body. The character and Velasco herself constantly challenge the limits of her physical ability, with cinematic tools including narrative, character definition, and camera angle underscoring the body, how it moves, and when it fails.

The opening scene of *¡El que no corre . . . vuela!* is an excellent example of how humor works in the India María films. La India María is introduced immediately, when she gets off a crowded bus that has just arrived in Mexico City from the countryside. Both the type of bus and the people disembarking are clearly from a rural area. The passengers descend one after another, clearing the way for the next person. But when La India María disembarks, she is overwhelmed and stumbles to a stop at the exit. The crowd of other passengers behind her eventually presses forward and roughly pushes her aside—literally shoving the character into the city. This poignant establishing scene and introduction to La India María foregrounds the character's physicality and also sets up a later gag, when she runs after a bus trying to jump onto the overcrowded stairs but falls and flips. The next instant a taxi drives by, splashing her with dirty water. La India María's struggles are the joke, but they also serve to contextualize the character in a bustling, excessive urban environment, visible as such through the character's distress. Spectators might also experience pleasure from the way in which the noise and high energy of the city reveal her inability to deal with daily urban routines. She is personified as a charming underdog, comparable to Charlie Chaplin's Little Tramp, enticing viewers to identify the character's plight with struggles that they themselves experience.

Numerous comments on YouTube clips of Velasco's films confirm Velasco's talent and the potential of her films to provoke laughter and entertain audiences. These online viewers often emphasize their appreciation of India María films with transcribed laughter: for example, "jejeje" or "hihi." An excellent example of how online viewers confirm the lasting entertaining quality of Velasco's films well after their releases can be seen in a comment by a user called "crosseto" on the opening scene of *¡El que no corre . . . vuela!* posted in October 2010:

> Jajaja!!!! No manches . . . a mi tambien me laten las pelis de "La India Maria" son la neta he, en esta peli me mie de risa cuando se baja del camion en movimiento en joda y se le va atrepar a un buey que lo estan rasurando en la peluqueria se ve bien curada esta escena muy buena pelicula . . . consumamos los mexicano jejeje!!![5]
> [Hee, hee, hee!!! No way. . . I also love the India María movies. So cool. In this film, she makes me pee laughing when she gets out of the moving bus, making a joke, then stumbling over a guy who is getting shaved in a barbershop. What a well-orchestrated scene, what a great film! Let's consume Mexican culture, heeheehee!]

This viewer also commented in Spanish on another bus gag from this film, pointing out the humor of Velasco's exaggerated gestures and slapstick performance when India María jumps out of a moving bus, fails to control her speed, stumbles into a barbershop, and ends up lying flat on a customer seated in a barber stool with shaving cream on his face. Staggering, La India María spins on the stool, crushing the man under her.

While "crosseto"'s comment clearly expresses his enjoyment of Velasco's slapstick performance and physicality, he also praises the film and calls for the consumption of Mexican culture, poking fun at existing debates and emphasizing national pride, with his closing "jejeje!!!" being a clear appropriation of Velasco's own tactics.

A HEROINE WORTH ADMIRING

Transgressing gender roles often provokes laughter. In India María's case, however, slapstick's emphasis on the body plays out in significantly different ways. While other slapstick performers, including Charlie Chaplin and Cantinflas, use comedy and physical humor to expose oppressive modes of representation, Velasco frequently structures these comic moments around gender. Like Chaplin's Tramp or Fortino Mario Alfonso Moreno Reyes's Cantinflas, she stages La India María in poses and caricatured actions that expose issues of class, but she also diverts quite radically from common representation of her gender. By repeatedly breaking with gender norms—by handling male props, appropriating status symbols, and invading spaces associated with men—she demands social and narrative agency.

In *La presidenta municipal*, for instance, the basic premise is that women have no place in the Mexican political arena. Even today the nation's key political positions are dominated by men. By entering municipal-

4.4. In *La presidenta municipal* (1975) La India María appropriates male props such as a gun and bandolier. Instead of making her look powerful, they become part of the film's running physical humor. (Diana Internacional Films, S.A. de C.V.)

level politics, La India María accesses a male domain where a poor rural woman seems out of place. This deviation alone leads to numerous comic moments. In a shaky attempt at disguise, India María arrays herself with an assortment of stereotypically male objects—for instance, she starts carrying a gun with a bandolier ammunition belt, slyly quoting a classic image of the Mexican revolutionary. In the end these objects do not lend her the authority that they represent but merely limit her freedom of motion. To give just one example, through a series of comical near-collisions, India María ends up "accidentally" striking a male colleague in the crotch with the barrel of her gun. Velasco is clearly playing with gendered connotations attributed to the objects, actions, and spaces, so that they—rather than La India María herself—become objects of ridicule. These comic scenes make the depicted clichés seem ludicrous and carry the humor a step further for the audience by fulfilling an underlying fantasy—in this case, hitting a man below the belt. Velasco deliberately uses self-ridicule

4.5. Posters and other promotional materials for *La presidenta municipal* enhance and exaggerate the film's motifs and foreground gender aspects. (Cineteca Nacional)

as a strategy, suggesting that in order to ridicule others she must first ridicule herself to earn self-awareness and ultimately laughter.

In *La presidenta municipal*, La India María changes dramatically as she gains agency and experience. At the opening of the film, she lives and works in a simple adobe hut. After her election to office, she moves into a luxurious presidential residence. While Velasco first accentuates the incongruity of the situation—La India María initially seems lost—she eventually gains confidence and takes over the space by working at her large desk, standing on the balcony looking over her town, and leading the annual fair. After a while, she feels comfortable in a bar, a bullring, and other spaces dominated by the town's men.

Promotional materials for Velasco's films also subvert traditional gender roles. The poster for *La presidenta municipal*, for example, pulls together cartoon scenes and stills from the film. The cartoons show India María bullfighting, dancing, falling in love, and being photographed in full revolutionary drag by a white tourist. The poster also contains a still from the actual film, which shows a scene from the bullfight. Like scenes in the film, the poster underlines India María's physical prowess and stages her "male" actions as spectacular moments or attractions, attesting to the character's unusual abilities as a woman. She more than transcends the limits of gender here: she demonstrates superhero-like powers that stand in stark contrast to the initial definition of the character as naive and clumsy. The advertising campaign for *La presidenta municipal* focuses explicitly on the importance of women in politics:

> "¡Los problemas municipales deben ser solucionadas por una mujer!"
> *La presidenta municipal*, en el año internacional de la mujer.
> ["Political municipal problems have to be solved by a woman!" *La presidenta municipal*, in the international year of the woman.] (publicity material for the film)

The intention of this newspaper advertisement is unmistakable and elicits clear expectations of the film. Potential viewers will anticipate seeing the story of a woman who succeeds in political office. In this sense, *La presidenta municipal* is a perfect illustration of many India María films, in which the character cleverly appropriates male props and spaces to play with, subvert, and—against all the odds—rise above social and gender roles.

La India María also creates laughter by subverting cinematic norms for expressions of women's sexuality. Images of dancing women are a common depiction of the sexualized female body (Balides 1993: 20). Mexican sexy movies usually stage dancing female bodies as a visual spectacle intended to attract male viewers. Velasco's India María comments on this convention by performing a dance routine in almost all of her films. The dance sequence lasts over ten minutes in *El coyote emplumado*, an exceptionally long scene. María flees from a gangster and incidentally passes through one of Acapulco's discos. To escape her pursuer, she tries to cross the dance floor, where she is invited to dance. Reluctantly at first, La India María starts moving her body, but soon she is gyrating her whole body—enthusiastically shaking her hips, rhythmically lifting her arms over her head, jumping back and forth, and rolling her shoulders. Her rapid, exaggerated movements are underlined by camera movements switching between high and low angles and recorded with a special lens multiplying her image and actions. La India María's movements allude to erotic dances exaggerated to an extreme. Overtly stressing the body as spectacle, this scene unmasks this norm for women's bodies in film and turns it into a comic transgression of both gender and spectacle.

Film critic Jorge Ayala Blanco (1989) harshly condemned Velasco for

4.6, 4.7, 4.8, AND 4.9. In *El coyote emplumado* (1983) La India María moves her body with manic, exaggerated gestures. In this excessively long dance sequence, special effects and lighting magnify the display of spectacle.

suppressing erotic dimensions of the India María character to create humor. I disagree with Blanco's critique. Velasco engineers comic moments not by desexualizing the character but by explicit exaggeration—and the character's (unfulfilled) sexual desire often becomes the joke. In *La presidenta municipal*, India María fancies a handsome American (*güero*). At every encounter between the two, her arousal is manifested in the movement of her braids.

With a mind of their own, La India María's braids slowly stiffen, rise, and stand straight out to the side—accented by a ratcheting sound underlining the movement. Such a depiction of female sexual desire is surprisingly explicit, in stark contrast to commonplace rose-toned depictions of women's desire—the cinematic trifecta of lip nibbling, hair tossing, and coy glances. Here the humor comes from the female character exposing her sexual desire in an embarrassingly public way, like a man's. At the core of both opposing representations of the character's sexuality—one neutralized, the other explicitly stressed—lie the pleasures (here comic) generated by human bodies on screen.

La India María remained single throughout her long history on the screen and only rarely even flirted with having a relationship or getting married. In fact, she generally expressed a rather critical view of marriage. In film and television dialogue, the character repeatedly pointed to the marital problems of the couples that she met. Velasco even recorded an album in the 1970s with a song about the suffering that marriage brings. These open criticisms of marriage are extremely unusual and highly surprising for women to express in a Mexican context. Yet this is one reason why women in particular admire the character. Many of my interviewees emphasized that they liked La India María because she does what she wants and refuses to let a man control her life.

Velasco's position as a woman in a male-dominated industry clearly shaped the reception of her films. In addition to her candid remarks about the challenges that she faced as a woman in Mexico's film industry, she often spoke out against sexism in general. When interviewed about her films, she frequently made good use of her celebrity to argue in favor of gender equality, as in this 1987 interview in *El Nacional*:

> Sucede que las mujeres—por el hecho de serlo—nos consideramos reprimidas. Los hombres por su parte, no creen en nuestras capacidades y eso no es verdad, el talento es característica de ambos sexos.
> [It happens that we women—just because of our sex—consider ourselves suppressed. Men, for their part, don't believe in our abilities, and that is simply not true, because talent is a quality shared by both sexes.] (Anonymous 1987c)

Time and again Velasco encouraged women to claim their own share of power (Anonymous 1994a). She repeatedly pointed out that more women

4.10. In *La presidenta municipal* (1975) La India María's braids rise when she is attracted by the handsome American.

should occupy key political positions, not only in her interviews but also through her films. Two of her films, *La presidenta municipal* and *Las delicias del poder*, produced more than twenty years apart, center on the political ascent of female protagonists. When launching *Las delicias del poder*, Velasco insisted on delivering the message that someday many women would rise to powerful positions and even the presidency (De la Cruz Polanco 1998), although she also stressed that she did not intend to enter politics herself. Instead she declared that she would continue conveying encouraging messages to women as a film director (Ramírez Hernández 1998).

In the late 1990s Velasco took a public stance on abortion—a highly sensitive topic in Mexico. She surprised many by declaring a pronounced pro-choice position on abortion—still illegal at the time—and harshly condemned the law for limiting women's access to family planning. Her statements show a notable level of empathy and concern for her female audience. Dangerous illegal abortions remained common throughout the 1990s (Leal and Pérez 1997). Mexico City decriminalized early-stage abortions in 2007, but the ban continues today in more than half of the Mexican states.

Velasco became notably more outspoken in the course of her career, as she earned public recognition and power in the film industry. Through her work and her public statements, she demanded more agency for herself and for all women. Velasco eventually gained the influence she sought by directing, contributing to scripts, and finally establishing her own production company. A similar process of empowerment is evident through her representation in the media over time. Due to her steady work in bringing media attention to women's rights, Velasco was invited as guest of honor to a 2007 gathering of Mexican women filmmakers in Tijuana (Fregoso and Iglesias 1998; Hernández 2007). Velasco was a rare example of a woman in the Mexican film industry whose success was owed largely to determination, business acumen, and self-awareness—not beauty. Just like the character India María, María Elena Velasco was able to surmount obstacles because she knew what she wanted and worked hard to achieve it.

Velasco's audiences—especially the women—emphasize the empowering aspects of both Velasco and her persona. They often claim that Velasco and La India María have been underestimated and defend her by explaining that even though the character might seem one-dimensional she is actually far more complex. There are many examples of interviews with women who support Velasco with comments like "Es una de nosotras" [She is one of us] or come to India María's defense by saying: "A lo mejor parece tonta, pero en realidad es muy inteligente y además es guapa"

[She might seem stupid, but she is actually very intelligent and pretty too]. Male interviewees often refer to the fact that their wives, grandmothers, and sisters like the character. One taxi driver even added: "La India María es la reina de mi vieja" [La India María is my wife's queen]. Younger women in particular, as well as Latinas living abroad in the United States, express an admiration for both the character and the film director—by choosing to identify with the character. Some young women go as far as actively promoting La India María by making YouTube clips of Velasco's films available online or appropriating variants of María's name as their avatars for online social networks.[6]

Interviewees' comments indicate a widespread admiration for the character of La India María that focuses on female identity. A shared experience among audience members of being undervalued as women seems to be key. The characterization of La India María—her disappointments, pratfalls, and stories that always lead to happy endings—is further complemented by Velasco's hard-earned position in the Mexican film industry and her media representation. These factors work together to empower fans and encourage their participation and appropriation. This type of active, fan-driven reception reflects the ability of India María films to uncover existing power structures and reveal their essential weakness—all through the medium of laughter.

Other Mexploitation characters also push cultural boundaries and provide audiences with satisfying models of resistance. Many characters in Mexploitation films foster fantasies of power through extreme violence, mocking authorities, and breaching clearly defined limits and laws. Like Velasco and her characterization of La India María, various other Mexploitation stars and characters push the boundaries of gender definitions. Particularly interesting is the character "Lola la trailera," played by the actress Rosa Gloria Chagoyán, famous for her violent border action films.[7] The pleasures of empowerment enjoyed by fans of Chagoyán's character and star image are akin to those provided by La India María and Velasco, although gunfire and gore take the place of comic pratfalls (Benamou 2009: 172). Film scholar Tina Vares (2001: 238–239) suggests that all violent women on screen have the potential to trigger such fantasies. Studies of blaxploitation films have taken a similar angle, arguing that films with action heroines favor alternative reception practices (Dunn 2008; Holmlund 2005; Keeling 2007; Sims 2006). These characters could thus be seen as projected fulfillments of what is desired and absent within the status quo, nourishing dreams of upward mobility and real-world struggles for social transformation.

A STAR JUST LIKE US

Numerous India María features tell stories of social oppression and subsequent class empowerment. In several films the character works as a maid in an upper-class household. Her refusal to acknowledge other characters' bad nature and her daily resistance to the condescending attitude of her employers create many comic moments—yet through her bumbling defiance she defeats her oppressors and voices her opposition to class and ethnic inequalities, thereby unmasking and transcending these artificial boundaries. In *La comadrita* La India María is introduced as a defenseless girl from Mexico's countryside who is forced to move to the city in order to make a living. The gap between social classes leads to numerous conflicts and comic moments, but the character consistently breaks out of the expected submissive position of a servant. In one scene she carries on a private phone conversation with a relative in the presence of her wealthy employers. She comfortably installs herself in an armchair, leans back, and confidently holds forth about the plans for her sister's marriage. By refusing to accept an inferior servant's position, La India María brings a comic touch to Mexican films' typically indifferent or demeaning depictions of household workers.

An article in the *New York Times* introduced India María to a broad US audience by emphasizing her popularity with the *pueblo*:

> Somewhere in the most remote hinterland of Mexico, there just might be a village whose residents have yet to see one of the many movies of La India María. But to most Mexicans, the woman with the long braids, bright native costume and guileless smile is a figure almost as familiar as the President, with admirers ranging from the chief executive down to the humblest peasant. (Rohter 1988)

The *New York Times* journalist went on to note La India María's popularity with blue-collar Mexicans, saying that "she provides a rare opportunity [for them] to see themselves and their daily routines portrayed in a sympathetic fashion" (Rohter 1988).

Not only does the character belong to the people, but the creative force behind the character—Velasco, as actress, director, and producer—deliberately presented herself in a similar light through the media. An analysis of newspaper articles demonstrates how, through clever sleight of hand, Velasco regularly adopted two positions. First, she presented herself as a champion of her audience. Then, by emphasizing her humility, she aligned herself with her viewers. In a 1989 interview Velasco pointed out that many people in Mexico are actually campesinos (farmers), who can identify with the character (Vélez 1989). She continued:

> Por eso, mi lucha por llegar a ser, la comparto con el público, que me ha apoyado siempre porque han estado conmigo en las buenas y en las malas. [For that reason, I share with my audience the struggle of becoming who I am today. They have always supported me, because they were with me through the good and the bad.] (El Soberbio 1989)

In many interviews across her career, Velasco emphasized that awards and honors did not mean much to her, because her main goal was to meet her audience's expectations:

> No busco premios ni reconocimientos de ningún tipo porque mi única y mayor satisfacción me la brinda el público con su cariño y su preferencia. [I don't want prizes or awards of any kind because the most important and only recognition comes from my audience, who have been loving and faithful.] (Avilés Duarte 1994)

Velasco went as far as to call her audience her trophy, a clear signal to her fans of how seriously she took them (Segoviano 1994). She continued to express this dedication even during a period when her audiences declined—indeed, she recommended that they spend their money on food rather than movies during tough economic times (Dávalos 1998: 14).

Contrary to her stance on women's issues, Velasco's attitude in the media regarding the question of political empowerment was quite controversial. In the beginning she maintained that her films were meant for pure entertainment (Pacheco 1988). Later she refused to make any divisive political statements to the press, but at the same time declared that she might have studied law or political science if she had not become an actress (V. H. Sánchez 1989). Even as late in her career as 1988, when her border-crossing film *Ni de aquí, ni de allá* came out, she made only understated comments about the problem that so many Mexicans could not make a living in their own country (Pacheco 1988). In my view, most of Velasco's statements on political issues were quite moderate. She pointed out social ills simply because she took her audience seriously. When she looked back at her achievements in 1999, she said: "Lo bonito es que con La India María he podido desahogar las cosas que nos incomodan a todos los mexicanos, sobre todo los campesinos" [What is beautiful is that

4.11. Flyer for a performance in which Velasco performed her sketches in front of live audiences and increased her social criticism. Most of the live events were free of charge. (Vlady Pictures)

through La India María I have been able to bring up uncomfortable topics and vent the worry of all Mexicans, especially the farmers] (Álvarez 1999). This is not to say that Velasco avoided taking a political stance entirely, particularly in front of smaller audiences in the live theater. In 1996 she characterized her theater sketches in this way: "Ante de todo mi teatro es crítica social" [Before anything else, my theater plays are social criticism] (Olvera 1996).

Reflecting her pronounced rapport with her audience, Velasco never saw herself as a high-maintenance star, but rather as a modest person—much like La India María (Hernández 1996). She pointed out that she was not rich and that she drove an inexpensive car, sometimes took the subway, liked to cook, and lived a simple life (Anonymous 1987a; Flores 2004; Gómezturja n.d.; Morales Valentín 2002). Throughout her career, she always emphasized her ordinariness, foregrounding her humility and simple tastes, such as her preference for traditional Mexican dishes like rice and beans (Garay 1996; Olaiz 1991; Salazar H. 1995). She even interrupted an interview once to tend to a pot of beans: "Déjame bajarle la lumbre a los frijoles" [Let me turn down the heat on the beans] (Olaiz 1991). Velasco also frequently discussed Mexican music and recorded several folksongs. Unlike other actors, she never received much attention for her recordings, but they nevertheless demonstrated her fondness for traditional music. Finally, Velasco admitted to never receiving any formal acting or film school training (Morales Valentín 2002; Pacheco 1988). With that statement she encouraged viewers with little education to pursue their goals, even if at first they seemed unreachable.

Particularly at the beginning of her career, Velasco cultivated a star image that scarcely diverged from her character. In interviews and other media encounters, Velasco framed herself—like La India María—as an ordinary Mexican woman who repeatedly uncovered through her ordinariness the already existing and oppressive power structures. Compounded by so many other similarities, Velasco's emphasis on a close relationship to her audience contributed to slippages between her character and persona. When I accessed Velasco's Wikipedia entry in 2010, it suggested that the character's image was exactly the same as Velasco's. The entry made this interesting observation: "Not much about Velasco's private life has been open to the public eye. She prefers to be seen by the public as the character that she usually plays in her movies."[8] Unlike many other film stars in Mexico and the United States, Velasco never made headlines with scandals or an extravagant lifestyle. When asked about her children or family, she said that she considered such personal matters private (Jiménez 2002; Pacheco 1988).

This correspondence between the character and the star's image is what film scholar Richard Dyer (2000a: 126) calls a "perfect fit," where all aspects of a star's image are reflected in the traits of the character that he or she plays.[9] Often perfect fits occur when scripts are developed and written expressly for a specific star. In the early years of Velasco's career the perfect fit worked in reverse. For Velasco, her character type created her celebrity and star image—so much so that the media, with Velasco's participation, initially equated the two. Although Velasco didn't belong to Mexico's lower class after her success, like her character, she expressed her sympathies for the less fortunate and underlined her modest tastes and lifestyle, leaving out facts that might not appeal to her audience or align her with India María. Velasco was not illiterate, for example; nor did she come from a rural background. As she continued to succeed in her career, she began to cultivate her own star image independent of the María character, stressing her traits as an intelligent, powerful, and outspoken woman. She spoke openly about gender issues and women in the film industry and ultimately staked out some carefully calibrated but important political statements.

In contrast to the usual process of star appropriation in which viewers negotiate their differences from the star's image (Stacey 2000: 149), media images of Velasco, even at a later point in her career, made it easy for her audience to exercise a class-based appropriation based on their similarity with her. Velasco's celebrity image was constructed through discourses of ordinariness and closeness to the *pueblo*—a marked difference from great Mexican film stars of the Golden Age, such as María Félix and Dolores Del Río.[10]

At the same time, Velasco embodied the image of an independent woman who knows what she wants, pursues clear goals, and reaches them—a star image with a rebellious touch. These aspects of her public persona coincided with her character, who always triumphs heroically at the end of the film. My interviews confirm that some viewers identify with La India María because of Velasco's closeness to both her character and the audience. These viewers see the character and star together as representatives of the fight for Mexico's underclass—a dynamic duo of (anti)heroines who constantly test the boundaries of power by questioning and denouncing entrenched hierarchic structures. Viewers described La India María in these heroic terms: "lucha contra la corrupción" [she fights against corruption] and "es la reina de los pobres" [she is the queen of the poor]. Importantly, viewers enjoy these fantasies of empowerment. They are especially attractive to audiences who cannot experience or enjoy them in everyday life (Stacey 2000: 149). Yet few viewers actually put their fantasies into practice. Those who do actively appropriate them always use the character's image and not the star's: by tweeting, for example, with India María as a pseudonym on Twitter in order to advocate for workers' rights.

Fans' deeply personal and committed reception of India María as the people's heroine is additionally supported by the viewing context. Interviewees reported that family and friends always cheer for La India María whenever she is in danger or being harassed by the police or other authorities. Viewers clearly both sympathize with La India María and admire her bravery in confronting and standing up to power. Interviewees share a sense of solidarity with a character that, like themselves, is marked as oppressed.

RACIST DEPICTION OR INDIGENOUS ROLE MODEL?

Journalists, critics, and scholars have supplied many explanations for La India María's success, yet one argument that always resurfaces points directly to the character's ethnicity. The Mexican film scholar Maricruz Castro Ricalde (2004a: 3) suggested that the character was enthusiastically embraced by television viewers because her image was among the first representations of indigenous characters to circulate widely. In the 1930s and 1940s, during the Golden Age of Mexican cinema, indigenous characters were mostly played by actors of European descent with "white" instead of indigenous features. La India María represents a clear departure from such practices: Velasco's appearance, from her facial features to her stature, is recognizably indigenous, despite her mestiza heritage. Writing in the early 1990s, Carmen Huaco-Nuzum (1992: 129) also suspected that La India María's ethnic characteristics made it easier for indigenous and mestizo audiences to identify with her.

While this line of argument seems plausible, I suggest that the reception of the character's ethnicity is far more complex and strongly linked to Velasco's celebrity persona. La India María reflects the interplay of meanings derived from the films, Velasco's persona, and the broader political context. While some viewers see her as a heroine, others—among them many film critics—see her representation of ethnicity as racist. The range of reactions shows how diverse interpretations of the character can be.

The first India María productions in the early 1970s launched a wave of polemical discussions about the character. People who consider Velasco's portrayal of La India María racist typically criticize her for perpetuating stereotypes of Indians that had been a staple of Mexican popular culture since the colonial era. Some people I interviewed in 2009 and 2010 strongly disapproved of the films and the character.[11] They saw Velasco's depiction of La India María as a racist stereotype endemic in "low-quality" films. When asked "¿Que opina usted de La India María?" [What do you think of La India María?], one man responded: "Es racista y se burla de los indígenas" [She is racist and makes fun of indigenous people]. Some said that the films simply offer yet another excuse to ridicule ethnic minorities. In fact, one interviewee wanted to stop our interview because she thought that I supported Velasco's representation of indigenous Mexicans.

Similarly, some critics strongly disapproved of the characterization. In an article in the newspaper *Excelsior*, journalist Ezequiel Barriga Chávez wrote (1988ba):

> Nada más racista en nuestro contexto que una película de la señora Velasco, en que lo indígena es envilecido en aras de un dudoso humor y los indios y las indias son representados como estúpidos y retrasados mentales que merecen nuestras burlas y nuestra risa. El que en una cinta de esta naturaleza el personaje de la India María constituya la heroína en nada modifica ese esquema clasista y racista.
> [There is nothing more racist in our context than a film by Señora Velasco, in which indigenous people are degraded to villains through dubious humor, depicted as stupid and mentally retarded people who deserve to be mocked and laughed at. Even if La India María is the hero in a film of this kind, that doesn't change the fact that it is classist and racist.]

Barriga Chávez points out an important dilemma of the India María character, if taken at face value: even as a conquering hero, he says, the character automatically reads as a negative stereotype because of her ethnicity. He does not consider the possibility that the exaggeration of all of India María's character traits—overtly linked to her ethnicity or not—could serve as a key to emancipation, if merely by raising awareness and recognition. In essence, he suggests that "poor" people pushed to the margins, whether by class or ethnicity, need to be depicted as suffering. Many Latin American films do precisely this: they depict the suffering of the indigenous people, without offering alternatives. Jorge Ayala Blanco (1989) shared Barriga Chávez's position, considering the character a tragic folkloristic figure.

This critique of the films prevailed through the 1990s. During the 2000–2006 presidency of Vicente Fox, his administration made an attempt to halt all India María films from further distribution because of their negative depiction of an ethnic stereotype. The outright censorship of such a popular media figure sparked a highly polemical discussion. A television documentary called *Las delicias de la India María* (The delights of India María) (2004) was filmed, and researchers weighed in on the debate. The author of a book about Mazahua women (Oehmichen Bazán 2005: 201) said:

> Una de ellas me dijo muy convencida que la dueña del taller era la India María, personaje cómico desarrollado por la actriz María Elena Velasco,

> difundido por Televicentro (hoy Televisa). Supuestamente la India María se había enriquecido a costa de las Mazahuas. Esta percepción no es tan equivocada si consideramos que el personaje representa a una comerciante ambulante vestido con el atuendo de las mujeres de San Antonio Pueblo Nuevo.
>
> [One of them (the indigenous market women) convincingly told me that the owner of the shop was La India María, the comic character developed by the actress María Elena Velasco and aired on Televicentro (today Televisa), who had made a fortune on the Mazahuas. In fact, this notion is not entirely false, because the character represents a street vendor dressed up like the women of San Antonio Pueblo Nuevo.]

This critic supported the censorship measure and condemned La India María as a racist representation of an ethnic minority brazenly exploited to make a profit.[12] Supported by the new administration, these voices encouraged an even more critical appropriation of the character and persona of La India María, but in the end Velasco's resistance to the planned ban succeeded. Her films have continued to be aired.

Critics concerned about racism in the films have a fair amount of ammunition. In *Duro pero seguro*, for example, La India María sells tacos in a television studio. A man forces her to change her vending location and hits her in the process. The next day the man wins the lottery, and soon rumors abound that beating La India María brings luck. Mayhem ensues, featuring comic scenes choreographed to show La India María being beaten in various ways by gleefully hopeful characters. Beyond the running gag of gratuitous violence against an indigenous character by white men, critics denounced the lack of sophistication in the character's depiction: naive throughout the film, she never speaks out against the prevailing racism and at first even accepts the beatings with relatively little fuss. With this placid acceptance of degradation and physical suffering, Velasco cleverly links the character to the Virgin Mary, exaggerating and parodying what was taken as a feminine norm during the Golden Age of Mexican cinema (De la Mora 2006: 28). But for La India María, unlike her predecessors, her newfound saintly status and virginal identity mostly cause problems, rather than opening up new opportunities or helping her to achieve her goals. In all of the films, many naysayers complain, the character's refusal to develop and improve her skills—to learn to read, for instance—and her stereotypical speech and appearance make her an outmoded and backward-looking depiction of an indigenous woman.

Unlike earlier film depictions of indigenous characters, however, La India María presents a deliberately exaggerated rendition of the proscribed characteristics, which serves both to reveal and to aggravate the negative stereotype. The public beating scene perfectly illustrates how India María films evoke such contradictory receptions—viewers might perceive them as hilarious or simply horrifying. The slapstick violence that brutalizes the character can be interpreted at face value, as accepting and condoning the mistreatment of an ethnic minority for the sake of amusement. It can be dismissed entirely as "just a joke." Conversely, the brutalized figure can become a symbol of spirited and ultimately successful resistance. By quoting clichés, Velasco presents the stereotype for what it is, pushes it even further, and encourages an ironic reflexivity. The India María character is reminiscent of satirical characters like Borat, played by English actor Sacha Baron Cohen, or characters played by the Brazilian star Carmen Miranda, who toy with the discomfort of viewers' witnessing—and therefore allowing—violence (López 1993: 77–78). The audience either becomes complicit or, when the suffering doesn't lead anywhere, must conclude that the violence is absurd and pointless—and therefore is a joke on the perpetrator. In the India María film the beatings are revealed as being senseless. The attack is on India María, but ultimately the humor is at the expense of those who were foolish enough to hurt her.

Velasco's film image was closely linked to the ethnic group of her character, although Velasco herself was mestiza, of mixed ethnicity. Notably, Velasco's remarks on La India María's ethnicity and her responses to the media's reception of the character gradually shifted over the course of her career. While she initially insisted that the character was inspired by the Mazahua ethnic minority and that her main goal was to entertain audiences, over the years Velasco began to comment on the situation of Mexico's indigenous population. There is no doubt that she gradually developed a deeper awareness and sensitivity to indigenous struggles, enabling her to take a clear stand in their favor.

Velasco did not voice a position until relatively late, however, in the 1990s, as the political situation in Chiapas came to a head when the North American Free Trade Agreement (NAFTA) came into effect. After the Zapatista uprising in 1994, she said: "Yo lo [el papel] hago por amor, respeto a mis raíces a mis queridos indígenas" [I play it (my part) out of love, respect for my roots and for my beloved indigenous people] (cited in Ruiz 1994). Some of her comments before this time seem rather uneasy and defensive:

> La interpretación de las llamadas marías, siempre ha sido con respeto, incluso, ellas me ven con cariño. Yo en lo personal deseo que mejoren en todo sentido, porque también son mexicanas.

> [Interpretation of the so-called Marías has always been done with respect, and what's more they themselves hold me dear. Personally, I hope that their situation improves, in all senses, because they too are Mexican.] (Anonymous 1992a)

In this 1992 interview, Velasco made the case for improving the situation of Mazahua women based on a common national identity, although she was also concerned with defending herself from charges of disrespect. Nevertheless, her defensive reaction turns a mirror to her critics by noting the labeling of Mazahua women as Marías and gently accusing journalists of perpetuating the very thing that they pretend to condemn.

From this point, Velasco began actively using her celebrity as a soapbox to advocate for better conditions for indigenous women (Cuéllar 1994; García López 1998; Hernández 1999; Notimex 1997; Pérez Albarrán 1994; Ruiz 1994; Salazar H. 1995; Segoviano 1994). Again and again when interviewed, she would stress the difficulties that Mexico's indigenous women face and emphasize that desolate living conditions had hardly improved over the years:

> En cuanto a los cambios que han experimentado las llamadas "Marías" que llegan a la capital, sin reflexionar mucho puntualizó, habrán cambiado de vestido, de lugar, a veces venden cerca de la Torre Latinoamericano, sus condiciones de vida siguen siendo las misma, lamentablemente. [As for the changes that the so-called "Marías" who come to the capital have experienced, without thinking too much—they might have changed their dress, their place, and at times they sell their merchandise near the Latin American Tower, but their living conditions unfortunately remain the same as before.] (Carreño Burgos 1994)

Here Velasco's call for change remained rather vague, but in another interview in the same year she promised indigenous Mazahua women her personal support (Grajales 1994). Among other ideas, she talked about opening a workshop where they could sell their merchandise (cited in Ruiz 1994). During the run of her 1994 theater show *México canta y aguanta* [Mexico sings and lives through rough times], Velasco underscored her social commitment by frequently inviting groups of Mazahua women to watch her performances (Garay 1994; Hernández 1996). The presence of indigenous people at theater performances was so uncommon that it remains a matter of speculation whether her invitation was a publicity stunt, an expression of solidarity, or both. When asked what she thought about the armed resistance in Chiapas and Guerrero, Velasco bluntly rejoined:

> ¡Ay, Dios mío! Creo que a todos nos mortifica saber que a los campesinos no se les da el lugar que realmente merecen. Las autoridades deberían brindarles toda la ayuda que necesitan para trabajar la tierra. Ellos, como todos los mexicanos, tienen derecho a vivir dignamente. A mí me da tristeza que sufran y que no les hagan caso.
> [Oh my God! I think we all suffer knowing that campesinos are not given what they really deserve. The authorities should give them all the help they need to work the fields. Like all Mexicans, they have the right to live in dignity. It makes me sad to know that they suffer and no one cares for them.] (Hernández 1996)

Yet when journalists dug deeper, she showed herself to be both funny and determined:

> Periodista: "¿Le gustaría platicar con Marcos?" Velasco: "¿Cuál Marcos? ¡Ah, el subcomandante! Primero que se quite eso que trae . . . ¡El pasamontañas! Ya luego nos entendemos. Sus intenciones son excelentes, muy buenas; hacer algo por los indígenas chiapanecos y, en general, por todos los del país es bueno. Pero ocultarse detrás de una máscara no es bueno."
> [Journalist: "Would you like to chat with Marcos?" Velasco: "Marcos who? Ah, the general! Well, first he should remove that thing he's wearing . . . The balaclava! Then we would understand each other. His intentions are excellent, very good; to do something for the indigenous people of Chiapas and more generally for the country is good. But to hide behind a mask is not appropriate."] (Hernández 1996)

In this 1996 interview Velasco at last plainly voiced her support for the indigenous struggle. Though she scoffed at Subcomandante Marcos (Rafael Sebastián Guillén Vicente)—a fellow mestizo who, like Velasco, acted as a spokesperson for the indigenous cause—she mostly disagreed with his choice to remain anonymous. Velasco was in something of a position to judge: like her, Marcos was primarily known by his pseudonym and his character functioned as a hero for the indigenous community. Two years later Velasco said that she would like to meet important women of the indigenous movement, such as Guatemalan Nobel Peace Prize winner Rigoberta Menchú and Comandante Ramona of the Zapatista National Liberation Army (Subcomandante Marco's superior), to get a better understanding of the struggles of indigenous people (García López 1998).

Some interviewers appreciated Velasco's support for indigenous people, but others were so harsh that it was hard for her to shake their accusations—and after all, the India María character didn't change with Velasco's more vocal public persona. Before and after Velasco's newfound political stance in the face of her critics, the press continued to attack India María films. When Velasco died in 2015, most obituaries did not mention her advocacy for indigenous rights or her depiction of an indigenous character but simply praised her for creating a folk character loved by the people.

Most India María films have been uploaded in short segments to websites such as YouTube, where they are watched and commented on by users in Mexico, in the United States, and around the world. These viewers actively negotiate interpretations and meanings through discussions that appear as comment threads next to uploaded clips of India María films and TV series. YouTube offers an ideal platform to create compensatory discourses. As shown in this book, the India María films as well as other Mexploitation films were harshly condemned by film critics across Mexican newspapers. In the 1970s and 1980s moviegoers lacked a public means to express their fondness for the films other than at screenings. YouTube and other online forums offer a platform to express opinions and articulate views that oppose those of film critics. Negative reactions are rare in online comment threads. Those that appear are often quickly deleted by the fan that posted the material. Negative comments frequently trigger counteraccusations and animated discussion defending India María films against judgments that contribute to the image of Mexploitation as being of "low quality."

These online discussions join the larger debate on whether La India María should be seen as a racist depiction or as a sign of indigenous pride. On YouTube Velasco's fans avidly defend La India María, constructing a counterdiscourse to harsh critical commentaries that view La India María as simply a racist depiction of an ethnic minority. The comments on YouTube also show that supporters of Velasco are informed and articulate about how and why her films are subversive and aim to counter the stereotypes about them. User "superculovacayin," for instance, commented on a clip of *¡El que no corre . . . vuela!* (1982) posted on YouTube in October 2010:

> No puede ser que el tal "naavehe" no comprenda una realidad que es la comedia basada en una problemática de México, esto no es racismo, al contrario es una película que exige que pongan atención al grupo campesino de forma cómica como la caricaturas en los periódicos y hay que homenajear el arte que hace María Elena Velasco porque se ve que a estudiado muy bien el personaje de La India María así que es mejor informarse mejor.

> [It can't be that user "naavehe" doesn't understand the style of comedy, which is based in Mexico's reality and the country's problems. This is not racism, on the contrary, it is a film that demands (that people) pay attention to Mexico's indigenous farmers in a entertaining way, much like caricatures in newspapers. You need to respect María Elena Velasco's art, because she has intensively studied the character La India María, really, you need to inform yourself better.]

My interviews revealed that Latinos residing in the United States, as well as younger viewers, were more likely to interpret Velasco's characterization of La India María as a direct criticism of ethnic discrimination and social injustice in Mexico more generally. Some viewers do perceive La India María as an exaggerated ethnic and social stereotype, but my interviews did not confirm the prevalent assumption that the character is loved and admired mainly for her ethnicity. On the contrary, interviewees gave other reasons for their admiration of the character—not a single person mentioned her ethnicity. Even upon direct questioning, they did not see her ethnicity as a decisive factor: her marginal economic and social positions, as well as her gender, were far more important. Many viewers enjoyed the style of films and stereotypical characters, which play with a worldwide prejudice against Mexico and Latin America as "underdeveloped." Several interviewees specifically mentioned being amused by films that parody economic restrictions and other characteristics of so-called underdeveloped nations, so they enjoy María's backward ways and economic struggle. In the vein of the famous Mexican film characters Cantinflas and El Chavo del Ocho, this subgenre of comedy offers a fantasy of economic and cultural underdevelopment and embraces a notion of anti-progress (Nasser 2008: 143, 158)—which many viewers familiar with these restrictions seem to find laugh-out-loud funny.

Initially I had worked from the assumption that people's reactions to the character's ethnicity would be linked to the viewers' own ethnic background: that indigenous viewers would generally rate the character more positively or negatively than white or mestizo viewers. I found no link between interviewees' ethnic roots and their interpretation of the character. A divide in reception emerged instead in terms of the distance from the production, whether geographic or generational. The long-standing polar reactions to La India María persist today, emphasizing the character's polysemous nature and the controversy that goes hand in hand with her marked ethnicity. For this reason she can be understood as both critiquing and perpetuating social injustices.

CHAPTER 5

CROSSING BORDERS: INDIA MARÍA'S DIASPORA

WHILE LIVING IN LOS ANGELES, I was astonished by the number of India María fans in the Latino community. I discovered that the cleaning lady at the university used a line of dialogue from an India María film as her cell phone's ringtone. During an evening gathering with politically active Chicano friends, I heard them use the India María line "coffee and donuts" as a shorthand for their differences from mainstream Americans. My hairdresser expressed her genuine admiration for the character, who like herself had gone through many struggles when she migrated from Mexico to the United States. In many places and contexts, I encountered India María fans and community-building references to Velasco's films.

India María films, television shows, and theater sketches have resonated and proliferated widely outside Mexico among the Latino community in a diaspora spreading through the United States and beyond. As Mexploitation's heyday drew to a close, Velasco's films were among the top rentals at video stores in Latino neighborhoods in the United States (Arbeláez 2001: 642; Barrios 1989). When María Elena Velasco performed her comic routines live before screenings in Latino movie theaters in the United States, seats would sell out quickly. Even today Velasco's films remain top rentals at video rental stores in the Los Angeles area, several of which I visited personally during my research stay in Los Angeles in 2009 and 2010. Video store employees in California and Texas told me that India María DVDs were frequently rented. Some stores even had multiple copies of some of her films. Velasco's ongoing popularity is also reflected on Spanish-language television channels that still air her films, alongside the hundreds of clips of her films available online.

The Latino community in the United States has actively appropriated Velasco's films for several key reasons. Interestingly, the India María films present realistic images of the border-crossing experience, which many fans say they personally understood and implemented as guidelines for their own border crossings. These cinematic images also reinforce existing border myths. In addition, Mexican migrants and Mexican Americans respond to the films as representations of Mexican identity that help them to express their sense of loss and longing for a homeland. Finally, as I have observed firsthand, viewers reenact scenes and stories, incorporating them into their own lives, and thereby contribute to their development beyond the cinema. These diasporic experiences and appropriations of India María films together constitute a cultural picture of Latinos in the diaspora.

At the core of all diasporic receptions lies La India María, a character marked indelibly by migration. As described in earlier chapters, in nearly every film La India María is an indigenous woman who migrates—usually to a major Mexican city—in order to make a living by selling fruit or working as a servant. This beloved character's status as a migrant has shaped numerous stories on migration that belong to what I consider a category: the adventurous migration journey with a guaranteed happy ending. Only two India María films are concerned with (illegal) migration across the national border with the United States—significantly, these films were her two blockbusters, *Okey, Mister Pancho* (1981) and *Ni de aquí, ni de allá* (1988). The theme of international migration in her other films, television shows, and theater plays is subtly woven into the stories, as, for instance, through the mention of migration policies such as the bracero program.[1]

IS THIS REAL?

It might seem peculiar that some viewers appropriate India María films as meaningful depictions of border-crossing experiences, since even Velasco often described her comedies as simple entertainment. Eight of the people that I interviewed for this study, however, strongly identified these comic depictions of immigration with their own personal experiences and memories of border crossing. When asked about how migration is portrayed in Velasco's films, some of the interviewees stated: "Exactamente así me pasó" [It's exactly what happened to me]. It is interesting to note that Velasco wrote the script for *Ni de aquí, ni de allá* based on migration anecdotes that she had heard at first and second hand. This kind of real-life inspiration might favor Velasco's choice to engage in what French film theorist Roger Odin (1990b: 130) called a "documentarizing" mode. As Odin has demonstrated, when the documentarizing mode of reception shapes a

5.1 AND 5.2. In *Ni de aquí, ni de allá* (1988) La India María experiences the typical difficult and degrading labor conditions of undocumented workers.

fictional narrative, spectators nevertheless assume that claims are being made about the real world. Odin has also argued that spectators participate in the documentarizing mode when they categorize the narrator as "real" and therefore partly responsible for the constructed discourse.

This documentarizing or real mode is at the heart of India María's diasporic reception. *Ni de aquí, ni de allá* strings together scenes portraying an illegal migrant worker, La India María, who tries to make a living in the United States. At first she works in a factory, where she must carry heavy cases. One day the *migra* [border patrol] bursts into the factory, and all the migrants flee. India María continues to tolerate difficult working conditions. She is shown waitressing and washing dishes at a Mexican restaurant in Los Angeles, but again things go terribly wrong. Modern kitchen equipment confuses her, a coffee maker explodes, and she again ends up fleeing the police. At yet another job she wears an oversized hen costume to advertise the fast-food chain Kentucky Fried Chicken. She bounces up and down in front of the restaurant in her feathered suit, while a promotional voice-over announces the crunchiness of the chicken and pedestrians stop to stare and laugh. Numerous scenes like this depict La India María as cheap labor. Each work experience is more degrading than the last, making oppression a fundamental aspect of her character. Yet India María stoically endures her submissive position—at least at first.

Audiences may give India María films a documentarizing reading in part because of their depiction of food. Food is not merely a commodity that India María advertises in the Kentucky Fried Chicken scene: unfamiliar food plays a key role in underlining the character's displacement, along with the fast-paced English that flies past her. India María knows only a

5.3. The border crossings in *Okey, Mister Pancho* (1981) are depicted in realistic detail. Here La India María is crossing the border on the bottom of a truck. (Diana Internacional Films, S.A. de C.V.)

few phrases in English. Her line "coffee and donuts," now famous among Latinos, is one of them. Through repetition these few words come to represent a host of limitations. Each time the character is hungry and tries to order food, she ends up eating sugary donuts with sweetened coffee. The absence of Mexican food and India María's limited diet become a running gag. In these scenes, Velasco plays with a disorienting experience of difference that many migrants can relate to and (as I discovered in some interviews) even perceive as "real."

In *Okey, Mister Pancho* the border crossing itself is depicted in numerous scenes. The film begins with La India María trying to obtain a visa for the United States. At the US embassy, she is informed about the documents she has to provide in order to travel legally to the United States. These items, ranging from a passport to bank statements and a credit card, are exactly the documents actually required of a Mexican at the US border. The scene alludes to increasingly strict migration laws enforced in the 1980s that made legal crossing into the United States more difficult for ordinary Mexican workers, who labor in a cash economy and frequently lack a passport or official identity documents. Here the film clearly depicts real-world conditions. When India María's visa application is later declined, she decides to cross the border illegally.

La India María's various border crossing attempts are shown in detail, from swimming across the Rio Grande to latching onto the underside of a truck, although the film's storyline does not require such precision. In contrast to the generally comic tone of the film, the border-crossing scenes stress the seriousness and violence of the situation—at times extreme. At some points, viewers might forget that they are watching a comedy. This slippage toward the genre of border-crossing drama is a deliberate decision: an important aspect of Velasco's storytelling that reveals her intention to evoke a reception of a "real" border crossing. Although many film viewers had already lived through this experience, one person interviewed stated that his grandmother advised him to learn about migration strategies before his illegal crossing by watching Velasco's two border crossing films, *Okey, Mister Pancho* and *Ni de aquí, ni de allá.*

Beyond the world of her films, Velasco produced an audiotape in the 1980s informing migrants about their legal rights in the United States. The case containing the tape reveals the purpose of the recording:

> María Elena Velasco "La India María"—Destacada actriz de cine, televisión y también conocida compositora de canciones quien en este casete se dedica a traer su inimitable estilo de humor con la intención de ayudarle a todos aquellos de habla hispana conocer sus derechos legales.
> [María Elena Velasco "La India María"—Renowned film and television actress and famous song composer, who dedicates herself in this recording to bringing you her inimitable style of humor with the intention of informing all Spanish speakers about their legal rights.] (from the cover of the audiotape "Sus derechos legales")

The recording consists of a conversation between India María and a migration expert.[2] Velasco plays a naive migrant who voices all imaginable concerns about migration. The expert answers her questions by informing her of her actual rights. Listeners are likely to identify with La India María, who voices their worries. Velasco used this recording to signal her "real" engagement with the concerns of migrants, precisely because this recording provides real help, beyond her supposedly light comedies. Significantly, the recording also allowed Velasco to reinforce her position as being *del pueblo* [of the people] and thus close to her audience.

In a number of interviews, Velasco declared that she tried to convey an accurate message about migration through her films:

5.4 AND 5.5. Felipe A. Salazar and María Elena Velasco recording materials for the audiotape "Sus derechos legales" [Your legal rights]. The recording might have encouraged reception in the documentarizing mode. (Vlady Pictures)

> Como en el caso de *Ni de aquí ni de allá*, tomando en cuenta el público que ve mis películas, traté de hacerles entender cuáles son los problemas de los mexicanos que van a los Estados Unidos . . . Había que estar en el pellejo de toda esta gente, para saber por qué se atrevan a jugarse la vida en una aventura, como lo es la de pasarse la frontera sin papeles.
> [As in the case of *Ni de aquí ni de allá*, taking into account the audiences of my films, I tried to make them aware of the problems that Mexicans face when migrating to the United States . . . You would have to be in their shoes to understand why they dare to risk their lives in the adventure of crossing the border without papers.] (A. C. Hernández 1988)

Here Velasco shows concern for an experience shared by her audience and many Mexicans and also uses her acting practice to understand it. Putting herself "in their shoes," she positions herself close to the migrant community. Like Velasco, other Mexploitation stars and characters (such as Chagoyán's *Lola la trailera*) have deliberately constructed an image based on empathy and shared identity with a diasporic audience. The Almada brothers, Mario and Fernando, also regularly emphasize that they themselves—like the characters that they portray—are originally from rural Mexico and still have a humble lifestyle. Mario Almada claimed to have frequently visited the border region where the stories in their films take place (cited in Iglesias 1991: 125). Like Velasco, he expressed his wish to accomplish more than just entertaining his audience: "Espero que la gente pueda aprender sobre los riesgos que hay en tratar de cruzar la frontera" [I hope that people will learn about the risks when trying to cross the border] (cited in Pérez 2005).

Mexploitation producers of other border adventure movies also saw their films as a means to unravel the inhumane treatment of Mexican migrants. Producer David Agrasánchez, for instance, stressed that his company hired a researcher to investigate the conditions of undocumented workers and their border-crossing experiences before film scripts were written (cited in Iglesias 1991: 76). These sorts of practices contribute to a documentarizing mode and point to the value of understanding India María comedies within the broader framework of border cinema.

REINFORCING BORDER STORIES

"Que fuerte, yo como La India casi me murió cruzando la frontera" [Crazy, I almost died crossing the border, just like La India], one interviewee told me. Like him, other interviewees used the India María films as a way to reinforce and at times glorify real-life border-crossing stories. Film scholar Norma Iglesias (1999: 235) observed this reception among migrants who have experienced displacement: the border action films present a means to revive memories of their migration journey. Two cornerstone principles define this reception. First, the film serves as a frame of reference for recounting numerous anecdotes about the border; second, it makes ritualized use of music.

Iglesias's book *Entre yerba, polvo, y plomo: Lo fronterizo visto por el cine mexicano* (1991) has made an important contribution to understanding Mexploitation cinema. Her analysis of border films does not directly coincide with categories of Mexploitation films as I define them, but she offers a genealogy of border films that indicates the long tradition of the genre and provides a useful reference frame and wider context that also includes India María films that deal with migration and the diaspora. Iglesias divides border cinema into three historic periods. The first period, from 1938 to 1969, was marked by thematic diversity, featuring different perspectives on migration, displacement, and labor exchange (Iglesias 1991: 23ff.). In the second period, from 1970 to 1978, border cinema enjoyed increasing popularity, cementing traditions that would eventually determine the depiction of certain kinds of border stories and characters like the coyote (human trafficker), the suffering migrant, and the immigration officer. The "Chicano" character—marked by the diaspora experience—gradually emerged as a popular type, while the theme of migration became more important and politically loaded (Iglesias 1991: 43). Finally, between 1979 and 1989, during the third and most productive period that Iglesias identified, plots increasingly focused on drugs, violent crimes, and other sensational aspects of the border.

The film *La banda del carro rojo* (1976) is one of the best-known examples of the third period. Though produced a little earlier, it served as a model for subsequent productions. Like many other border films, it depicts the border region as a lawless zone where drug lords dictate the rules, while migrants are exposed and vulnerable to extreme violence. Violence functions as an excessive spectacle, with brutal, long-running action scenes that display the toll of violence in broken bodies and graphic carnage.

These loving and notably gruesome depictions of violence clearly direct spectators' focus away from the narrative to the displayed attractions. Violent spectacles influence reception significantly, since they glorify the region's lawlessness and likely prevent a more realistic, measured reception otherwise shaped by a documentarizing mode.

Iglesias (1991: 67) argues that border films' use of excessive violence, oversimplification, and repetition of stories during the third period—along with repeated casting of the same actors—helped to construct and affirm the border-crossing experience, which through media consumption has been converted into a "myth." Although her use of the term "myth," like the depictions that she criticizes, is somewhat exaggerated, the films reaffirm a simplified notion of the border as a zone without laws and the experience of its crossing as a heroic act. The India María border films, *Okey, Mister Pancho* and *Ni de aquí, ni de allá*, fall in this third period of border cinema, among popular films that helped build the border-crossing myth.

Unlike violent border action films like *La banda del carro rojo*, India María border comedies are appropriate entertainment for the whole family. But the border zone that India María passes through on her "adventurous journey" does resemble the typical depiction of the area as a lawless zone, where rules are not respected. The difference in Velasco's general approach is evident in an otherwise potentially disturbing scene from *Okey, Mister Pancho*, when India María crosses through the borderlands and is picked up by a truck driver who harasses and tries to rape her. Sexual violence against onscreen women is a common way to represent the violence of the border region. The way in which Velasco stages the attempted rape scene in *Okey, Mister Pancho*, however, diverges significantly from the norm. Instead of glorifying the violence, Velasco's style and method of exaggeration focus on the ridiculous. While she presents a spectacular fight, special effects such as fast motion produce a bizarre distancing. When the rapist rips off La India María's clothes, explicitly marked low camera angles reveal her knee-length bloomers embellished with red hearts. As she strikes at her rapist with acrobatic slapstick moves and screams for help, an Indian comes to her rescue with a bow and arrows. The accumulating clichés, filming techniques, and mere fact of enacting rape as a comic spectacle have a strongly alienating effect—the violent excess becomes overtly and deliberately unreal.

The attempted rape scene in *Okey, Mister Pancho* goes well beyond reaffirming the border region as a dangerous zone. It categorically questions normative depictions through their alteration, making them the object of the gag. Interestingly, Velasco's slapstick performance entirely reduces the character to her body. Even as slapstick functions to shift the notion of the dangerous border zone to the absurd, this less voyeuristic enactment may trigger a general discussion of violence against migrant women. In other films about the border experience, the crossing leaves visible marks on the

5.6. In *Okey, Mister Pancho* (1981) the depiction of a "comic" rape scene plays with and ruptures the notion of the border as a "dangerous zone." (Diana Internacional Films, S.A. de C.V.)

bodies of migrants. All four protagonists in *La banda del carro rojo* are permanently disfigured and riddled with gunshots. In several films La India María repeatedly insists on showing—but never actually reveals to the camera—the marks left on her body by violent migration experiences. Pointing to scars that she never discloses is another way to question and transgress established representations of the border zone's dangers. Instead of glorifying the sufferings, La India María constantly points them out, parodying a victim mentality and signaling the negative implications that these visible and invisible scars carry for daily life.

Aside from the violence typical of the period, the use and exaggeration of stereotyped characters is also a strategy of the border action films. It is debatable, however, whether the repetition of these characters (and actors) contributes to the cementing and securing of their respective stereotypes or whether their obviousness leads instead to a critical questioning of what they represent. When India María encounters prostitutes, coyotes, or the *migra*, Velasco sets up a confrontation with schematically reduced types determined by their physical traits as well as by their actions. Viewers might categorize these depictions as the affirmation of stereotypes, while at the same time they might be revealed as such. In *La banda del carro rojo* and many other border films, in contrast, these character types are less ambivalent in their depiction and function as a means of reaffirming the anecdotes of the border region. In both cases, characters like these are all reduced to their physicality and a display of attractions that is symptomatic for border action films in general (Rohrer 2009c: 29, 30).

Along with the cemented character types and scenarios typical of the third period of border films, the use of music, specifically Mexican ballads or *corridos*, functions in favor of a reception that reaffirms Iglesias's observations on the border "myth." In fact, there doesn't seem to be a single border action film without a *corrido*. Film scholar María Herrera-Sobek has analyzed the various applications of Mexican ballads in border films. Not only is the ballad ubiquitous in border films but entire films are often based on these *corridos*. In these cases, songs significantly shape the development of the storyline. In other cases, the music has the dramaturgical function of revealing parts of the story or even providing additional information on the film's plot. *Corridos* also can be inserted as foreshadowing agents priming the audience for events to come. These extradiegetic clues might be of political, economic, or psychological nature, providing details on characters or historical settings (Herrera-Sobek 1998: 230).[3]

Velasco's use of *corridos* in India María films does not differ from their use in border action films. The title ballad "Ni de aquí, ni de allá" both restates the title of the film and establishes its main topic. It is played twice, as extradiegetic commentary at the beginning and the end of the film. The song refers to a common saying that reflects a feeling of cultural displacement and in-betweenness experienced by many migrants. Velasco's *corrido* is one of many musical interpretations of the familiar saying. Among recent examples, the Mexican American rapper Jae-P rhymes his 2003 version of "Ni de aquí, ni de allá" with lines about the homeland and his alienation from it, while Chilean folksinger and performer Nutria NN reflects on his diasporic experience on his 2014 album *No Man's Land*, presenting alternate interpretations of the border-crossing experience.

Popular Mexican ballads are key elements in the story of a film and at the same time are appropriated by viewers to reinforce their shared diasporic identity. This type of active reception occurs particularly with films where *corridos* are performed by a band and displayed as spectacles—this display encourages viewers to sing along. In *Okey, Mister Pancho*, for instance, India María herself sings a *corrido* on a small stage and performs a dance. When the film opened, Velasco also released a recording of songs, mostly from the *Okey, Mister Pancho* soundtrack. The use of traditional tunes in the film and its promotion reinforced the attention to creating a myth around the border region, along with broader cultural themes of the songs such as traditional food, migration, poverty, and the nation. The songs were a means for Velasco to engage in an even closer relationship with her audience. In a similar way, producers of border action films promoted their title songs, often releasing albums concurrently with the films. The title song "La banda del carro rojo," for instance, became and remains a popular hit that played a key role in building the audience for border action films.[4]

Along with their resonances within border films, Mexican ballads were an intrinsic part of the viewing context of the films. When India María movies opened, Latino theaters in the United States commonly hired live bands and singers to play *corridos* before the screening when Velasco was not present to perform songs herself. Numerous exhibitors also organized singing contests between shows. Such activities clearly indicate the active engagement of Velasco's audience and the audience of Mexploitation films more generally.

Through my interviews and attendance at public and private screenings, I discovered that some viewers sing along to popular songs that they often know by heart—and some also make short remarks on their personal border-crossing experiences, whether in front of the TV at home or at a theater screening. This sort of active audience engagement is common across Latin America and is not limited to cult consumption (McCulloch 2011). The active viewing context can be framed within Frank Kessler's (2006: 59) *dispositif* of the cinema of attractions, where spectacles are displayed both onscreen and in the exhibition venue. From this perspective, the film's very function is determined differently from that of normative cinema—if viewers are already familiar with the story of the films, they can concentrate on other activities such as singing along, discussing their own experience, and sharing stories with other audience members. Talking with companions about the stories or characters on-screen and sharing personal experiences and struggles in their daily lives was a means for migrants to become familiar with customs and manners of their new country. The exchanges with other audience members created strong feelings of unity, which are also connected to the films.

In venues screening Mexploitation films, including the India María films, such extrafilmic practices were actively encouraged. Exhibitors spared no effort to transform the theatergoing experience into a carnival-like event. In some US theaters viewers were actively encouraged to come on the stage to perform a song between screenings or to sing along with the popular tunes. Iglesias (1999: 242) observed numerous organized and informal activities during screenings of border action films. She noted that the film seemed to be the least important thing going on in the theater. Whistling, chattering, and jokes were commonly audible, and the audience sometimes applauded when something thrilling happened on screen. The *Los Angeles Times* journalist Lee Grant (1982) wrote about Latino theaters of the Mexploitation era in Los Angeles, California: "On Sunday, the noise level was pretty high. Babies cried, older children ran up the aisles or played video games in the lobbies. Inside lighting was kept less than pitch-black. At the concession stands *churros* were sold alongside hot dogs, nachos next to popcorn."

Chicano scholar Adán Avalos (2009: 185) recalled the theaters of his childhood: "I vividly remember a trip to a dilapidated movie theater in Fresno, California. For the price of admission, my parents got free or reduced-rate counsel from a paralegal in an upstairs office next to the projectionist. While my parents and other Mexican illegal migrants obtained assistance with the challenge of legalizing their status in the United States, we children were captivated by the film." His memories, dating back to the late 1970s and the 1980s, characterize the period when moviegoing formed part of the daily lives of Mexican migrants. While Avalos nostalgically remembered theatergoing as part of his childhood, his parents might have perceived the films and moviegoing experience in the documentarizing mode: they received legal counsel, watched at least part of the films, and talked with other migrants about their experience and legal challenges. The theaters provided them with a public space where they satisfied both their need for social interaction with people having similar experiences and their desire for a temporary escape from everyday reality. Iglesias (1999: 240) considers moviegoing to be a social ceremony that helps spectators to feel less lonely in the face of their foreign and undocumented status, noting that most interviewees went to the theater without even knowing what film was going to be screened. Her research is limited to border action films, but it is likely that a broader group of Mexploitation films similarly built a shared diasporic identity for Mexican migrants far from home.[5]

A sense of unity among migrants was not only created at theaters: watching Mexploitation films together on the small screen at home tied many migrant families. Most of the people I interviewed recalled numerous Sunday afternoons spent watching India María films and other Mexploitation fare in their living rooms with friends and family, repeating lines, singing along, talking back to characters and making fun of them,

5.7. In this late 1960s photo taken at the Victoria, a Latino theater in Texas run by the Ruenes family, the audience awaits the screening. (Photo by Rick Ruenes)

and at times expressing their amusement about how poorly the films were crafted. Interviewees said that they saw these films over and over on TV, VHS, or DVD until they almost knew them by heart. The ritual of watching Mexploitation movies with loved ones strongly shaped both diaspora identities and family bonds.

REMEMBERING MEXICO

For the expatriate Mexican community in the United States, getting together with family, friends, and other migrants to view India María films at movie theaters or on the small screen for decades has been a popular way to keep an active link to the homeland and strengthen ties within the Latino community. Popular and traditional tunes are a major trigger for a reception based on migrants' nostalgia for home. Significantly, film ballads reminded many interviewees of Mexico. A few migrants I interviewed said that they enjoy singing along to film music, particularly in Spanish. One man even remarked that the films did not matter much—for him the popular songs were more important. A reception stressing the homeland is not restricted to those India María films that tell border stories or feature an adventurous migration journey. Any of Velasco's films will evidently do the trick, since they all contain memorable familiar songs and in various ways foreground national identity or Mexicanness.

A common way in which Mexican films have stressed national identity is through references to Mexico's past, mainly by glorifying the accomplishment of Indian ancestors—the Mayans and Aztecs. The films of Mexico's Golden Age celebrated Mexico's pre-Hispanic past by staging stories with noble Indians as protagonists, but India María films function quite differently. In numerous films, among them *El coyote emplumado* and *La presidenta municipal*, La India María makes a living by selling duplicates of archaeological treasures to gringos (a derogatory but widely used term for Americans). She sells artifacts of the past, commodities that have come into demand in international markets. Instead of glorifying the past, Velasco's films seem to confront spectators with a critical and explicitly commercial examination of Mexico's relationship with its history. An example illustrating this claim can be found in *El coyote emplumado*. The main story develops around an original artifact that gets lost after being mixed up with one of its duplicates fabricated by María and her grandfather. The fact that the items being sold are false and puts the real value of the originals slyly into question.

An archaeologist figures prominently in the film. He stands as a symbol for Mexico's national consciousness and repeatedly stresses that Mexicans must acknowledge and cherish their national heritage. His scripted lines are didactic and aim at reassuring Mexicans of the country's richness. By reminding Mexicans to be proud of their nation and appreciate its cultural heritage instead of selling it to foreigners, the character points to a concept of shared Mexicanness aimed at fostering national unity. *Las delicias del poder* contains a similar message: it is La India María herself who prevents the sale of a cultural heritage site. Once again the story unfolds in a small rural town. Right in the middle of a politician's speech, a woman gives birth to twin girls. When the mother dies, the politician adopts one of the newborns. As an adult, one sister (played by Velasco) runs for president of the Partido Único Feminino (PUF) women's party, but is severely injured during the campaign. Her twin sister, La India María (also played by Velasco), still lives in the countryside. Through a series of comic misadventures, she is forced to cover for her twin as a cosmopolitan woman and politician. But unlike her sophisticated sister, she understands the needs of the Mexican people and lives up to her promises. Most importantly, she protects one of the most sacred sites of Mexico's indigenous heritage, preventing US investors from converting the Teotihuacán archaeological site and its several pyramids into a Teotihualandia theme park.

The circular narration of the "adventurous migrations" common in Mexploitation comedies—featuring journeys that eventually lead the India María protagonist back to her hometown—reinforces nostalgia for the homeland, whether Mexico itself or the idealized Mexican countryside. In keeping with the perfect fit between her character and media persona, Velasco regularly stressed in interviews that she was proud to be Mexican and heavily stressed the nation's need to preserve *lo mexicano* [Mexicanness]. She lamented that so many Mexicans had to leave to work abroad simply because they couldn't make a living in Mexico (Rohrer 2008, 2009a). At the same time, Velasco's overt condemnation of the conditions that many Mexicans workers have to face was a nod to her viewers and their loved ones who had left Mexico precisely because of the difficult economic situation. Mexploitation exhibitors and producers took a similar stance. They argued that the cinema was a way for Mexicans living in the United States to maintain active ties to their home. The producer Rubén Galindo Jr., who worked and lived in Texas, explained that Mexploitation films are received differently abroad than within Mexico's borders—with a much stronger emphasis on nationalism:

> En México pueden no sentir que están perdiendo México porque al fin y al cabo están ahí, en su país, pero los que estamos fuera donde el cine es una de nuestras vías de contacto con México, con nuestras raíces. ¿Qué vamos hacer?
> [In México people don't realize that they are getting out of touch with Mexico because they are still there, in their country; for us, however, we are away from home and films remain one of the last links to Mexico, to our roots. What are we supposed to do?] (Iglesias 1991: 68)

As one answer to Galindo's wistful question about how to handle the absence of Mexican culture in the United States, some US exhibitors named their theaters after patriotic heroes and landmarks. Theaters across the United States named Azteca, Maya, Zapata (after the revolutionary hero Emiliano Zapata), or Popocatépetl (Mexico's most famous volcano) celebrate Mexico's history and unique geography (Agrasánchez 2006: 11). The names of US theater venues foregrounded the Mexican nation for a community far from home.

Together with a viewing context specific to the United States, India María films—supported by Velasco's image in the media—serve expatriate Mexicans as links to the past and vehicles for remembering a homeland. Interestingly, this aspect of Mexicanness was not emphasized by viewers living within Mexico. It was particularly clear at a geographic distance for Mexicans who lived in the United States. This reception is not unique to India María films or even Mexploitation films but can be observed through a wide range of Mexican films and music. The language and national specificity of these cultural products bind audiences to their sense of a homeland. Film historian Rogelio Agrasánchez Jr. (2006: 8), son of a prolific Mexploitation producer, posed a similar argument in his study of films from Mexico's Golden Age of cinema, pointing out that people experience stronger patriotic feelings when displaced simply because they constantly miss their national customs. Iglesias (1999: 235) goes further to suggest that border films, in particular, ease the feeling of loss of the homeland and strengthen individual understanding of national belonging. She concurs with film scholar Hamid Naficy's (2001: 13–14) understanding of diaspora: nostalgia for a homeland restores a sense of community, often by idealizing the lost home. Diaspora also maintains a sense of difference over a long period.

La India María has clearly been received differently in the United States than in Mexico. In the United States the films have been a nostalgic means for migrants to remember their homeland and bathe in the sounds of their language and also to establish a sense of unity in the diaspora. In Mexico interviewees were more skeptical about national pride—and their reasoning went back to the films themselves. Some felt that the India María films were rather critical of Mexico, with the character fighting against everyday corruption, nepotism, and abuses of power.

PROUD TO BE LATINO

When hybrid forms of culture emerge, they reflect the diasporic experience of migrants and first-generation Americans: *ni de aquí, ni de allá* (neither from here nor from there). Among Latinos in the United States, I have observed a diasporic reception of Mexican films and other cultural productions that embrace in-betweenness as a point of pride and as a source of identity that is more forward-looking than nostalgic.

The film *Ni de aquí, ni de allá*—with its manifold receptions and appropriations—has had a strong impact in Mexico but continues to hold special meaning for migrants in the United States. Objects clearly marked as American are used as props in the film and function in contrast to La India María's Mexicanness, to emphasize the character's displacement. At the end of the film María returns to Mexico by bus, passing an official border crossing, wearing flashy sneakers and carrying a bag emblazoned "I love Los Angeles" in one hand and a radio in the other—objects that clearly indicate their origin and her arrival from the "rich" North. Her ability to acquire these objects suggests hybridization—India María has participated in a process of adaptation characteristic of the experience of Latinos in the United States.

As noted earlier, in this film La India María only eats donuts and drinks coffee simply because she doesn't know the English words for other dishes. The line "coffee and donuts" pronounced with a heavy Spanish accent has become a wry catch phrase used by Latinos in Los Angeles (and possibly in other parts of the United States) over the years to lament their inability to get basic services, in part because of limited English. More importantly, when used by Latinos themselves, the phrase underlines their awareness of being out of step with the American mainstream, even for people who have not seen the film *Ni de aquí, ni de allá*. When asked what the phrase meant to them, interviewees all responded that they are proud of their Mexican background. To them, the phrase is not degrading. On the contrary, like La India María's comic style, it is always a self-deprecating joke—an ironic, self-aware declaration that constructs identity through difference. The use of humor to unmask cultural belonging is quite effective, as it creates a sense of community by laughing together about a foreign environment and the real challenges that it presents.

Posters and other promotion for *Ni de aquí, ni de allá* contained similar cues stressing an identity built on in-betweenness and difference. The lobby cards promoting *Ni de aquí, ni de allá* are a series of five posters. While the frame with the cartoon scenes remains the same for the whole series, each poster has different stills on the right. In the cartoon Uncle Sam—patriotic icon of the United States—and an equally caricatured Mexican revolutionary are pulling La India María by her signature braids to their side of the border, drawn as a thin white line. The first still in the poster shows La India María sitting in a donut shop eating the unfamiliar American food. In the bottom still she is the center of a fracas in a Mexican restaurant. This depiction of La India María torn between cultures, cuisines, and identities stresses her displacement and subsequent in-betweenness.

Statements by interviewees such as "I am both Mexican and American" affirm hybridity, where the experience of in-betweenness is not perceived as negative. Such statements demonstrate a hybrid identity marked by multiculturalism, a culturally complex category of shared identity that

5.8. The lobby card for the film *Ni de aquí, ni de allá* (1988) alluded to cultural hybridity and a sense of in-betweenness. (Cineteca Nacional)

is commonly expressed online. Some YouTube users choose avatars and user names to identify themselves as fans of La India María and make Velasco's movies widely accessible across national borders. Other users post comments on the film clips that reflect their identity as proud Latinos. They appropriate Velasco's films according to their own needs by commenting on them, an exchange that describes a shared experience written in Spanish permeated with English terms—an insider's dialect commonly called Spanglish.

Most clips receive passionate and often lengthy comments. In October 2010 an exemplary online dialogue responding to a clip of the final scene from *Ni de aquí, ni de allá* makes many different receptions evident in a single comment thread. While "omarzamora10001" comments directly on the scene, expressing tongue-in-cheek admiration for India María's new sneakers worn with her traditional outfit, "abner7949" identifies with the character because of her status as an undocumented worker: "How sad if you think that we only want to work, I am also illegal." User "piscodelcocdv89" wants to know the title of the final song: "¿Cómo se llama la canción que sale al final?" Finally, some people complain about the dialogue's many mistakes in the use of language, possibly reflecting their discomfort with an in-betweenness where neither Spanish nor English dominates. Also, quite frequently comments in English express appreciation for the user who posted the films online.

In a different thread, a user named "metono" thanks "PrincessSheik7" for uploading India María film clips and expresses her effusive affection for the character.

> Ay no mancheesssssssss, estuve buscando pelis de la india maria y no encontraba aki gracias x subirla!!! Me encanta es mi idola JEJEJEJEJE. Desde que soy una niña las veia y casi me las se de memoria. Sube mas plisssss. Gracias :D :D :D[6]
> [Wow, no joke, I have been looking for films of La India María and didn't find them here. Thank you for uploading!!! I love her, she is my idol HAHAHAHAHA. Since my childhood, I have watched her films and I almost know them all by heart. Please upload more! Thank you. :D :D :D.] (discussion on YouTube in October 2010 triggered by a clip)

This comment also provides a good example of how a mixture between English and Spanish occurs. When "metono" uses the English word "please" to request more clips, she spells it phonetically ("plisssss") to emphasize her Spanish accent. Another user who writes in English and identifies himself on his channel as a Latino living in San Diego expresses his admiration for the character: "heeheheh, I love u India Maria u r so cute."

Fans also request information on this forum about where to buy La India María DVDs. According to user comments, India María films are more widely distributed in the United States than in Mexico. In one comment, a user jokes about how the films themselves have migrated, saying that a reverse nostalgia is at work: India María fans miss Mexico, but Mexico misses its expatriate Latinos.

These and hundreds of other comments on uploaded clips of Velasco's films communicate users' underlying desire to belong to a Latino community across borders—even by simply declaring themselves to be fans of La India María. Seeing familiar clips on YouTube might trigger feelings of pride, akin to Benedict Anderson's (2006) concept of an "imagined community." He introduced this term to explain the mechanism of belonging apart from face-to-face interactions: an imagined community is a set of people who share a socially constructed identity even though they have often never met (Anderson 2006: 6). This concept needs to be applied and situated clearly within a defined historical and cultural context. The dialogue threads quoted above clearly show how a cultural text only becomes meaningful when put into context. For the India María films, receptions reflecting themes of in-betweenness that ultimately trigger Latino pride emerge through YouTube and other online forums nearly twenty years after the films' first releases. Commenting on individual scenes (cut short because of YouTube guidelines) functions like a replay function in home video viewing and strengthens the imagined diasporic community—a set of people who have never met but share a common experience and work together to build a shared identity through their interactions. Furthermore, through active participation and transformation, members of the community become producers of popular culture who actively renegotiate cultural meaning. As with most Internet forums, community membership is stressed; in this case, user members contribute (with loose, informal Spanglish and shared shorthand conventions), transforming Velasco's films into objects of Latino identity.

Sometimes the way viewers appropriate India María films to foreground Latino identity goes well beyond just commenting online. Short bits or phrases taken from India María films are distributed as multimedia clips, frequently as message or ringtones for cell phones. Some online viewers film themselves doing short India María sketches or reenact scenes from the films and upload their efforts to YouTube for public viewing and comment. Users' responses to their edits are generally highly positive, encouraging them to continue putting their videos online. One notably clever and cheeky appropriation is a live drag show in San José that features a transvestite dressed as India María who attracts audiences of all ages.[7]

Similar practices can be observed with other Mexploitation films and stars, especially border action films such as *La banda del carro rojo*. Fans of these movies have also reenacted scenes repeatedly and produced slideshows, and *corridos* covered by different bands have been turned into clips for wide distribution online.

The India María films actively encourage a diasporic reception, which is one reason for their ongoing success in the United States. Migration is stressed throughout the entire filmic practice: in the films, promotional materials, distribution, and viewing context as well as by the director, María Elena Velasco, who also contributed her informative recording for migrants. A diasporic audience is naturally affected by the depiction of migration in India María films, as the interviews with Latinos in the United States confirmed. Many interviewees mentioned aspects of their own migration experience. The diasporic receptions outlined earlier (supposedly "real," "reinforcing the border myth," foregrounding the nation, and Latino pride), while distinct, should not be understood as isolated from one another. All four categories are porous, hybrid, and, most importantly, always shifting. People who recently emigrated from Mexico tend to appropriate films under the documentarizing regime or use them to remember their homeland, while Latinos living in the United States for longer or who grew up there favor appropriations that elicit pride, reinforce identity, and produce a sense of community.[8]

INDIA MARÍA AND MEXPLOITATION TODAY

MEXPLOITATION PRODUCTION DIDN'T grind to a sudden halt, but gradually fewer films were produced with Mexico's economic crisis in the late 1980s and 1990s (MacLaird 2013: 32, 33). Numerous private companies ultimately stopped their Mexploitation production entirely, while other producers tried to supplement their income with commercials. Some Mexploitation insiders launched new products. The performer Pedro Fernández—whose stage name points to two famous singers and actors, Pedro Infante and Vicente Fernández—introduced his own tequila brand Solo para Machos [For Men Only], reaffirming his image as a womanizer (Orso 2001). Other producers ramped down their production but continued to make some films or shifted to producing for television. María Elena Velasco is one of the few prolific producers who stayed committed to the film business, regularly directing and acting after Mexploitation's heyday in the late 1970s and 1980s. The new economic reality touched Velasco as well: instead of shooting one film nearly every year, after 1990 Velasco produced one film every four to six years until her death in 2015.

Today India María films continue to air on television and are available on DVD and as video on demand. Pirated copies still circulate within the United States and across Latin America. More recently, many of Velasco's films have been uploaded to YouTube and other online platforms, where fans eagerly watch and comment on them.[1] Some online users even produce short clips of their own renditions of India María. Interestingly, the distribution of these materials online is widely appreciated within the online fan community.

Other Mexploitation films also continue to be widely available online as well as on legal and pirated DVDs and VoD. The popular film *La banda del carro rojo* (1976) is a typical example: it is available in its entirety online and as a variety of clips, ranging from the original song performed by the band Los Tigres del Norte to selected scenes, including the final showdown, a restaging of the song.

While relatively few Mexploitation films continued to be produced for the big screens—among them the India María films—some performers kept their characters alive exclusively on television. The most prominent example is Roberto Gómez Bolaños (called Chespirito) with his two well-loved characters, the orphan El Chavo del Ocho and the antihero El Chapulín Colorado. The strategy worked for Gómez Bolaños: he continued his successful career on the small screen until his death in November 2014. In 2005 he received an honorary doctorate in El Salvador. A year later Mexican president Vicente Fox even dedicated a series of postage stamps to El Chavo del Ocho and El Chapulín to honor the career of Bolaños and officially recognize these characters as icons of the Mexican nation (Nasser 2008: 126).

As the low-budget film industry ebbed, new characters and formats emerged on television. Some bear obvious parallels to La India María in terms of aesthetics, character traits, and plots. The Colombian *telenovela Yo soy Betty, la fea* [I am ugly Betty] (1999–2001) and its sequel *Eco Moda* (2001–2002) strongly echo the India María films and television series. The *telenovela* reached vast audiences across Latin America, the United States, and Europe. According to the trade journal *Variety*, when first aired it reached over 80 million viewers in Latin America alone (Sutter 2001). After the success of the Mexican series in Spanish, a US English-language adaptation *Ugly Betty* aired from 2006 to 2010, along with adaptations in other languages in the Philippines, France, Germany, and elsewhere.

The stories all center on a hard-working and intelligent woman, Betty, who is employed as the personal assistant of a beauty magazine editor. Just like La India María, Betty is clumsy and doesn't dress like a businesswoman. The *telenovela* revolves around the question of female "beauty." The opening credits show close-ups of female body parts, such as eyes and lips. Images of "beautiful" women are interwoven with images of Betty, who stands out as the Other or the Ugly: she wears braces, has visible facial hair, and has heavy eyebrows. The depiction of Betty and her other "ugly" friends who work for the company raises questions like those posed by the India María films, centering on race, class, and power constellations.[2]

Although Betty's skin is darker than that of many *telenovela* stars, in the US series the character never transgresses the dominant notion of female beauty, in marked contrast to the India María films. In the end Betty

6.1 AND 6.2. Like La India María, Betty in the US adaptation *Ugly Betty* (2006–2010) of the telenovela *Yo soy Betty, la fea* (1999–2001) is depicted as the Other. She becomes the object of constant ridicule by her "beautiful" co-workers. In the end, however, she succeeds as a businesswoman.

is transformed into a "beautiful" woman; her braces are removed, her eyebrows are plucked, and she is provided with fashionable new clothes. Her transformation ultimately leads to her professional advancement and allows her to become the president of the company. Unlike La India María, Betty never challenges existing power constellations; nor does she stay true to her working-class roots. Instead she becomes a member of the middle class by adapting to the rules, a well-worn formula for rags-to-riches stories.

Interestingly, the character Betty targeted not only a wide Latino audience but in particular the gay community (Benavides 2008: 2012). Similarly, several gay men that I talked with are avowed India María admirers. Two of these men cited La India María's Otherness and marginality as one reason why she is beloved by this community. Velasco's excessive performance may also have turned La India María into a "camp" character. The Mexican director Julián Hernández, for example, genuinely admires La India María and feels that the character is inspiring for his own films centering on gay characters such as *Mil nubes de paz, cercan el cielo, amor, jamás acabarás de ser amor* (*A Thousand Clouds of Peace*) (2004), *El cielo dividido* (*Broken Sky*) (2006), and *Rabioso sol, rabioso cielo*

(*Raging Sun, Raging Sky*) (2009). In fact Hernández even played a minor role in Velasco's last film, *La hija de Moctezuma*.

A few new cinematic forms of Mexploitation have evolved since the late 1990s. Many Spanish-language films produced in the United States—particularly popular among Latinos—closely resemble Mexploitation films in their story formulas, style, and character types. The stories are often set in Mexico, but the films' production values are often much lower than during the heyday of Mexploitation. Few of them are exhibited at theaters; instead, they are released straight to DVD or VoD. These newer Mexploitation-style productions minutely recycle scripts and conventional character types. The film *La del moño colorado* (The girl with the red ribbon) (1998, directed by José Antonio Chávez) makes obvious reference to La India María. It tells the story of an indigenous girl who moves to the city to make a living. Overwhelmed by the city's hectic pace, the clumsy girl maneuvers herself into numerous adventures. The story could come directly from an India María film—and the character is costumed exactly like La India María. An unknown starlet, Valeria Gallort, imitates María's tone of voice, accent, and lines. Production values for *La del moño colorado* are incredibly low, even by Mexploitation standards. It is clear at a glance that the film was produced with practically no budget.

Similar movies filmed in the United States are no longer set in Mexico but instead recount the adventures of Latinos living in America. A good example is *Tortillas Again?* (2006, directed by Paul and Sergio Ramirez). Set in Los Angeles, the story concerns a Latino family struggling to survive. They play the lottery, hoping to improve their financial situation. One day they pick the lucky numbers, but the lottery ticket is accidentally lost in a homemade tortilla. In the end the family realizes that money alone won't make them happy. Like many previous Mexploitation films *Tortillas Again?* aims at entertaining a working-class audience. All the dialogue is in English and only the music and some catch phrases are in Spanish, but the look of the film strongly evokes the Mexploitation style, although it was entirely shot and produced in the United States.

The same holds true for *A Day without a Mexican* (2004, directed by Sergio Arau). The comedy plays with the fantasy of what would happen if all the Mexican workers suddenly disappeared from the state of California. It shows the striking effects of the absence of the Mexican population: the trash is no longer collected, children are left without care, and the state soon finds itself in total chaos. The film contains a political message in line with earlier Mexploitation border films, underlining the vital importance of the undocumented labor force.

6.3. The film *La del moño colorado* (1998) copies earlier India María films, borrowing liberally from the character, setting, and dialogue.

For the production *Nacho Libre* (2006, directed by Jared Hess) the US distributor Paramount even got on board. *Nacho Libre* nods to familiar elements of low-budget comedies and wrestling films, but provides a contemporary setting in the United States. Ignacio (played by Jack Black), a cook at a monastery, transforms himself at night into a *luchador* in tight pants: our unlikely hero Nacho. To save the monastery's orphanage, Nacho challenges Mexico's most fearsome wrestlers. Production values here are visibly higher than in Mexploitation films. Both *Nacho Libre* and *A Day without a Mexican* are available in Spanish and English, whereas most earlier Mexploitation films were only released in Spanish. The availability of the films in both languages clearly points to their aim of reaching wider audiences, including second- and third-generation US Latinos.

Renowned Latino filmmaker Robert Rodriguez is proudly inspired by Mexploitation. From the beginning of his career, Rodriguez, a native Texan of Mexican descent, has positioned himself as an independent film industry rebel and producer of low-budget films, even as his early successes allowed him to work with stars like Antonio Banderas and co-direct with Quentin Tarantino. At the beginning of his career, Rodriguez regarded the production mode of low-budget Mexican films as the only way open to him to produce a feature film, which is how he hit on the idea of making a border action film for the Spanish-language video market. Rodriguez borrowed piles of VHS films from a local Latino video rental shop and set himself the goal of making something similar—only better and cheaper (Rodriguez 1995: 6–7). The result was Rodriguez's first low-budget film production, *El Mariachi* (1992). It cost $7,000 to produce and was financed with money that Rodriguez earned as a pharmaceutical test subject (1995: 10). Rodriguez was solely responsible for the film's directing, production, camera work, special effects, and editing. With the Mexploitation production mode as his model, he recruited actors and props from his circle of friends and large family.

Although Rodriguez originally planned to release the film directly on video, Columbia Pictures unexpectedly took on distribution of *El Mariachi* and financed its postproduction. When *El Mariachi* won the Audience Award at the 1993 Sundance Film Festival, its Latino director—only twenty-three years old at the time—stepped into the limelight. He proved that films can be made in the United States with a very limited budget and a small team and gave fresh momentum to independent filmmakers with his do-it-yourself attitude (Horsley 1999: 249-270). At the time of the release, US media didn't connect his first film, *El Mariachi*, with Mexploitation, even though the parallels in the production mode, the story, and the characters are obvious. Although his film budgets were much higher after the success of *El Mariachi*, Rodriguez never abandoned his Mexploitation-style production mode that involves his extended family. He has produced many of his films (*Spy Kids 1–3* [2001–2003], *Once upon a Time in Mexico* [2003], *Machete* [2010], and others) through his own production company in Austin, Texas, far from the Hollywood scene. He continues to do the editing, sound tracks, and special effects himself in his garage. He also produces short clips that he calls *10 Minute Film School* that offer advice for amateur filmmakers. His goal is to prove that anyone can make films, using creativity to make up for what they lack in money. Like Rodriguez's first feature-length film *El Mariachi* (1993), *Desperado* (US, 1995), the sequel *Once upon a Time in Mexico* (2003), and his *Machete* films (2010 and 2013) follow the same story formula found in numerous border films. *Machete* presents a myriad of visual excesses and attractions: gallons of blood are shed, body parts are hacked off, and nakedness is displayed as a spectacle. Rodriguez's films remain an exception because of their widespread success with international audiences. Mexploitation films, in particular the films of La India María, have not reached comparable international success. Rodriguez's films speak to a large transnational audience, because they smartly combine elements of mainstream cinema with Mexploitation elements. His films resemble fighter-adventure blockbusters like *Rambo: First Blood* (US 1982/MX 1983, directed by Ted Kotcheff), but Rodriguez's heroes are working-class Latinos. Their stories are set in the border region and feature exciting Mexploitation attractions, such as a flashy machete fight in which members of a gang of the powerful elite are slashed and subdued.

Aurora Martínez (commonly known and credited as "Rory"), one of the most prolific straight-to-DVD producers and directors living in the

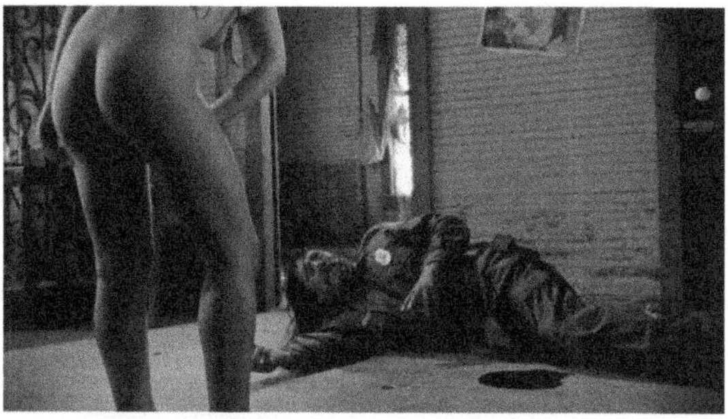

6.4 AND 6.5. In the film *Machete* (2010) spectacular scenes with action and nudity enrich the story.

United States but producing in Mexico today, follows the low-budget production and distribution scheme that appealed to Rodriguez in his early days. Since the 1980s Martínez has worked with star performers like the Almada brothers, famous since the emergence of Mexploitation in the late 1960s and early 1970s. Most of her films are entirely shot in Mexico. In a career spanning three decades, she has directed, produced, and acted in more than seventy films—most of them depicting extreme violence and border-crossing adventures. Although Martínez, like María Elena Velasco, is one of the few women to succeed in the Mexploitation film business, her work has not yet attracted any attention from film critics and film studies scholars. I hope that future research will shed some light on her career.

Throughout this book I have outlined similarities between India María and other Mexploitation films to situate La India María within a broader realm of a historic period. It would be interesting to research parallels between films with similar aesthetic features from different countries. Mexploitation cinema shares some interesting similarities with Nigerian mainstream cinema, called Nollywood, and Brazil's parodies and sexy movies of the 1970s, the *pornochanchadas*. Besides parallels in the aesthetics, they are also similar in their production mode, exhibition practices, and reception.

Although María Elena Velasco's prolific career came to a sudden end with her death in May 2015, her films continue to circulate around the world. Some will hate and others admire the India María character and her creator, but I believe that Velasco's contribution to the Mexican film industry will gradually be recognized and celebrated. The numerous obituaries published after her death primarily acknowledge La India María and Velasco's success at shaping her over nearly five decades. Some journalists also mention her achievements as a director and producer (Anonymous 2015; Cane 2015). This gives me confidence that Velasco's accomplishments not only as an actress but also as a filmmaker and producer will at long last earn the recognition that they deserve. I hope that this book will do its part.

Tonta tonta, pero no tanto (Stupid stupid, but not that much) (MX, shot in 1971, released in 1972) by Fernando Cortés. La India María migrates to Mexico City, where she works as a maid. She prevents the theft of valuable jewels and foils an insurance scam.

Pobre pero . . . ¡honrada! (Poor but honorable) (MX, shot in 1972, released in 1973) by Fernando Cortés. Does La India María possess supernatural powers to cure illnesses? Her mysterious healings suggest that she does.

La madrecita (The little nun) (MX, shot in 1973, released in 1974) by Fernando Cortés. La India María saves a Catholic convent in an unconventional way.

La presidenta municipal (The municipal president) (MX, shot in 1974, released in 1975) by Fernando Cortés. La India María is elected mayor by accident. Once in office, she imposes her own rules on rich people and on the male population.

El miedo no anda en burro (Fear doesn't ride a donkey) (MX, shot in 1973, released in 1976) by Fernando Cortés. La India María stays at a haunted house. In order to protect a cat, she must fight an arsenal of monsters.

Duro pero seguro (Hard but safe) (MX, shot in 1974, released in 1978) by Fernando Cortés. La India María is selling tacos at a television studio when a rumor spreads that hitting her brings good luck. The beatings begin.

La comadrita (The child's godmother) (MX, shot in 1975, released in 1979) by Fernando Cortés. Working as a maid in an upper-class household, La India María proves that she knows how to ride a motorbike, play soccer, and perform other physical feats.

Sor Tequila (Sister Tequila) (MX, shot in 1977, released in 1980) by Rogelio A. González. As Sister Tequila, La India María is transferred to a small town, where the local priest has established a repressive regime. She fights him with unorthodox methods.

Okey, Mister Pancho (MX, shot in 1979, released in 1981) by Gilberto Martínez Solares and María Elena Velasco. La India María unknowingly smuggles diamonds across the border to the United States and lives through various adventures.

¡El que no corre . . . vuela! (Who doesn't run, flies) (MX, shot in 1981, released in 1982) by Gilberto Martínez Solares. La India María is arrested for selling fruit in the streets of Mexico City. She fights exploitative women in jail and after she is freed.

El coyote emplumado (The feathered coyote) (MX, shot in 1982, released in 1983) by María Elena Velasco. La India María and her grandfather go to Acapulco to sell counterfeit Mayan artifacts. They end up being persecuted by a gang of scoundrels.

Ni Chana, ni Juana (Neither Chana nor Juana) (MX, shot in 1982, released in 1985) by María Elena Velasco. Twins separated at birth (both played by Velasco) reunite, leading to a series of entanglements.

Ni de aquí, ni de allá (Neither from here nor from there) (MX, shot in 1987, released in 1988) by María Elena Velasco. La India María migrates to the United States and tries to make a living. She ends up being constantly on the run.

Se equivocó la cigüeña (The stork was wrong) (MX, shot in 1992, released in 1993) by María Elena Velasco. La India María accidentally steals a fair-skinned baby and is pursued by the police.

Las delicias del poder (The delights of power) (MX, shot in 1996, released in 1999) by Iván Lipkies. The confusion of two twin sisters (both played by Velasco) leads to political uprisings.

La hija de Moctezuma (Moctezuma's daughter) (MX, shot in 2011, released in 2014) by Iván Lipkies. La India María is called by the Aztec god Moctezuma to save Mexico's indigenous heritage.

FILMOGRAPHY

Italicized film title translations indicate an English-audience release; otherwise, English titles appear in roman.

Albures mexicanos (MX, 1975), (Mexican jokes) by Alfredo B. Crevenna
¡Ay María qué puntería! (TV, MX, 1998), (María, what an aim!) by María Elena Velasco
Bellas de noche (MX, 1975), (Beauties of the night) by Miguel M. Delgado
Born in East L.A. (US, 1987/MX, 1988) by Cheech Marin
Contrabando y traición (MX, 1977), (Contraband and treachery) by Arturo Martínez
Day without a Mexican, A (US/MX, 2004) by Sergio Arau
Deadly Trackers, The (US, 1973/MX, 1974) by Barry Shear
Desperado (US, 1995) by Robert Rodriguez
Duro pero seguro (MX, 1978), (Hard but safe) by Fernando Cortés
Eco Moda (TV, Colombia, 2001–2002), (*Eco Moda*, US, 2001) by Mario Ribero Ferreira
El analfabeto (MX, 1961), (The illiterate) by Miguel M. Delgado
El barrendero (MX, 1982), (The street sweeper) by Miguel M. Delgado
El Chanfle (MX, 1979) by Enrique Segoviano
El chapulín colorado (TV, MX, 1973), (The crimson grasshopper) by Enrique Segoviano
El chapulín colorado 3D (MX, 2013), (The crimson grasshopper 3D) by Roberto Gómez
El chavo del ocho (TV, MX, 1972–1979), (The lad from the eighth) hosted by Televisa
El cielo dividido (MX, 2006), (*Broken Sky*, US, 2006) by Julián Hernández
El coyote emplumado (MX, 1983), (The feathered coyote) by María Elena Velasco
El fugitivo de Sonora) (MX, 1989), (The fugitive from Sonora) by Alfredo B. Crevenna
El Mariachi (MX/US, 1992) by Robert Rodriguez
El miedo no anda en burro (MX, 1976), (Fear doesn't ride a donkey) by Fernando Cortés
El padrecito (MX, 1964), (*The Little Priest*, US, 1965) by Miguel M. Delgado
¡El que no corre . . . vuela! (MX, 1982), (Who doesn't run, flies) by Gilberto Martínez Solares
El rey del tomate (MX, 1963), (The tomato king) by Miguel M. Delgado
El siete machos (MX, 1951), (*Seven Men*, US, 1954) by Miguel M. Delgado
El terror de la frontera (MX, 1963), (Terror of the border) by Zacarías Gómez Urquiza
El último túnel (MX, 1987), (The last tunnel) by Servando González
Emilio Varela vs Camelia la texana (MX, 1980) by Rafael Portillo
Gatilleros del Río Bravo (MX, 1984), (Gunmen of the Rio Grande) by Pedro Galindo III
Huapango (MX, 2004) by Iván Lipkies
La banda del carro rojo (MX, 1976), (The red car gang) by Rubén Galindo
La comadrita (MX, 1979), (The child's godmother) by Fernando Cortés
La del moño colorado (MX, 1998), (The girl with the red ribbon) by José Antonio Chávez
La guerra de los sexos (MX, 1978), (The war of the sexes) by Raúl de Anda Jr.

La hija de Moctezuma (MX, 2014), (Moctezuma's daughter) by Iván Lipkies
La ilegal (MX, 1979), (The illegal) by Arturo Ripstein
La ley Simpson me viene Wilson (MX, 1988), (The Simpson law makes me Wilson) by José Loza
La loba (MX, 1965), (*The She-Wolf*, US, 1966) by Rafael Baledón
La madrecita (MX, 1974), (The little nun) by Fernando Cortés
La mujer murciélago (MX, 1968), (The batwoman) by René Cardona
La nave de los monstruos (MX, 1960), (*The Ship of Monsters*, US, 1961) by Rogelio A. González
La presidenta municipal (MX, 1975), (The municipal president) by Fernando Cortés
La pulquería (MX, 1981), (The pulque tavern) by Víctor Manuel Castro
La pulquería II (MX, 1982), (The pulque tavern II) by Víctor Manuel Castro
La rielera (MX, 1988), (The railroad woman) by Raúl Fernández
La risa en vacaciones 1–8 (MX, 1988–1996), (Holiday laughs) by René Cardona Jr.
Las amantes del señor de la noche (MX, 1986), (Lovers of the lord of the night] by Isela Vega
Las braceras (MX, 1981), (The female emigrants) by Fernando Durán Rojas
Las delicias de la India María (TV, MX, 2004), (The delights of La India María) by Televisa
Las delicias del poder (MX, 1999), (The delights of power) by Iván Lipkies
Las del talón (MX, 1978), (The high-heeled ones) by Alejandro Galindo
Las fabulosas del reventón II (MX, 1983), (The fabulous women of the wild party II) by Fernando Durán Rojas
Las ficheras: Bellas de noche II parte (MX, 1977), (The B girls: beauties of the night part II) by Miguel M. Delgado
Las luchadoras contra el robot asesino (MX, 1969), (Wrestling women versus the murderous robot) aka *El asesino loco y el sexo* (The mad killer and sex) by René Cardona
Las luchadoras contra la momia (MX, 1964), (*Wrestling Women versus the Aztec Mummy*, US, 1965) by René Cardona
Las luchadoras vs el médico asesino (MX, 1962), (*Doctor of Doom*, US, 1963) by René Cardona
Lola la trailera (MX, 1983), (*Lola the Truck Driving Woman*, US, 1985) by Raúl Fernández
Lola la trailera 2 (MX, 1986), (Lola the truck driving woman 2) by Raúl Fernández
Lola la trailera 3 (MX, 1991), (Lola the truck driving woman 3) by Raúl Fernández
Los días de los albañiles (MX, 1985–1990), (Day of the bricklayers) by Gilberto Martínez Solares
Machete (US/MX, 2010) by Robert Rodriguez
Machete Kills (US/MX, 2013) by Robert Rodriguez
María Candelaria (Xochimilco) (MX, 1944), (*Portrait of Maria*, US, 1944) by Emilio Fernández
Mataron a Camelia la texana (MX, 1978), (They have killed Camelia the Texan) by Arturo Martínez
Mil nubes de paz, cercan el cielo, amor, jamás acabarás de ser amor (MX, 2004), (*A Thousand Clouds of Peace*, US, 2004) by Julián Hernández
Misterio en las Bermudas (MX, 1979), (Mystery in the Bermuda Triangle) by Gilberto Martínez Solares

Mojado . . . pero caliente (MX, 1989), (Wet . . . but hot) by Rafael Portillo
Muerte en Tijuana (MX, 1991), (Death in Tijuana) by Hernando Name
Nacho Libre (US/MX, 2006) by Jared Hess
Navajeros (Spain, 1980), (Criminals with knives) by Eloy de la Iglesia
Ni Chana, ni Juana (MX, 1985), (Neither Chana nor Juana) by María Elena Velasco
Ni de aquí, ni de allá (MX, 1988), (Neither from here nor from there) by María Elena Velasco
Noches de cabaret (MX, 1978), (Carnival nights) by Rafael Portillo
Nos reimos de la migra (MX, 1984), (Poking fun at the border patrol) by Víctor Manuel Castro
Okey, Mister Pancho (MX, 1981) by Gilberto Martínez Solares and María Elena Velasco
Once upon a Time in Mexico (US/MX, 2003) by Robert Rodriguez
Perdida (MX, 2009), (Loss) by Viviana García Besné
Picardía mexicana (MX, 1978–1997), (Spicy Mexican sayings) by Abel Salazar
Pobre pero . . . ¡honrada! (MX, 1973), (Poor but honorable) by Fernando Cortés
Rabioso sol, rabioso cielo (MX, 2009), (*Raging Sun, Raging Sky*, US, 2009) by Julián Hernández
Rambo: First Blood (US, 1982/MX 1983) by Ted Kotcheff
Rambo III (US/MX, 1988) by Peter MacDonald
Revista musical Nescafé (TV, MX, 1972), (Nescafé show) by Telesistema Mexicano S. A.
Santo contra el asesino de la televisión (MX, 1981), (Santo versus the murderer of TV) by Rafael Pérez Grovas
Santo contra las mujeres vampiro (MX, 1962), (*Samson versus the Vampire Women*, US, 1963) by Alfonso Corona Blake
Santo en la frontera del terror (MX, 1981), (Santo on the border of terror) by Rafael Pérez Grovas
Se equivocó la cigüeña (MX, 1993), (The stork was wrong) by María Elena Velasco
Siempre en domingo (TV, MX, 1969–1998), (Always on Sunday) hosted by Raúl Velasco on Televisa
Simplemente María (TV, Peru, 1969–1970), (Simply María) by Carlos Barrios Porras
Solo para damas (MX, 1981), (For ladies only) by Fernando Durán Rojas
Sor Tequila(MX, 1980), (Sister Tequila) by Rogelio A. González
Soy chicano y mexicano (MX, 1975), (I am Chicano and Mexican) by Tito Novaro
Spy Kids 1–3 (US/MX, 2001–2003) by Robert Rodriguez
Superzan y el niño del espacio (MX, 1973), (Superzan and the space boy) by Rafael Lanuza
Tacos al carbón (MX, 1972), (Grilled tacos) by Alejandro Galindo
Tívoli (MX, 1975) by Alberto Isaac
Tonta tonta, pero no tanto (MX, 1972), (Stupid stupid, but not that much) by Fernando Cortés
Tortillas Again? (US, 2006) by Paul and Sergio Ramirez
Ugly Betty (US, 2006–2010) by Silvio Horta
Una gallina muy ponedora (MX, 1982), (A hen that lays a lot of eggs) by Rafael Portillo
Viento negro (MX, 1965), (Black wind) by Servando González
Yo soy Betty, la fea (TV, Colombia, 1999–2001), (Ugly Betty) by Fernando Gaitán

NOTES

INTRODUCTION

1. Ivette Eugenia Lipkies goes by the nickname Goretti. On Wikipedia and in the International Movie Database (IMDb), Goretti and Ivette are listed separately. This is not correct. Velasco only has one daughter.

2. Hereafter called Diana Films.

3. For publications on the Golden Age, see Noble (2005), Mora (2005), and Monsiváis (1999). Acevedo-Muñoz (2003) focuses on the work of director Luis Buñuel. For particular focus on gender aspects, see Hershfield (1996, 2001). For contemporary filmmaking, see Haddu (2007), Wood (2006), and González Vargas et al. (2006). For an overview of the broader Latin American context, see Shaw (2007), Shaw and Dennison (2005), and Stock (1997). For an overview of Mexican film history, consult the essays in Paranaguá (1995).

4. For my research, I understand spectatorship in terms of its manifold tensions between "actual viewers," who are historically and locally determined by viewing practices, race, gender, class, and institutions, and theoretical "spectators" fashioned by the text. I thus use the grid of multiculturalism proposed by the film scholars Ellah Shohat and Robert Stam (1994: 347). In addition, I draw from reception theories by French scholar Roger Odin (1990a) and cultural studies scholar John Fiske (1995).

CHAPTER 1: LA INDIA MARÍA

1. Piporro was famous for his northern slang [*norteño*] and his rural attitudes. He appeared in a series of big box-office hits as well as Mexican knockoffs of Hollywood monster films, all the while maintaining his character type (García Riera 1998: 223). Resortes appeared in hundreds of Mexican comedies and *telenovelas* [TV soap operas] over a span of more than seventy years.

2. Meriche was of Polish and Russian origin. He passed away in 1974 when Velasco was already a well-known performer. She later established her own production company and gave it her husband's first name.

3. During each of my research trips to Mexico, I asked people in the streets about their favorite characters and what media they knew them from.

4. María Elena Velasco and Raúl Velasco were not related.

5. I have not analyzed all shows but have limited myself to the materials accessible at no or low cost: Iván Lipkies placed at my disposal numerous videos of the show *Siempre en domingo* and *Revista musical Nescafé*. He also recorded parts of the television sitcom *¡Ay María qué puntería!*

6. Rumor has it that Velasco was banned from *Siempre en domingo* because of a political joke (Pelayo 1985). Although she never confirmed this, chances are that her social criticism, disguised in the form of comedy, was carefully monitored by Telesistema Mexicano (Televisa), which was closely aligned to the Partido Revolucionario Institutional (PRI: Institutional Revolutionary Party) (Castro Ricalde 2004b: 204).

7. Iván Lipkies claims that there are two reasons why his mother rarely appeared on television later in her career. First, because television vetoed Velasco and her character; second, because she was fully committed to her feature films.

8. Gunning (1986: 64) defines the cinema of attractions by its ability to show. In his view, it is a form of "exhibitionist" cinema, because it directly addresses spectators and enters into a relationship with them, for example, through the actors' looks at the camera, the displays of bodies (often full nudity), or magic tricks, held together in a rudimentary way through the succession of events (Gunning 1986: 64, 65, 1989: 10). "Rather than a desire for an (almost) endlessly delayed fulfillment and a cognitive involvement in pursuing an enigma, early cinema, therefore, attracts in a different manner. It arouses a curiosity that is satisfied by surprise rather than narrative suspense" (Gunning 2004: 44).

9. According to the historical record, La Virgen de Guadalupe appeared to the first literate convert and indigenous "peasant," Indio Juan Diego, in 1531 and was officially declared authentic by the Catholic Church a century later. A Spanish bishop recognized that the apparition of La Virgen de Guadalupe had the potential to convince the Catholic Church that Mexico's indigenous people had souls and hence could be saved. The apparition of the Virgin in indigenous form served as a bridge between indigenous pre-Hispanic beliefs and Christianity. Over time a veritable cult developed around the Virgin that combined indigenous and Christian practices (Hershfield 1996: 22). Even today La Virgen de Guadalupe occupies an important moral position in Mexico. Every year on her name day hundreds of thousands of believers crawl on their knees to visit her shrine in Mexico City.

10. I speak of ethnicity and not "race," a term that is misleading within the Mexican context. Contrary to race, ethnicity is defined not only by the color of the skin; it includes an emphasis on cultural practices and beliefs (O'Sullivan et al. 1994: 107f.). According to statistics from the Mexican government, approximately 12 million Mexicans identify as indigenous—about 10 percent of the nation's population. A majority of Mexicans define themselves as mestizos, people of mixed indigenous and Spanish descent (see cdi.gob.mx/indicadores2015/#/6). Sixty-two indigenous languages are officially recognized in Mexico, and many of these are still spoken today. Despite their considerable number, indigenous people rarely occupy political offices or executive positions.

11. Indigenous people (many of them Mazahuas) began migrating to the cities earlier. In the 1960s this trend increased, due to poor rural living conditions and the effects of industrialization and governmental policies favoring urban areas.

12. In Mexico *Simplemente María* boasted TV ratings of 56 percent, and some episodes even surpassed the ratings for the soccer world championship. In Peru the average rating for this *telenovela* was 85 percent (Rogers and Singhal 1999: 32–33). Public support of the show reached extreme proportions. For example, after the Peruvian press announced the heroine's marriage in a future episode, over ten thousand fans dressed up for the occasion and congregated at the church where the wedding scenes were to be shot (Rogers and Singhal 1999: 25). After the original Peruvian version—an adaptation of an Argentinian *radionovela* [radio soap opera] (1967–1968)—five different TV versions of *Simplemente María* (including a Mexican version) were produced and broadcast, and each one was a popular success (Rogers and Singhal 1999: 39).

13. The film historian David Wilt (1996b) suggests dividing films with indigenous

protagonists into the following six categories. Indigenous people are presented on the silver screen either as members of an advanced civilization or as barbarians. Wilt also identifies a third category that depicts what he terms "contemporary Mexican Indians." These films focus on the history of oppression and the clash of cultures. A fourth category consists of films illustrating the lives of notable indigenous figures such as Benito Juárez, the Virgin of Guadalupe, and Juan Diego. The fifth category, which Wilt calls "primitive savages," depicts indigenous people as wild savages who live in the Mexican jungle, far away from civilization. The last category is comedies. Here Wilt singles out La India María as the most important figure of all.

14. In order to assess Velasco's performance, I refer to Richard Dyer's definition: "Performance is what the performer does in addition to the actions/functions she or he performs in the plot and the lines she or he is given to say. Performance is how the action/function is done, how the lines are said" (cited in Pearson 1992: 5). As signs of performance, he lists facial expressions, voice, gestures, posture (how someone is standing or sitting), and body movement (all activities).

CHAPTER 2: MEXPLOITATION

1. In recent years, blaxploitation has repeatedly been the subject of academic research. Besides more general introductions by authors such as Howard (2008) and Walker et al. (2009), many studies center on aspects of race in relation to their audience (Benshoff 2000; Kraszewski 2002; Lawrence 2008; Sévéon 2008) or on aspects of gender (Holmlund 2005; Keeling 2007; Sims 2006).

2. Muñoz continued her acting career and played numerous roles across genres.

3. Today these films would probably be released as NC-17 in the United States.

4. The Internet Movie Database (IMDb) lists over 364 titles for Mario Almada and 155 credits as an actor for Fernando Almada (August 25, 2016).

5. Scholar Norma Iglesias has analyzed a large corpus of Mexican films, centering on stories set in—or closely related to—the border region. She offers a more general definition: the plot—or a significant part of it—unfolds on the US/Mexican border; the film itself presents characters living in that region and is also often produced there; and the story deals with Mexicans living in the United States and the ensuing cultural clashes (Iglesias 1999: 234). Iglesias also observes that the majority of border films have become known for their cheap look, combined with a high level of popularity. However, her judgment of Mexploitation films, like that of Mexican critics, is highly negative. She denies them any cultural value and condemns the often violent and sexist plots, along with the stereotypical characters that they depict.

6. The low-budget mode of production originated during a time of economic growth, also referred to by historians as El Milagro Mexicano [the Mexican Miracle, 1930–1970]. Inflation rates were relatively stable until 1976, when the country experienced a massive devaluation of the peso. The subsequent economic crisis culminated in the 1980s.

7. It has also been argued that the reason for authorizing films with sexually promiscuous content might be that the state gained revenues from their distribution and exhibition (Maciel 1999: 211).

8. All of these scholars have published numerous articles and books on Mexican cinema that have become key references for Mexican film history. For my research, I

draw widely from their scholarship. However, I am fully aware of their political and ideological standpoint as well as their particular interest in auteur cinema.

9. Simultaneously, filmmakers and intellectuals across Latin America decided to unite and use film as a means to express their political opinions. Argentine filmmakers Fernando Solanas and Octavio Getino wrote a manifesto entitled *Tercer Cine* [Third cinema] (1976). Brazilian filmmaker Glauber Rocha published several pamphlets on the Cinema Novo [New Cinema]. Cuban Julio García Espinosa speaks of Cine Imperfecto [Imperfect Cinema] (Espinosa 2003). All these movements (Mexicans, Argentineans, Brazilians, and filmmakers from other Latin American nations) tried to set themselves apart from Hollywood (that is, first cinema) to find their own cinematic language. Many also drew on nonprofessional actors and were often overtly political. However, the different movements varied considerably.

10. It still remains unclear how the company managed to thrive during these years.

11. David Wilt has generously provided me a list of hundreds of Mexican straight-to-video productions. Although the list is not complete, according to Wilt, it gives an idea of the extensive volume of straight-to-video productions.

12. The number of Mexploitation films produced in the 1980s and early 1990s is extremely difficult to calculate. As a point of departure, I looked at statistics and lists of privately produced films, most of which can be considered Mexploitation. However, the sources at my disposition vary considerably. García Riera (1998: 331), for example, counts 107 films in 1980 and 63 films in 1986. Numbers provided by the industry's magazine *Cámara* are significantly higher. This is mainly because foreign productions shot in Mexico were also included in the statistics by *Cámara*, as were films by Mexican directors shot abroad. In 1988, for example, García Riera calculates a total of 76 films in 1988. *Cámara* (1989: 23) counts a total of 125 films in 1988, however, of which 10 percent are foreign productions shot in Mexico. *Cámara* (1987c: 16) also declares that in 1986 alone 8 films were produced in the United States, some of which were never released in Mexico. Not included in García Riera's or *Cámera*'s calculations are television productions (mainly Televicine, the film branch of Televisa) and straight-to-video productions. Similarly, films produced or directed by Mexican immigrants living in the United States are not part of the corpus. To understand the boom completely, production modes such as television, straight-to-video, co-productions, and so forth need to be considered and analyzed in detail. Limitation to either a certain form of distribution or exhibition or adherence to a single national industry would fall short and draw an incomplete or even inadequate picture.

13. During these difficult economic times, loans were given to the Mexican state as well as to private entrepreneurs, mainly by the United States. In the mid-1980s Mexico's foreign debts were already at around 80 billion US dollars (*Cámara* 1987b: 23). To what extent the film producers profited from foreign support, however, is uncertain.

14. During the presidential term of Luis Echeverría the Universidad Nacional Autónoma de México (UNAM) was the sole producer of independent films. Under José Lopéz Portillo (1976–1982) the independents gained strength (King 2000: 140).

15. Valdés mostly played a stereotypical Mexican American, who attracted attention with his flashy clothing and slang.

16. See, for example, Hershfield and Maciel (1999), Medrano Platas (1999), Rashkin (2001), and Solís (1990).

17. Ramírez Berg (1992: 37) notes that the average cost per film in the 1940s was roughly the same as in the 1970s, taking the inflation rate into account. In addition, salaries for motion picture workers were raised, which implied that producers had to cut back in other areas or simply made less profit.

18. For all sources indicating costs only in Mexican pesos, I used the historic exchange rate provided by the Global Financial Data database (globalfinancialdata.com). The exchange rate used was a quarterly yearly average of the Mexican peso.

19. Rogelio Agrasánchez Jr. provided me with copies of data from his father's company. The originals are in Harlingen, Texas, in his private collection (Agrasánchez 1971–1984).

20. I was generously given access to production cost figures for all features produced by Diana Films (ranging from budgets to shooting schedules and correspondence). In the original documents all costs are indicated in old Mexican pesos. For clarity, I have calculated the equivalent value in US dollars based on the historic exchange rate provided by the Global Financial Data database (globalfinancialdata.com): *Tonta tonta, pero no tanto* (shot in 1971, released in 1972): 1,117,750 Mexican pesos ($94,200); *Pobre pero . . . ¡honrada!* (shot in 1972, released in 1973): 1,199,000 Mexican pesos ($95,920); *La madrecita* (shot in 1973, released in 1974): 1,219,650 Mexican pesos ($97,572); *La presidenta municipal* (shot in 1974, released in 1975): 1,074,099 Mexican pesos ($85,927); *El miedo no anda en burro* (shot in 1973, released in 1976): 1,197,760 Mexican pesos ($95,825); *Duro pero seguro* (shot in 1974, released in 1978): 1,498,039 Mexican pesos ($65,703); *La comadrita* (shot in 1974, released in 1979): 1,925,300 Mexican pesos ($84,442); *Sor Tequila* (shot in 1977, released in 1980): 5,374,898 Mexican pesos ($226,789); *Okey, Mister Pancho* (shot in 1979, released in 1981): 6,027,899 Mexican pesos ($241,112); *¡El que no . . . corre vuela!* (shot in 1981, released in 1982): 8,051,00 Mexican pesos (around $80,000 depending on the time of the year transactions were made; extremely high inflation rates make it difficult to set a reliable dollar value).

21. By the early 1990s Televisa had even become the main distributor for theatrical releases of Mexican films in its home market (Getino 1998: 129).

22. The film premiered at the Morelia International Film Festival in Michoacán in 2013, although it was not part of the official program. The film was released in theaters in Mexico in 2014.

CHAPTER 3: BOX-OFFICE MONEYMAKERS AND SMALL-SCREEN HITS

1. Miguel Contreras Torres (1960) uncovers the business practices of Jenkins in his book *El libro negro del cine mexicano* and accuses Jenkins of destroying the Mexican film industry with his monopoly.

2. As an exception, *Sor Tequila* was distributed by Clasa-Mohme.

3. Exact numbers for Mexico are calculated for the time between 1983 and 1990. Attendance dropped additionally in the following two years.

4. In the United States 18 percent fewer people attended the movie theaters during the same time (Getino 1998: 27). The difference between Latin America and the United States is striking. In the United States attendance at theaters dropped shortly after the introduction of television, while throughout Latin America the process took sig-

nificantly longer and was most noticeable after the mid-1980s (García Canclini et al. 1994: 161).

5. Carlos Monsiváis (1994) writes that during the Golden Age audiences were united, all watching the same films, in the same cinemas. His idealistic understanding of the audience, however, can be questioned. I would argue that people have always attended cinemas in their neighborhoods, which were clearly inhabited by a rather unanimous class.

6. *Piojito* also means caressing the hair to soothe or relax somebody, so the nickname of the theater points to the rundown facility while also indicating that this is a place where viewers will feel comfortable and loved.

7. Often the films were exhibited in these theaters several months or years after they premiered in Mexico City (Valenzuela Arce 1994: 309).

8. Diana Films provided me with a list of theaters in which the films were screened or Velasco performed.

9. Articles that mention her box-office success include Anonymous 1985a and Camargo 1993.

10. Available box-office figures, the numbers of copies circulating, and the attributed "popularity" awards testify to La India María's extraordinary success with the audience.

11. Ugalde Romero (1982a: 11) observed the gradual increase in copies and even speaks of a new trend assuring producers of recouping their investments over a shorter time. I propose that the increasingly unstable economic situation led to this exhibition practice. Producers simply tried to assure revenues before the Mexican peso was significantly lower in value.

12. Articles announcing or commenting the reruns include Anonymous 1987c and Barriga Chávez 1991.

13. In Mexico, in contrast, drive-ins were the dernier cri, offering an unusual viewing experience at a very high cost and exclusively showing Hollywood fare (*Cámara* 1978a: 20; Romero and Bertol 1981: 10).

14. In 1994 Velasco had to share the award with the actors of *La risa en vacaciones* (Holiday laughs) (1994, directed by René Cardona Jr.) for the first time (Anonymous 1995: 3). After her success with *Ni de aquí, ni de allá*, she was awarded a prize sponsored by the Mexican newspaper *El Heraldo* for her career defending an innocent form of humor (Anonymous 1989b; El Soberbio 1989; V. H. Sánchez 1989).

15. I came to this conclusion based on interviews, old television programs, and ratings as well as video rental hit lists.

16. Responding to this trend, some cinema exhibitors installed video rental stores or simply sold videos in the lobby of their theater. The Agrasánchez family, for example, offered a selection of about 300 videos (Rohrer 2010d). The exhibitor Ramón Medrano, who owned several cinemas, did not run a video business himself, but his son opened one (Rohrer 2010b). The industry journal writes "No hay una gran diferencia entre vender palomitas de maíz y vender una cinta de video" [There is no big difference between selling popcorn and selling videos] (*Cámara* 1984d: 15). Not all of these entrepreneurial endeavors were successful, however, and few of them actually lasted. They can be seen as attempts to react to the new exhibition trends.

17. No reliable statistics exist for the 1980s for either video rental stores or piracy.

Data provided for the early to mid-1990s show that almost 10,000 video rental stores were counted in Mexico, with a higher density in the cities than in the countryside (García Canclini et al. 1994: 161).

18. The video rental stores in Mexico City were often integrated in libraries. This automatically attracted different customers.

19. María Arbeláez (2001: 642) created a hit list of popular movies through a survey conducted in communities where the majority of the population was either Mexican born or of Mexican descent. Most films mentioned center on stars such as Rosa Gloria Chagoyán, the Almada brothers, Angélica Chaín (Camelia La Texana), and La India María. Following in popularity are films with Cantinflas and other stars of the classical era.

20. According to interviews that I conducted in Texas, exhibitors believed that the Simpson-Rodino law had no influence. Exhibitors in other states, however, do talk about its impact (Rafael Pérez Grovas in Iglesias 1991: 102).

21. This holds true for both 1984 and 1990, when Sánchez Ruiz conducted his study.

22. Interviewees from the working class enjoyed *telenovelas*, action series, and comedies the most (Sánchez Ruiz 1993: 236; see also Quintal Avilés and Reyes Domínguez 1994: 278). Cable television did not play a pivotal role in the exhibition of Mexploitation films in Mexico. Introduced in 1986, it offered a predominantly US content. The service was very expensive, so only consumers with a higher income subscribed to it (García Canclini et al. 1994: 220).

23. Televisa's hegemonic position was found to be illegal in 1987. The company was forced to reduce its shares significantly and thereby lost control over Univisión (Sinclair 2004: 14). In the following years, Hallmark ended up running Univisión (Sinclair 1999: 106, 107).

24. Although Latinos were an increasingly important consumer group, it took a while until the Hispanic Television Rating System was introduced in the early 1990s (Sinclair 2004: 13). The US networks were also reluctant to launch channels aimed at Latino audiences. By the early 1990s they finally penetrated the Spanish-language market by introducing their own Latino channels. CNN transmitted its program in the United States as well as across Latin America. Time-Warner launched its own movie channel, HBO Olé. Later Discovery, Fox Latin America, MTV Latino, and others joined the market (Sinclair 1999: 114–115).

25. In the late 1970s and throughout the 1980s major political and financial turmoil destabilized the banking sector in Argentina, Bolivia, Chile, Colombia, Costa Rica, Ecuador, El Salvador, Guatemala, Honduras, Nicaragua, Panama, and Uruguay (Carstens 2004: 4).

26. The numerous spelling errors in the publicity texts are eye-catching.

CHAPTER 4: HATED BY CRITICS, LOVED BY THE PEOPLE

1. I carried out the interviews mainly in 2009 and 2010, during my research stay in Mexico and in the United States. In Mexico I interviewed seven taxi drivers, one hairdresser, five market women, two cleaners, and one gardener. In the United States I interviewed three teachers, three hairdressers, two library clerks, two cleaners, three

farmworkers, and one gardener. The interviewees were all between twenty-five and sixty years old and all of Mexican descent. At first I recruited interviewees through organizations such as farmworkers' unions and businesses, but I soon realized that many interviewees felt uncomfortable and only gave rudimentary answers. I can only speculate about the reasons for their discomfort: quite possibly they felt like objects of investigation; this distance might have been worsened by my status as a white European, and a female at that. In response, I adjusted my method of gathering data. Instead of conducting scheduled interviews indoors, I went out into the field and talked with people in the streets and other public places. I began each conversation by explaining that I believe these films are interesting and valuable objects of research. I think that my affirmative statement at the beginning of the interviews was particularly important to the people who liked the films but were reluctant to show their enthusiasm. Despite the drawbacks of a subjective approach, I believe that claims about reception must rely on the candid testimony of individual viewers.

2. The linking of critics and scholars, and at times even filmmakers, needs to be contextualized within the Grupo Nuevo Cine, a group of critics and filmmakers formed in the 1970s, which fostered films that brought Mexico's realities to the screens. Several film critics belonged to that group, produced films, and worked at universities.

3. In the course of my research, I have discovered only a few private collectors or fans who kept Velasco materials, while the producers themselves and the archives did not consider the materials worth filing.

4. The terms "cult," "paracinema," and "trash" are often used interchangeably, although differences exist. "Cult films" are often defined by their subcultural ideology, which regards filmmakers, films, or spectators as being in opposition to the mainstream (Jancovich et al. 2003: 1). "Trash" generally describes a category of films either explicitly rejected or simply ignored by legitimate film culture (Sconce 1995: 535). Some film scholars have placed "trash" within the realm of poststructuralism, building on the assertion that individuals construct rather than receive meaning (Cartmell et al. 1997: 2). Jeffrey Sconce (1995: 535) describes "paracinema" as a particular reading protocol, "a counter-aesthetic turned subcultural sensibility devoted to all manner of cultural detritus." Paracinema thus functions through its ironic strategy and its aspiration to achieve the status of a countercinema, which seeks to promote alternative preexisting visions of cinematic art by questioning the legitimacy of reigning aesthetic discourses and by attacking the criteria used to define "high-quality" films in order to establish a film canon (Sconce 1995: 536).

5. Missing accents and incorrect spellings are part of the original online comments.

6. Unlike visiting viewers of YouTube clips, people who comment on Youtube are relatively easy to trace because they have accounts that provide some basic information about themselves. The majority of commenters analyzed identified as Mexican residents. The second largest group of users lives in the United States, and most of them have a Mexican or Latino background. Other contributors are from Peru, Panama, Argentina, Chile, Honduras, and other Latin American countries as well as from Spain. Their ages range from fourteen to forty-four, with a majority of younger users.

7. For an introduction to Lola, see chapter 2.

8. From en.wikipedia.org/wiki/Mar%C3%ADa_Elena_Velasco. The entry has been edited since I consulted it (on October 11, 2010), removing this material.

9. Dyer (2000a: 124, 2000b: 121, 2004: 3ff.) has thoroughly studied celebrity phe-

nomena. In 1979 he was analyzing what makes Hollywood stars in terms of their production and how their image is reflected in the characters they depict.

10. Unlike these two stars, Velasco never attracted fans beyond the Latino community. On the image of other Latino stars, see Hershfield (2001), Perriam (2005), and Thornton (2010).

11. Three interviewees (all male) were highly negative about the character. One man belonged to an indigenous movement group, another worked as a hairdresser in Los Angeles, and the third was a scholar.

12. During my research I came across one article accusing the character of not being racist enough. According to its author, indigenous people are supposedly much more repulsive than the India María character shows (Montes de Oca Heredia 1993).

CHAPTER 5: CROSSING BORDERS

1. The bracero program was a series of laws and political agreements between Mexico and the United States. It was introduced during World War II to regulate labor force exchange between the two countries and allowed Mexicans to work legally in the United States, mostly in agriculture. Consequently, over one hundred thousand laborers left Mexico (Agrasánchez 2006: 31). The bracero program ended in 1964 due to harsh criticism. Nevertheless, the term "bracero" is still used in Mexico to refer to migrant workers.

2. Unfortunately I was not able to find a playable copy of the tape. The information used here is based on the information given to me by María Elena Velasco.

3. In some cases, *corridos* have even spawned serial movies. The ballad *Camelia la texana* (also by Los Tigres del Norte), for example, inspired numerous border films based on the character Camelia, all of them with melodramatic elements. *Contrabando y traición* (Contraband and treachery) (1977, directed by Arturo Martínez) was released in 1977. *Mataron a Camelia la texana* (They have killed Camelia the Texan) (1978, directed by Arturo Martínez) followed. The list of titles continues with *Emilio Varela vs Camelia la texana* (1980, directed by Rafael Portillo) and many more. The similarity of the films' titles is striking and suggests that only slight story variations were made. In fact, all *Camelia la texana* serial movies are almost identical.

4. Music was a key element in Mexican cinema before the emergence of Mexploitation. During the Golden Age of Mexican cinema, for instance, monthly magazines such as *La Novela Cine-Gráfica* aimed at familiarizing the public with upcoming films through film songs and lyrics (Agrasánchez 2006: 40; Anonymous 1947). By the time films premiered, people already knew the lyrics of the songs and selections of dialogue before entering the theater. Although I am not aware of such magazines published to promote Mexploitation films, these practices surely shaped the way in which committed viewers engaged with the movies that they enjoyed.

5. Despite the existence of scattered observations, no systematic research exists on the viewing conditions and side activities for Mexploitation films. The existing information is restricted to comments by some journalists and scholars of Latin American cinema.

6. Spellings left as in the original comment.

7. See frictionmagazine.com/artful/artists/rosemarie_print.html.

8. The number of people interviewed for this study was limited to thirty, so caution

has to be applied to avoid generalizations when analyzing these essentially anecdotal findings. The lack of previous scholarship on the production and reception of Velasco's films is clearly a drawback of this study.

EPILOGUE: INDIA MARÍA AND MEXPLOITATION TODAY

1. Three types of materials can be found online. First, recurrent clips of India María feature films in which Velasco plays the leading role are uploaded. Each clip is accompanied with several user comments, ranging from scene-related comments to fan statements. Moreover, users have defined key scenes that they consider particularly funny or interesting and posted them online. Material on La India María apart from the feature films can also be found, including excerpts from the television shows *Siempre en domingo* (1971), *Revista musical Nescafé* (1972), and *¡Ay María qué puntería!* (1998). There is also a short television documentary on María Elena Velasco and amateur recordings of her appearances at public events such as *ferias* [fairs].

2. The film scholar Yeidy M. Rivero (2003: 67) has examined the reception of *Yo soy Betty, la fea* by using two focus groups of Latinas with different ethnic backgrounds, all living in the United States. Most of the women agreed that Betty does not correspond to mainstream notions of beauty: her skin is darker and she is from the lower end of the social scale. At the same time, her body is not hypersexual/sensual—a common depiction of Latina women. All participants enjoyed the depiction of Betty, however, because she represented an alternative to dominant depictions of Latina women. This corresponds to my findings about the reception of La India María. Dolores Tierney (2013: 18) further argues that Betty's marked ethnicity is categorized as beautiful at the end of the series and therefore transgresses common representations of Latinas on television.

BIBLIOGRAPHY

Acevedo-Muñoz, Ernesto R. 2003. *Buñuel and Mexico: The Crisis of National Cinema.* Berkeley: University of California Press.

Agrasánchez, Rogelio. 2006. *Mexican Movies in the United States: A History of the Films, Theaters, and Audiences, 1920–1960.* Jefferson, NC: McFarland & Co.

Agrasánchez, S. A. 1971–1984. "Production Files." Harlingen: Agrasánchez Film Archive, Folder Production.

Alemán, Gabriela. 2009. "At the Margin of the Margins: Contemporary Ecuadorian Exploitation Cinema and the Local Pirate Market." In Victoria Ruétalo and Dolores Tierney (eds.), *Latsploitation, Exploitation Cinemas, and Latin America*, 261–274. London, New York: Routledge.

Altman, Rick. 2002. "The American Film Musical as Dual-Focus Narrative." In Steven Cohan (ed.), *Hollywood Musicals: The Film Reader*, 41–51. London, New York: Routledge.

Álvarez, Ethel. 1998. "Promete una 'delicia.'" *Reforma*, December 17, 1998, 13.

———. 1999. "Las delicias de ser María: La India le tira a lo 'grande.'" *Reforma*, January 3, 1999.

Amador, Carlos. 1983. "México y su nueva esperanza." *Cámara: Órgano Informativo de la Cámara Nacional de la Industria Cinematográfica* 4 (26): 33.

Ampudia Girón, Manuel. 1980. "Carta de despedida." *Cámara: Órgano Informativo de la Cámara Nacional de la Industria Cinematográfica* 2 (11): 12–19.

Anderson, Benedict. 2006. *Imagined Communities.* London, New York: Verso.

Anonymous. 1947. *La novela cine-gráfica.* Los Angeles: Orbe Publications.

———. 1975. "La India María." *El Chicano*, May 1, 1975.

———. 1976. "La India María: Star at Magic Mountain's Mexican Independence Day Celebration." *El Chicano*, September 2, 1976.

———. 1985a. "La India conquista nuevo cine." *Novedades*, August 15, 1985.

———. 1985b. "¿Que no gane con Lola? ¡Ja, Ja, Ja . . . !" *Cinema Teatro* 1 (4): 4–5.

———. 1987a. "Concluyó La India María el rodaje de *Ni de aquí, ni de allá.*" *El Nacional*, March 1, 1987.

———. 1987b. "La India María deja su personaje de 16 años: María Elena Velasco interpretará a una maestra del conservatorio." *El Heraldo*, August 25, 1987.

———. 1987c. "Reestrenan en el DF un filme de la India María." *El Nacional*, January 20, 1987.

———. 1989a. "La India María: Los intelectuales no me quieren, ¡pero el pueblo sí!" *Super Musical*, April 19, 1989.

———. 1989b. "María Elena Velasco recibirá nuestro trofeo, por 35 años de carrera artística: Un caso insólito." *El Heraldo*, February 17, 1989.

———. 1992a. "Las 'Marías' me ven con mucho cariño: María Elena Velasco." *Tribuna*, February 28, 1992.

———. 1992b. "No soy ahorrativa: La India María." *El Sol del Mediodia*, March 31, 1992.

———. 1994a. "Comercialismo, traba en el cine: India María." *Últimas Noticias*, May 11, 1994.

———. 1994b. "Faltan mayores programas humorísticos." *Últimas Noticias*, May 10, 1994.

———. 1995. "Cine." *La Opinión*, January 18, 1995.

———. 1997a. "Apantallará La India María." *Novedades*, August 1, 1997.

———. 1997b. "No hay necesidad de recurrir a lo vulgar: La India María." *El Sol de México*, August 19, 1997.

———. 2015. "Murió la actriz María Elena Velasco, intérprete de 'La India María.'" *Univision.com*, May 1, 2015.

Arbeláez, María S. 2001. "Low-Budget Films for Fronterizos and Mexican Migrants in the United States." *Journal of the Southwest* 43: 637–657.

Arnaud, Fabián. 1979. "El cine y la television están hermanados en todo el mundo." *Cámara: Órgano Informativo de la Cámara Nacional de la Industria Cinematográfica* 1 (5): 6–7.

Arredondo, Arturo. 1999. "*Las delicias del poder.*" *Novedades*, January 15, 1999.

Avalos, Adán. 2009. "The Naco in Mexican Film: *La banda del carro rojo*, Border Cinema, and Migrant Audiences." In Victoria Ruétalo and Dolores Tierney (eds.), *Latsploitation, Exploitation Cinemas, and Latin America*, 185–197. London, New York: Routledge.

Avilés Duarte, Abel. 1994. "La popular actriz India María hará una temporada en el Teatro de Variedades Blanquita." *Excelsior*, April 20, 1994.

Aviña, Rafael. 1999. "Se lanza la India María." *Reforma*, January 1, 1999.

Ayala Blanco, Jorge. 1986. *La condición del cine mexicano (1973–1985)*. Mexio City: Editorial Posada.

———. 1989. "La India María y las atrofias de la farsa." *El Financiero*, May 3, 1989.

———. 1991. *La disolvencia del cine mexicano: Entre lo popular y lo exquisito*. Mexico City: Editorial Grijalbo.

———. 1994. "La comicidad picahuye." In Jorge Ayala Blanco (ed.), *La eficacia del cine mexicano*, 414–417. Mexico City: Grijalbo.

Azteca Films, Inc. 1980. "Listing of Theaters." Harlingen: Agrasánchez Film Archive, Folder Spanish Theaters, 1980.

Balides, Constance. 1993. "Scenarios of Exposure in the Practice of Everyday Life: Women in the Cinema of Attractions." *Screen* 1 (34): 19–37.

Barriga Chávez, Ezequiel. 1988a. "Desde la butaca: *El coyote emplumado.*" *Excelsior*, July 28, 1988.

———.1988b. "Desde la butaca: *Ni de aquí ni de allá.*" *Excelsior*, February 26, 1988.

———. 1991. "Desde la butaca: *Sor Tequila.*" *Excelsior*, August 5, 1991.

———. 1993. "Desde la butaca: *Se equivocó la cigüeña.*" *Excelsior*, August 22, 1993.

Barrios, Gregg. 1989. "The BIG MIX Video: So Many Video Stores, So Many Languages . . . " *Los Angeles Times*, February 5, 1989.

Beer, Amy Barnes. 2001. "From the Bronx to Brooklyn: Spanish-Language Movie Theaters and Their Audiences in New York City, 1930–1999." Unpublished manuscript at Northwestern University, Evanston, Illinois.

Benamou, Catherine L. 2009. "Con amor, tequila, y gasolina: Lola the Truck Driver and Screen Resistance in cine fronterizo." In Victoria Ruétalo and Dolores Tierney (eds.), *Latsploitation, Exploitation Cinemas, and Latin America*, 171–184. London, New York: Routledge.

Benavides, Hugo O. 2008. *Drugs, Thugs, and Divas: Telenovelas and Narco-Dramas in Latin America*. Austin: University of Texas Press.

Benshoff, Harry M. 2000. "Blaxploitation Horror Films: Reappropiration or Reinscription?" *Cinema Journal* 29 (2): 31–50.

Bertaccini, Tiziana. 2001. *Ficción y realidad del héroe popular.* Mexico City: Dirección Heneral de Culturas Populares e Indígenas del Consejo Nacional para la Cultura y las Artes, Universidad Iberoamericana.

Betacourt, Javier. 1999. "*Las delicias del poder.*" *Proceso*, January 19, 1999.

Betanzo, Alejandra. 1998. "De Office Boy a la TV: Raúl Velasco, pardrino del espectáculo." *Etcétera* 271 (9): 19.

Blanco Borelli, Melissa. 2008. "'¿Y ahora qué vas a hacer, mulata?': Hip Choreographies in the Mexican Cabaretera Film *Mulata* (1954)." *Women & Performance: A Journal of Feminist Theory* 18 (3): 215–233.

Borja, Hiram. 1975. "Dictamen guión cinematográfico titulado *La Comadrita.*" Report. Mexico City, Secretaria de Gobernación.

———. 1976. "Dictamen relativo al guión cinematográfico titulado *Sor Tequila.*" Report. Mexico City, Secretaria de Gobernación.

Cabildo, Miguel. 1976. "Agrasánchez desbaratará su companía y Arturo Martínez se irá a filmar a otro país por el boicot a sus cintas." *Últimas Noticias*, April 22, 1976.

Cámara. 1978a. "Balance de la industria cinematográfica." *Cámara: Órgano Informativo de la Cámara Nacional de la Industria Cinematográfica* 1 (1): 16–20.

———. 1978b. "Balance de la industria cinematográfica nacional." *Cámara: Órgano Informativo de la Cámara Nacional de la Industria Cinematográfica* 1 (3): 21.

———. 1980. "Utilización de salas de exhibición en la República Mexicana." *Cámara: Órgano Informativo de la Cámara Nacional de la Industria Cinematográfica* 2 (14): 16.

———. 1982. "Los precios de entrada." *Cámara: Órgano Informativo de la Cámara Nacional de la Industria Cinematográfica* 3 (21): 12.

———. 1984a. "El mercado hispanoparlante." *Cámara: Órgano Informativo de la Cámara Nacional de la Industria Cinematográfica* 5 (36): 4–11.

———. 1984b. "El reto: La reconquista." *Cámara: Órgano Informativo de la Cámara Nacional de la Industria Cinematográfica* 5 (36): 2.

——— 1984c. "Estadística." *Cámara: Órgano Informativo de la Cámara Nacional de la Industria Cinematográfica* 5 (35): 14.

———. 1984d. "Una pantalla grande + una pantalla pequeña = mayores utilidades." *Cámara: Órgano Informativo de la Cámara Nacional de la Industria Cinematográfica* 5 (35): 15.

———. 1987a. "Editorial." *Cámara: Órgano Informativo de la Cámara Nacional de la Industria Cinematográfica* 6 (50): 1.

———. 1987b. "Inciertos avances económicos para la industria cinematográfica mexicana." *Cámara: Órgano Informativo de la Cámara Nacional de la Industria Cinematográfica* 6 (49): 20–23.

———. 1987c. "Pese a la crisis, la producción fílmica mexicana no redujo su presencia en la economía durante 1986." *Cámara: Órgano Informativo de la Cámara Nacional de la Industria Cinematográfica* 6 (49): 15–16.

———. 1989. "Producción fílmica nacional (1983–1988)." *Cámara: Órgano Informativo de la Cámara Nacional de la Industria Cinematográfica* 7 (55): 23–25.

Camargo, Ricardo. 1993. "*Se equivocó la cigüeña*: Éxito en taquilla: La India María supera a Gloria Trevi." *El Nacional*, August 22, 1993.

Campbell, Joseph. 2004. *The Hero with a Thousand Faces*. Princeton/Oxford: Princeton University Press.

Cane, Miguel. 2015. "El viaje a la felicidad de María Elena Velasco." *Milenio.com*, May 3, 2015.

Carreño Burgos, Marcela. 1994. "Espectáculo de La India María en teatro de revista que exalta nuestro folclor." *Novedades*, April 20, 1994.

Carro, Nelson. 1984. *El cine de luchadores*. Mexico City: Universidad Nacional Autónoma de México.

Carstens, Augustin G., Daniel C. Hardy, and Ceyla Pazarbasioglu. 2004. "Banking Crises in Latin America and the Political Economy of Financial Sector Policy." Unpublished paper for the seminar Governments and Banks: Responsibility and Limits, IDB Annual Meetings in Lima, Peru, March 28, 2004.

Cartmell, Deborah, I. Q. Hunter, Heidi Kaye, and Imelda Wheelhan (eds.). 1997. *Trash Aesthetics: Popular Culture and Its Audience*. London, Chicago: Pluto Press.

Castro Ricalde, Maricruz. 2004a. "Campo mexicano y urbe estadounidense en flujo: La India María y el cine popular." In *Memorias del VII Congreso Internacional de la Asociación Internacional de Semiótica Visual (CD)*, 1–20. Mexio City: Tecnológico de Monte Rey.

———. 2004b. "Popular Mexican Cinema and Undocumented Immigrants." *Discourse* 24 (1–2) (Winter–Spring): 194–213.

———. 2006. "Imágenes y representaciones en el periodismo de izquierda en México." *Realidades Comunicativas* 9 (2): 77–90.

———. 2007. "El cine popular mexicano y la representación del indígena: *El coyote emplumado* de María Elena Velasco, la India María." In *Actas del XV Congreso de la Asociación Internacional de Hispanistas*, 629–639. Mexico City: FCE, AIH, Tecnológico de Monterrey, El Colegio de México.

Chiquet, Nora Marín. 1996. "María Elena Velasco retirará a La India María para hacer otros personajes." *El Universal*, September 2, 1996.

Clark, Jennifer S. 2009. "Liberating Bicentennial America: Imagining the Nation through TV Superwomen of the Seventies." *Television & New Media* 10 (5): 434–454.

Clark D'Lugo, Carol. 2008. "La India María vs. Cantinflas and El Santo: Identity Construction within Aspects of Race, Gender, and Class in Popular Mexican Cinema." In Guy H. Wood (ed.), *Cine-Lit VI: Essays on Hispanic Film and Fiction*, 4–15. Corvallis, OR: Cine-Lit Publications.

Contreras Torres, Miguel. 1960. *El libro negro del cine mexicano*. Mexico City: Contreras Torres.

Cuéllar, Juan Carlos. 2003. "'La India María' se las bailó en 'La hora pico.'" *El Universal*, February 15, 2003.

Cuéllar, Sara. 1994. "Una 'India' en la ciudad." *Siglo 21*, November 14, 1994.

Dávalos, Patricia E. 1987. "Sergio Klainer, el nuevo galán de La India María." *Sol de México*, January 3, 1987.

———. 1998. "La India María seguirá haciendo cine con huaraches y enaguas." *La Crónica de Hoy*, September 15, 1998.

De la Cruz Polanco, Fabián. 1998. "La India María cristaliza el sueño de muchas mujeres y divierte con *Las delicias del poder*." *El Heraldo de México*, December 18, 1998.

———. 2002. "María Elena Velasco La India María está lista para su regreso al cine." *El Heraldo de México*, September 3, 2002.

De la Fuente, Luis. 1974. "Llaman de Hollywood a La India María." *El Universal*, March 30, 1974.

De la Mora, Sergio. 2006. *Cinemachismo: Masculinities and Sexuality in Mexican Film*. Austin: University of Texas Press.

———. 2009. "'Tus pinches leyes yo me las paso por los huevos': Isela Vega and Mexican Dirty Movies." In Victoria Ruétalo and Dolores Tierney (eds.), *Latsploitation, Exploitation Cinemas, and Latin America*, 245–257. London, New York: Routledge.

De la Vega Alfaro, Eduardo. 1985. "Cine de traficantes y traficantes del cine." *Pantalla* 2: 24–26.

———. 1999. "The Decline of the Golden Age and the Making of the Crisis." In Joanne Hershfield and David Maciel (eds.), *Mexico's Cinema: A Century of Film and Filmmakers*, 165–191. Wilmington: Scholarly Resources.

Dever, Susan. 2003. *Celluloid Nationalism and Other Melodramas: From Post-Revolutionary Mexico to Fin de Siglo Mexamérica*. Albany: State University of New York Press.

Diana Internacional Films, S.A. de C.V. 1981. "*Okey, Mister Pancho* U.S. Revenues." Production folder, Mexico City.

Díaz, Sergio, et al. 2008. *Historia de la producción cinematográfica mexicana, 1979–1980*. Guadalajara/Mexico City/Veracruz: Universidad de Guadalajara/CONACULTA, IMCINE/Universidad Veracruzana.

Díaz-Zambrana, Rosana, and Patricia Tomé (eds.). 2012. *Horrorfílmico: Aproximaciones al cine de terror en Latinoamérica y el Caribe*. San Juan, Puerto Rico: Isla Negra Editores.

Dunlap, Richard H. 1974. "Letter to Producer" (Fernando de Fuentes). Archive of Diana Internacional Films, S.A. de C.V., Los Angeles.

Dunn, Stephane. 2008. *"Baad Bitches" and Sassy Supermamas: Black Power Action Films*. Urbana: University of Illinois Press.

Dyer, Richard. 1986. *Heavenly Bodies: Film Stars and Society*. London, New York: Routledge.

———. 1993. *The Matter of Images: Essays on Representations*. London, New York: Routledge.

———. 2000a. "Stars and 'Character.'" In Joanne Hollows, Peter Hutchings, and Mark Jancovich (eds.), *The Film Studies Reader*, 124–128. London: Arnold.

———. 2000b. "Stars as Images." In Joanne Hollows, Peter Hutchings, and Mark Jancovich (eds.), *The Film Studies Reader*, 121–124. London: Arnold.

———. 2004. *Heavenly Bodies: Film Stars and Society*. London, New York: Routledge.

———. 2010. "Understanding Characters." *Projections: The Journal for Movies and Mind* 4 (1): 16–40.

Elizondo, Jorge. 1991. "Investigación: Exhibición en México." *Pantalla* 15: 2–36.

El Soberbio, Tarquino. 1989. "A La India María no le agrada el cine de malas palabras, aunque reconoce su mérito: María Elena Velasco regresa a la TV con un buen equipo de escritores." *El Heraldo*, February 20, 1989.

———. 1994. "La India María regresa al Blanquita con la intención de divertir." *El Heraldo de México*, April 20, 1994.

Espinosa, Julio García. 2003. "For an Imperfect Cinema" (1983). In K. J. Shepherdson, Andrew Utterson, and Philip Simpson (eds.), vol. 3 of *Film Theory*, 314–324. London, New York: Routledge.

Fernández Escareño, Itzia Gabriela. 1996. "Diez estudios de caso de directoras de largometrajes de ficción: Dentro de los canones industriales, en la historia del cine mexicano." Unpublished manuscript, Universidad Autónoma Metropolitana, Mexico City.

Fernández Reyes, Álvaro. 2004. *Santo el Enmascarado de Plata: Mito y realidad de un héroe mexicano moderno*. Mexico City: Conaculta.

Fiske, John. 1995. *Understanding Popular Culture* (1989). London, New York: Routledge.

Flores, Bertha Alicia. 2003. "¡Viva La India María! ¡Viva el humor blanco!" *Ovaciones*, January 13, 2003.

Flores, R. Elizabeth. 2004. "Obsesiva y carismática." *El Universal*, November 1, 2004.

Fregoso, Rosa Linda. 1999. "Recycling Colonialist Fantasies on the Texas Borderlands." In Hamid Naficy (ed.), *Home, Exile, Homeland: Film, Media, and the Politics of Place*, 169–192. London, New York: Routledge.

———. 2003. *MeXicana Encounters: The Making of Social Identities on the Borderlands*. Berkeley: University of California Press.

Fregoso, Rosa Linda, and Norma Iglesias. 1998. *Miradas de mujeres: Encuentro de cineastas y videoastas mexicanas y chicanas*. Tijuana, Mexico: Colegio de la Frontera Norte.

Galeana, Edgar. 1988. "La India María también es campeona en el vídeo." *Ovaciones*, July 3, 1988.

Galindo, Alejandro Colectivo. 1987a. "El cine mexicano y sus crisis, primera parte." *Dicine* (19): 12–13.

———. 1987b. "El cine mexicano y sus crisis, segunda parte." *Dicine* (20): 12–15.

Galindo, Rosa. 1990. "En la línea cómica no es fácil la calidad: María Elena Velasco." *El Universal*, October 2, 1990.

Garay, Adriana. 1994. "En el tradicional teatro Blanquita, la gran revista musical con puritito sabor a *México canta y aguanta* con la inigualable India María." *Cuestión*, June 15, 1994.

———. 1996. "Escoge doble 'identidad.'" *Reforma*, March 17, 1996.

García Canclini, Néstor, and Déborah Holtz. 1994. *Los nuevos espectadores: Cine, televisión, y vídeo en México*. Mexico City: IMCINE, Consejo Nacional para la Cultura y las Artes, Dirección General de Publicaciones.

García Canclini, Néstor, Déborah Holtz, and Ana Rosas Mantecón. 1994. "La ciudad de México: Cinéfilos y videófilos." In Néstor García Canclini and Déborah Holtz (eds.), *Los nuevos espectadores: Cine, televisión, y vídeo en México*, 159–227. Mexico City: IMCINE, Consejo Nacional para la Cultura y las Artes, Dirección General de Publicaciones.

García López, Patricia. 1998. "María Elena Velasco regresa a la TV con una serie cómica, luego de 18 años de ausencia." *El Heraldo*, January 3, 1998.

García Riera, Emilio. 1998. *Breve historia del cine mexicano: Primer siglo, 1897–1997*. Mexico City, Zapopan: Ediciones Mapas, Instituto Mexicano de Cinematografía.

García Tsao, Leonardo. 1990. "Un fenómeno llamado India María." *El Nacional*, May 24, 1990.

Getino, Octavio. 1998. *Cine y televisión en América Latina: Producción y mercados.* Santiago de Chile: División de Cultura Universidad ARCIS LOM Ediciones.

Getino, Octavio, and Fernando Solanas. 1976. "Towards a Third Cinema." In Bill Nichols (ed.), *Movies and Methods*, 44–64. Berkeley: University of California Press.

Goldin, Greg, and Marc Cooper. 1986. "Hollywood, Mexico: Striking Gold on the Silver Screens of Los Angeles." *Los Angeles Times Magazine: Hollywood, Mexico at Theaters near You*, January 12, 1986.

Gómez Ocampo, Gilberto. 1997. "The Persistence of Vision: Going to the Movies in Colombia." In Ann Marie Stock (ed.), *Framing Latin American Cinema: Contemporary Critical Perspectives*, 174–183. Minneapolis: University of Minnesota Press.

Gómezturja, Elvira. n.d. "María Elena Velasco desmiente que sufra cáncer." *TVnotas.*

González Vargas, Carla, Nelson Carro, and Leonardo García Tsao. 2006. *Las rutas del cine mexicano contemporáneo, 1990–2006.* Mexico City: CONACULTA Landucci.

Grajales, Ulises. 1994. "Una escuela." *El Sol de México*, June 18, 1994.

Grant, Barry K. 2008. "Science Fiction Double Feature: Ideology in the Cult Film." In Ernest Mathijs and Xavier Mendik (eds.), *The Cult Film Reader*, 77–78. New York: McGraw-Hill.

Grant, Lee. 1982. "El Jefe of Broadway's Film Houses." *Los Angeles Times*, November 26, 1982.

Greene, Doyle. 2005. *Mexploitation Cinema: A Critical History of Mexican Vampire, Wrestler, Ape-Man, and Similar Films, 1957–1977.* Jefferson, NC: McFarland & Co.

———. 2007. *The Mexican Cinema of Darkness: A Critical Study of Six Landmark Horror and Exploitation Films, 1969–1988.* Jefferson, NC: McFarland & Co.

Gunning, Tom. 1986. "The Cinema of Attraction: Early Film, Its Spectator and the Avant-Garde." *Wide Angle* 8 (3–4): 63–70.

———. 1989. "'Primitive' Cinema: A Frame-up? Or the Trick's on Us." *Cinema Journal* 28 (2): 3–12.

———. 2004. "Now You See It, Now You Don't: The Temporality of the Cinema of Attractions" (1993). In Lee Grieveson and Peter Krämer (eds.), *The Silent Cinema Reader*, 41–50. London, New York: Routledge.

Gutiérrez, Ramón. 1996. "The Erotic Zone: Sexual Transgression on the U.S.–Mexican Border." In Avery F. Gordon and Christopher Newfield (eds.), *Mapping Multiculturalism*, 253–262. Minneapolis: University of Minnesota Press.

Gwenllian-Jones, Sara, and Roberta E. Pearson (eds.). 2004. *Cult Television.* Minneapolis: University of Minnesota Press.

Haddu, Miriam. 2007. *Contemporary Mexican Cinema, 1989–1999: History, Space, and Identity.* Lewiston, NY: Edwin Mellen Press.

Hall, Stuart. 1994. "Cultural Identity and Diaspora." In Laura Chrisman and Patrick Williams (eds.), *Colonial Discourse and Post-colonial Theory: A Reader*, 392–403. New York: Columbia University Press.

———. 1997. "The Spectacle of the 'Other.'" In Stuart Hall (ed.), *Representation: Cultural Representations and Signifying Practices*, 223–290. London: Sage in association with the Open University.

Heredia, Juanita. 2008. "From Golden Age Mexican Cinema to Transnational Border Feminism: The Community of Spectators in *Loving Pedro Infante.*" *Aztlán: A Journal of Chicano Studies* 33 (2): 37–59.

Hernández, Alejandro Salazar. 1996. "María Elena Velasco jubila a su personaje: En octubre filmará la útima película de La India María." *El Nacional*, September 3, 1996.

Hernández, Arturo C. 1988. "Los intelectuales hacen un cine que por desgracia no gusta a la gente: La taquillera India María." *Ovaciones*, February 15, 1988.

Hernández, Elizabeth. 2004. "Vuelve 'La India María' a la television mexicana." *El Universal*, May 8, 2004.

Hernández, Hugo. 1988. "Algún día morirá La India María." *El Sol de México*, April 6, 1988.

Hernández, Jesús. 1999. "Para votar echo un volado: María Elena Velasco." *El Financiero*, January 3, 1999.

Hernández, Minerva. 2007. "Honorarán a La India María y a otras mujeres del cine." *Reforma*, July 10, 2007.

Herrera-Sobek, María. 1998. "Undocumented Mexican Immigrants Films and the Mexican/Chicano Ballad." In David R. Maciel and María Herrera-Sobek (eds.), *Culture across Borders: Mexican Immigration and Popular Culture*, 227–258. Tucson: University of Arizona Press.

Hershfield, Joanne. 1996. *Mexican Cinema, Mexican Woman, 1940–1950*. Tucson: University of Arizona Press.

———. 1999. "Race and Ethnicity in the Classical Cinema." In Joanne Hershfield and David Maciel (eds.), *Mexico's Cinema: A Century of Film and Filmmakers*, 81–97. Wilmington, DE: Scholarly Resources.

———. 2001. "Dolores del Río Uncomfortably Real: The Economics of Race in Hollywood's Latin American Musicals." In Daniel Bernardi (ed.), *Classic Hollywood, Classic Whiteness*, 139–156. Minneapolis: University of Minnesota Press.

———. 2008. *Imagining la Chica Moderna: Women, Nation, and Visual Culture in Mexico, 1917–1936*. Durham, NC: Duke University Press.

Hershfield, Joanne, and David Maciel (eds.). 1999. *Mexico's Cinema: A Century of Film and Filmmakers*. Wilmington, DE: Scholarly Resources.

Holmlund, Chris. 2005. "Wham! Bam! Pam! Pam Gries as Hot Action Babe and Cool Action Mama." *Quarterly Review of Film and Video* 22 (2): 97–112.

Horsley, Jake. 1999. *The Blood Poets: A Cinema of Savagery, 1958–1999*. Lanham, MD: Scarecrow Press.

Howard, Josiah. 2008. *Blaxploitation Cinema: The Essential Reference Guide*. Guildford, Surrey: FAB Press.

Huaco-Nuzum, Carmen. 1992. "*Ni de aquí, ni de allá*: Indigenous Female Representation in the Films of María Elena Velasco." In Chon A. Noriega (ed.), *Chicanos and Film: Essays on Chicano Representation and Resistance*, 127–138. New York: Garland.

Hudson, Dale. 2010. "Sepancine Conference 2009, 5º Congreso Internacional de Teoría y Análisis Cinematográfico (5th International Congress on Film Theory and Analysis)." *Scope* 16: February–March 2010 (first published in his blog in October 2009). nottingham.ac.uk/scope/issues/2010/february-issue-16.aspx.

Huerta, César. 2004. "Suena ya su *Huapango*: Retorno al cine María Elena Velasco." *Reforma*, January 15, 2004.

Iglesias, Norma. 1991. *Entre yerba, polvo, y plomo: Lo fronterizo visto por el cine mexicano.* Tijuana, Mexico: El Colegio de la Frontera Norte.

———. 1999. "Reconstructing the Border: Mexican Border Cinema and Its Relationship to Its Audience." In Joanne Hershfield and David R. Maciel (eds.), *Mexico's Cinema: A Century of Film and Filmmakers*, 233–248. Wilmington, DE: SR Books.

Jancovich, Mark. 2002. "Cult Fictions: Cult Movies, Subcultural Capital and the Production of Cultural Distinctions." *Cultural Studies* 16 (2): 306–322.

Jancovich, Mark, Antonio Lazario-Reboll, Julian Stringer, and Andy Willis (eds.). 2003. *Defining Cult Movies: The Cultural Politics of Oppositional Taste.* Manchester, NY: Manchester University Press.

Jenkins, Henry. 2013. *Textual Poachers: Television Fans and Participatory Culture.* New York: Routledge.

Jiménez, Heriberto. 2002. "Guarda en el baúl a La India María." *El Universal*, July 21, 2002.

Jiménez Patiño, Juan. 1987. "Primer Plano: Gilberto Martínez Solares." *Pantalla* 9: 15–18.

Joseph, Gilbert M., Anne Rubenstein, and Eric Zolov. 2001. *Fragments of a Golden Age: The Politics of Culture in Mexico since 1940.* Durham, London: Duke University Press.

Keeling, Kara. 2007. *The Witch's Flight: The Cinematic, the Black Femme, and the Image of Common Sense.* Durham, NC: Duke University Press.

Kessler, Frank. 2006. "The Cinema of Attractions as Dispositif." In Wanda Strauven (ed.), *Cinema of Attractions Reloaded*, 57–69. Amsterdam: Amsterdam University Press.

King, John. 2000. *Magical Reels: A History of Cinema in Latin America.* London, New York: Verso.

Klain, Stephen. 1980a. "Mexican Conglom in U.S. Toehold." *Variety*, March 26, 1980.

———. 1980b. "Televicine Rolls Yank Hispanic Link." *Variety*, May 28, 1980.

Kraszewski, Jon. 2002. "Recontextualizing the Historical Reception of Blaxploitation: Articulations of Class, Black Nationalism, and Anxiety in the Genre's Advertisements." *Velvet Light Trap* 50: 48–61.

Laing, Heather. 2000. "Emotion by Numbers: Music, Song and the Musical." In Bill Marshall and Robynn Stilwell (eds.), *Musicals: Hollywood & Beyond*, 5–13. Portland: Intellect Books.

Lawrence, Novotny. 2008. *Blaxploitation Films of the 1970s: Blackness and Genre.* London, New York: Routledge.

Leal, Alejandro, and Verónica Pérez. 1997. "Lo que piensa María de María y las Marías." *Epóca*, September 26, 1997.

Le Guern, Philippe. 2004. "Towards a Constructivist Approach to Media Cults." In Sara Gwenllian-Jones and Roberta E. Pearson (eds.), *Cult Television*, 3–25. Minneapolis: University of Minnesota Press.

Levi, Heather. 1999. "On Mexican Pro Wrestling: Sport as Melodrama." In Toby Miller and Randy Martin (eds.), *Sport Cult*, 173–188. Minneapolis: University of Minnesota Press.

———. 2001. "Masked Media: The Adventures of Lucha Libre on the Small Screen." In Gilbert Joseph, Anne Rubenstein, and Eric Zolov (eds.), *Fragments of a Golden*

Age: The Politics of Culture in Mexico since 1940, 330–372. Durham, NC: Duke University Press.

Lipkies, Iván. 2010. "Email Re: Pregunta disco" (Mexico City), October 11, 2010.

List, Christine. 1992. "Self-Directed Stereotyping in the Films of Cheech Marin." In Chon A. Noriega (ed.), *Chicanos and Film Essays on Chicano Representation and Resistance*, 183–194. New York: Garland.

López, Ana M. 1993. "Are All Latins from Manhattan?: Hollywood, Ethnography and Cultural Colonialism." In Ana López, John King, and Manuel Alvarado (eds.), *Mediating Two Worlds: Cinematic Encounters in the Americas*, 67–80. London: BFI.

———. 1995. "Our Welcomed Guests: Telenovelas in Latin America." In Robert C. Allen (ed.), *To Be Continued . . . Soap Operas around the World*, 256–275. London, New York: Routledge.

Maciel, David. 1999. "Cinema and the State in Contemporary Mexico, 1970–1999." In Joanne Hershfield and David Maciel (eds.), *Mexico's Cinema: A Century of Film and Filmmakers*, 197–232. Wilmington, DE: Scholarly Resources.

Maciel, David, and María Herrera-Sobek (eds.). 1998. *Culture across Borders: Mexican Immigration and Popular Culture*. Tucson: University of Arizona Press.

MacLaird, Misha. 2013. *Aesthetics and Politics in the Mexican Film Industry*. New York: Palgrave Macmillan.

Márquez, Carlos F. 2009. "El cine de La India María, comedia ligera con crítica política según Rohrer." *La Jornada*, October 4, 2009.

Martí, Gabriel. 1980. "Incremento de la producción fílmica en 1980." *Cámara: Órgano Informativo de la Cámara Nacional de la Industria Cinematográfica* 2 (14): 9–12.

Mayne, Judith (2004), "Immigrants and Spectators." In Thomas Schatz (ed.), *Hollywood 3: Social Dimensions: Technology, Regulation and the Audience*, 355–365. London, New York: Routledge.

McCulloch, Richard. 2011. "'Most People Bring Their Own Spoons': The Room's Participatory Audience as Comedy Mediators." *Participations: Journal of Audience and Reception Studies* 8 (2): 189–218.

Medina de la Serna, Rafael. 1988. "Poco público menos cine." *Dicine* 24: 6–9.

Medrano Platas, Alejandro. 1999. *Quince directores del cine mexicano*. Mexico City: Plaza y Valdés.

Mendoza de Lira, Alejandra. 1998. "Las diabluras de 'La India María' en TV." *El Universal*, January 3, 1998.

Monaco, Paul. 2001. *History of the American Cinema: The Sixties, 1960–1969*. New York: Charles Scribner's Sons.

Monsiváis, Carlos. 1994. "Vino todo el pueblo y no cupo en la pantalla (notas sobre el público del cine en México)." In Carlos Monsiváis and Carlos Bonfil (eds.), *A través del espejo: El cine mexicano y su público*, 49–97. Mexico City: Ediciones del Milagro.

———. 1999. "Cantinflas and Tin Tan: Mexico's Greatest Comedians." In Joanne Hershfield and David Maciel (eds.), *Mexico's Cinema: A Century of Film and Filmmakers*, 49–79. Wilmington, DE: Scholarly Resources.

Montes de Oca Heredia, Raúl. 1993. "*Se equivocó la cigüeña*, sigue con lo mismo, nada nuevo." *Novedades*, July 12, 1993.

Mora, Carl J. 2005. *Mexican Cinema: Reflections of a Society, 1896–2004*. Jefferson, NC: McFarland & Co.

Morales Valentín, Emilio. 1998. "Invita La India María a compartir *Las delicias del poder*." *El Universal*, December 18, 1998.

———. 2002. "Niega La India estar enferma." *El Universal*, February 11, 2002.

Mottram, James. 2006. *The Sundance Kids: How Mavericks Took Back Hollywood*. London: Faber and Faber Limited.

Naficy, Hamid. 2001. *An Accented Cinema: Exilic and Diasporic Filmmaking*. Princeton: Princeton University Press.

Naficy, Hamid, and Teshome H. Gabriel (eds.). 1993. *Otherness and the Media: The Ethnography of the Imagined and the Imaged*. Chur, Switzerland: Harwood Academic Publishers.

Nasser, Jaime Javier. 2008. "Exporting Tears and Fantasies of (Under)Development: Popular Television Genres, Globalization, and Nationalism in Mexico after World War II." Dissertation, University of Southern California, Los Angeles.

Noble, Andrea. 2005. *Mexican National Cinema*. London, New York: Routledge.

Noriega, Chon A. 1992. "Between Weapon and Formula: Chicano Cinema in Its Contexts." In Chon A. Noriega (ed.), *Chicanos and Film: Representation and Resistance*, 141–167. Minneapolis: University of Minnesota Press.

———. 2001. "'Waas Sappening?': Narrative Structure and Iconography in *Born in East L.A.*" In Matthew Tinkcom and Amy Villarejo (eds.), *Keyframes Popular Cinema and Cultural Studies*, 186–202. London, New York: Routledge.

Notimex. 1997. "María Elena Velasco, La India María prepara su próxima película *Las delicias del poder*." *La Crónica de Hoy*, November 4, 1997.

Obscura Gutiérrez, Siboney. 1997. "Cinco actrices cómicas en la época de oro del cine mexicano." Master's thesis, Universidad Nacional Autónoma de México, Mexico City.

Odin, Roger. 1990a. *Cinéma et production de sense*. Paris: Armand Colin.

———. 1990b. "Dokumentarischer Film—Dokumentarisierende Lektüre." In Christa Blümlinger (ed.), *Sprung im Spiegel: Filmisches Wahrnehmen zwischen Fiktion und Wirklichkeit*, 125–146. Vienna: Sonderzahl.

Oehmichen Bazán, Cristina. 2005. *Identidad, género y relaciones interétnicas: Mazahuas en la ciudad de México*. Mexico City: Universidad Nacional Autónoma de México.

Olaiz, Lupita. 1991. "Dinastías: María Elena Velasco proviene de una familia musical." *El Sol de México*, July 6, 1991.

Olvera, Marco Antonio. 1996. "Adiós a La India María: María Elena Velasco dejará el personaje." *Universal Gráfico*, August 31, 1996.

Orso, Felipe. 2001. "La farandula." *La Opinión*, October 16, 2001.

O'Sullivan, Tim, John Hartley, Danny Saunders, Martin Montgomery, and John Fiske. 1994. *Key Concepts in Communication and Cultural Studies*. London, New York: Routledge.

Pacheco, Arturo. 1987. "Realizaron escenas de la nueva cinta de La India María en California." *El Nacional*, January 21, 1987.

———. 1988. "No hago cine de crítica social ni política porque mi función es divertir al público: La India María." *El Heraldo*, February 17, 1988.

Paranaguá, Paulo Antonio. 1995. *Mexican Cinema*. London: British Film Institute.

———. 1998. "Of Periodizations and Paradigms: The Fifties in Comparative Perspective." *Nuevo Texto Crítico* 10 (21/22): 31–44.

Pearson, Roberta E. 1992. *Eloquent Gestures: The Transformation of Performance Style in The Griffith Biographs Films.* Berkeley: University of California Press.

Pelayo, Aivia R. 1985. "La India María regresa a la TV." *TV y Novelas* (August).

Pendás, Ignacio. 1973. "Distribución de *Tonta tonta, pero no tanto* en Venezuela." Sent to Juan Baudera Molina. Unpublished report on the box-office performance after the film's release. Caracas, Venezuela.

Peralta, Freddy. 1999. "Santo: The Silver Masked Man of Mexican Cinema." In Rogelio Agrasánchez (ed.), *Mexican Horror Cinema: Posters from Mexican Fantasy Films*, 31–35. Harlingen: Agrasánchez Film Archive.

Pérez, Roberto, Jr. 2005. "Mario Almada en plena acción en su próxima película." *La Prensa de San Antonio*, February 27, 2005.

Pérez Albarrán, Jorge. 1994. "Celebran 200 representaciones de *México canta y aguanta.*" *El Heraldo*, September 3, 1994.

Pérez Turrent, Tomás. 1990. "El humor en el cine mexicano." *Pantalla* 11: 24–27.

———. 1995. "The Studios." In Paulo Antonio Paranaguá (ed.), *Mexican Cinema*, 133–144. London: British Film Institute.

Pérez Turrent, Tomás, and Gillian Turner. 1977. "Mexico." In Peter Cowie (ed.), *International Film Guide*, 207–209. London: Tantivy Press.

Perriam, Chris. 2005. "Two Transnational Spanish Stars: Antonio Banderas and Penélope Cruz." *Studies in Hispanic Cinemas* 2 (1): 29–45.

Quintal Avilés, Fanny, and Guadalupe Reyes Domínguez. 1994. "Mérida: Ver cine en una ciudad de provincia." In Néstor García Canclini and Déborah Holtz (eds.), *Los nuevos espectadores: Cine, televisión, y vídeo en México*, 262–297. Mexico City: IMCINE, Consejo Nacional para la Cultura y las Artes, Dirección General de Publicaciones.

Ramírez, Roberto. 1984. "Declara la actriz cómica La India María: Todos los que participan en el cine nacional, deben colaborar para que la industria mejore su situación." *Excelsior*, September 2, 1984.

———. 1985. "Expresa María Elena Velasco La India María: Deben los productores olvidar el comercialismo y tener amor por su trabajo para realizar buenos filmes." *Excelsior*, October 14, 1985.

———. 1987. "Affirma La India María, quien tendrá un personaje distino: Hay que hacer un esfuerzo por realizar mejores cintas." *Excelsior*, November 20, 1987.

Ramírez Berg, Charles. 1992. *Cinema of Solitude: A Critical Study of Mexican Film, 1967–1983.* Austin: University of Texas Press.

Ramírez Hernández, Rocio. 1998. "La India María regresa al cine." *Novedades*, December 18, 1998.

Rashkin, Elissa J. 2001. *Women Filmmakers in Mexico: The Country of Which We Dream.* Austin: University of Texas Press.

Rashotte, Ryan. 2015. *Narco Cinema: Sex, Drugs, and Banda Music in Mexico's B-Filmography.* New York: Palgrave Macmillan.

Reyna Bernal, Horacio. 1987. "Tiene a la baja la duración de las películas mexicanas en cartelera." *Cámara: Órgano Informativo de la Cámara Nacional de la Industria Cinematográfica* 6 (50): 38–39.

Rivero, Yeidy M. 2003. "The Performance and Reception of Televisual 'Ugliness' in *Yo soy Betty la fea.*" *Feminist Media Studies* 3 (1): 65–81.

Rodriguez, Robert. 1995. *Rebel without a Crew: Or How a 23-Year-Old Filmmaker with $7,000 Became a Hollywood Player.* New York: Plume.

Rogers, Everett M., and Arvind Singhal. 1999. *Entertainment-Education: A Communication Strategy for Social Change*. Mahwah, NJ: L. Erlbaum Associates.
Rohrer, Seraina. 2008. Interview with María Elena Velasco, Mexico City.
———. 2009a. Interview with María Elena Velasco, Mexico City.
———. 2009b. "Stereotyping in the Films of La India María." *Journal of Latino-Latin American Studies* 3 (3): 54–68.
———. 2009c. "Weder von hier noch von dort: Die Grenze USA-Mexiko, ein beliebter Schauplatz für Filme." *Rosa* (39): 28–30.
———. 2010a. Interview with Héctor Benítez, Harlingen, Texas.
———. 2010b. Interview with Ramón Medrano, Harlingen, Texas.
———. 2010c. Interview with Rick Ruenes, Brownsville, Texas.
———. 2010d. Interview with Rogelio Agrasánchez, Harlingen, Texas.
———. 2011. "La India María: Das Spiel mit einer stereotypen (Helden-)Figur der mexikanischen Populärkultur." In Robert Blanchet et al. (eds.), *Serielle Formen: Von den frühen Film-Serials zu aktuellen Quality-TV- und Online-Serien*, 399–415. Marburg, Germany: Schüren.
Rohter, Larry. 1988. "Film Version of Everyman Wins Mexico." *New York Times*, November 6, 1988.
Romero, Víctor Manuel. 1981. "Producción de películas en 1980." *Cámara: Órgano Informativo de la Cámara Bacional de la Industria Cinematográfica* 3 (15): 13.
Romero, Víctor Manuel, and Elena Bertol. 1981. "El público en el D.F." *Cámara: Órgano Informativo de la Cámara Nacional de la Industria Cinematográfica* 3 (18): 9–10.
Rosas, Mario A. 1974. "Carta solicitud clase de torero y karate." Letter sent by Fernando Cortés. Archive of Diana Internacional Films, S.A. de C.V., Los Angeles.
Ruétalo, Victoria, and Dolores Tierney (eds.). 2009. *Latsploitation, Exploitation Cinemas, and Latin America*. London, New York: Routledge.
Ruiz, Silvia. 1994. "La India María muda de piel para encarnar nuevos personajes." *Universal Gráfico*, June 18, 1994.
Salazar H., Alejandro. 1995. "La fama y la vida son efímeras." *El Nacional*, August, 3, 1995.
Sánchez, Francisco. 1989. *Crónica antisolemne del cine mexicano*. Veracruz: Universidad Veracruzana.
Sánchez, Víctor Hugo. 1989. "María Elena Velasco, La India María, prepara su autobiografía, luego de 15 años de estrella." *El Heraldo*, March 19, 1989.
Sánchez Ruiz, Enrique E. 1986. "La agenda televisiva en México y Guadalajara." *Cuadernos: Revista de Ciencias Sociales*, n.s. 2: 33–42.
———. 1993. "Guadalajara: Cine, televisión y vídeo." In Néstor García Canclini and Déborah Holtz (eds.), *Los nuevos espectadores: Cine, televisión y vídeo en México*, 228–261. Mexico City: IMCINE, Consejo Nacional para la Cultura y las Artes, Dirección General de Publicaciones.
———. 2000. "La televisión y el sector audiovisual mexicano: Breve examen de flujos asimétricos." *Revista Universidad de Guadalajara* 20: 55–62.
Schaefer, Eric. 1999. *"Bold! Daring! Shocking! True!": A History of Exploitation Films, 1919–1959*. Durham, NC: Duke University Press.
Sconce, Jeffrey. 1995. "'Trashing' the Academy: Taste, Excess, and an Emerging Politics of Cinematic Style." *Screen* 36 (4): 534–553.

Secretaría de Gobernación. n.d. "Dictamen relativo al guión cinematográfico intitulado Okey, Mister Pancho." Mexico City, Secretaría de Gobernación.

Segoviano, Rogelio. 1994. "La India María, reina de la taquilla." *El Nacional*, November 30, 1994.

Sévéon, Julien. 2008. *Blaxploitation: 70's Soul Fever.* Paris: Bazaar & Co.

Shaw, Deborah. 2007. *Contemporary Latin American Cinema: Breaking into the Global Market.* Lanham, MD: Rowman & Littlefield.

Shaw, Lisa, and Stephanie Dennison. 2005. *Latin American Cinema: Essays on Modernity, Gender and National Identity.* Jefferson, NC: McFarland & Co.

Shohat, Ella, and Robert Stam. 1994. *Unthinking Eurocentrism: Multiculturalism and the Media.* London, New York: Routledge.

Sims, Yvonne D. 2006. *Women of Blaxploitation: How the Black Action Film Heroine Changed American Popular Culture.* Jefferson, NC: McFarland & Co.

Sinclair, John. 1999. *Latin American Television: A Global View.* Oxford, New York: Oxford University Press.

———. 2004. "From Latin Americans to Latinos: Spanish-Language Television in the United States and Its Audience." *Revista Fronteras: Estudios Mediáticos* 6 (1): 7–20.

Solís, Teresa H. 1990. "Cineastas mexicanas." *Pantalla* (12): 24–27.

Sontag, Susan. 1999. "Notes on Camp." In Fabio Cleto (ed.), *Camp: Queer Aesthetics and the Performing Subject*, 53–65. Edinburgh: Edinburgh University Press.

Stacey, Jackie. 2000. "Feminine Fascinations: Forms of Identification in Star-Audience Relations." In Joanne Hollows, Peter Hutchings, and Mark Jancovich (eds.), *The Film Studies Reader*, 147–154. London: Arnold.

Stevenson, Mark. 2001. "Mexico's Invisible Issue." *Seattle Times*, February 26, 2001.

Stock, Ann Marie (ed.). 1997. *Framing Latin American Cinema: Contemporary Critical Perspectives.* Minneapolis: University of Minnesota Press.

Suárez Ojeda, Gustavo. 1992. "Nunca dejaré de interpretar a La India María, es mi personalidad." *Cine Mundial*, July 28, 1992.

Sutter, Mary. 2001. "*Ugly Betty* Turns Tables on Telenovela Formula." *Variety* 54: 22–28.

Syder, Andrew, and Dolores Tierney. 2005. "Importation/Mexploitation; or, How a Crime-Fighting, Vampire-Slaying Mexican Wrestler Almost Found Himself in an Italian Sword-and-Sandals Epic." In Jay Schneider and Tony Williams (eds.), *Horror International*, 33–55. Detroit: Wayne State University Press.

Taves, Brian. 1993. "The B Film: Hollywood's Other Half." In Tino Balio (ed.), *Grand Design: Hollywood as a Modern Business Enterprise, 1930–1939*, 313–350. History of the American Cinema, 5. New York, Toronto: Maxwell Macmillan International.

Tetzpa Zayaz, Jamie. 1987. "Cancine otorgó la taquilla de oro a La India María: Fue considerada la artista más exito en el cine nacional." *El Nacional*, April 8, 1987.

Thornton, Niamh. 2010. "YouTube: Transnational Fandom and Mexican Divas." *Transnational Cinemas* 1 (1): 53–57.

Tierney, Dolores. 2007. *Emilio Fernández: Pictures in the Margins.* Manchester, UK, and New York: Manchester University Press.

———. 2013. "Ugly Betty's Latina Body: Race, Ethnicity, Class and Gender in Contemporary Mexico." *Film, Fashion & Consumption* 2 (1): 7–23.

———. 2014. "Mapping Cult Cinema in Latin American Film Cultures." *Cinema Journal* 54 (1): 129–134.

Tuñón, Julia. 1998. *Mujeres de luz y sombra en el cine mexicano: La construcción de una imagen, 1939–1952*. Mexico City: El Colegio de México/Instituto Mexicano de Cinematografía.

Ugalde Romero, Victor Manuel. 1982a. "La exhibición masiva en el área metropolitana." *Cámara: Órgano Informativo de la Cámara Nacional de la Industria Cinematográfica* 3 (23): 11.

———. 1982b. "Los espectadores se ausentan." *Cámara: Órgano Informativo de la Cámara Nacional de la Industria Cinematográfica* 3 (25): 3–4.

———. 1983. "Resumen de la producción de películas mexicanas en 1982." *Cámara: Órgano Informativo de la Cámara Nacional de la Industria Cinematográfica* 4 (26): 3–5.

Valencia, Sofia L. 1992. "Productora y cine-directora, actriz realmente consentida La India María, María Elena Velasco." *Diaro de México*, June 5, 1992.

Valenzuela Arce, José Manuel. 1994. "Tijuana: La recepción audiovisual en la frontera." In Néstor García Canclini and Déborah Holtz (eds.), *Los nuevos espectadores: Cine, televisión, y vídeo en México*, 298–329. Mexico City: IMCINE, Consejo Nacional para la Cultura y las Artes, Dirección General de Publicaciones.

Vares, Tina. 2001. "Action Heroines and Female Viewers: What Women Have to Say." In Martha McCaughey and Neal King (eds.), *Reel Knockouts: Violent Women in the Movies*, 219–243. Austin: University of Texas Press.

Vélez, Maria Luisa. 1989. "Millones de cine espectadores se identifican con La India María." *Novedades*, July 8, 1989.

Vergara, Francisco. 1972. "Otra película para Machuchal." *El Nuevo Día*, October 6, 1972.

Vieyra, Alberto. 1987. "La India María regresó a los estudios de cine." *Cine Mundial*, January 21, 1987.

Villaseñor, Eleazar. 1994. "Llega a 200 representaciones *México canta y aguanta*." *El Universal Gráfico*, September 2, 2010.

Walker, David, Andrew J. Rausch, and Chris Watson. 2009. *Reflections on Blaxploitation: Actors and Directors Speak*. Lanham: Scarecrow Press.

Wasko, Janet, and Mary Erickson. 2008. *Cross-Border Cultural Production: Economic Runaway or Globalization?* Amherst, MA: Cambria Press.

Wilt, David E. 1996a. "Horror Films from South of the Border." *Cinefantastique* 27 (10): 40.

———. 1996b. "Images of Indians in Mexican Cinema." *Mexican Film Bulletin* 3 (3): 1–5.

———. 1998. "Masked Men and Monsters." In Pete Tombs (ed.), *Mondo Macabro: Weird and Wonderful Cinema around the World*, 137–147. New York: St. Martin's Griffin.

———. 2004. *The Mexican Filmography, 1916–2001*. Jefferson: McFarland & Co.

———. 2009. "Based on a True Story: Reality-Based Exploitation Cinema in Mexico." In Victoria Ruétalo and Dolores Tierney (eds.), *Latsploitation, Exploitation Cinemas, and Latin America*, 158–170. London, New York: Routledge.

Wood, Jason. 2006. *The Faber Book of Mexican Cinema*. London: Faber and Faber.

Zimmermann, Patricia. 2009. "Mujeres, perro negro, 2 de octubre." *FLEFF* (blog), October 6. ithaca.edu/fleff/blogs/open_spaces/mujeres,_perro_negro,__2_de_octubre/.

Zúñiga Barba, Félix. 1989. "La India María piensa ya colgar los huaraches." *Novedades*, April 16, 1989.

INDEX

NOTES: Page number in *italics* represent people, places, and topics mentioned in photograph captions. Phrases enclosed in square brackets represent direct translations. Italicized film title translations indicate an English-audience release; otherwise, English titles appear in roman.